JEREMIAH

HIS TIME AND HIS WORK

JEREMIAH

HIS TIME AND HIS WORK

BY

ADAM C. WELCH, D.D.

GREENWOOD PRESS, PUBLISHERS
WESTPORT, CONNECTICUT

Library of Congress Cataloging in Publication Data

Welch, Adam Cleghorn, 1864-1943.
Jeremiah, his time and his work.

Reprint of the ed. published by Oxford University Press, London.
Includes index.
1. Jeremiah, the prophet. 2. Bible. O.T. Jeremiah--Criticism, interpretation, etc. I. Title.
BS580.J4W4 1980 224'.2'0924 80-17188
ISBN 0-313-22609-1 (lib. bdg.)

Reprinted in 1980 by Greenwood Press,
A division of Congressional Information Service, Inc.
88 Post Road West, Westport, Connecticut 06881

Printed in the United States of America

10 9 8 7 6 5 4 3 2 1

PREFACE

THE title chosen for this book is intended to define in some measure its aim. It is not a commentary on Jeremiah: it seeks to set the prophet in close relation to his period and to construe his message in this light.

Thus Jeremiah comes at the close of a long prophetic succession, and is always conscious of the past. Much which he has to say is not novel. But he brings to full and explicit utterance what had previously been dimly suggested, and he combines into a unity sporadic principles flung out by other men in their great moments. He sums up a movement in which he has no real successor.

Again, he appeared at a period, about the external and internal conditions of which we are exceptionally well informed. We can watch the hopes and fears of the nation in one of the great hours of its destiny. And we can recognize what religious aims were stirring men's minds. They were busy with a reform, the origin of which is still debated, but the issue of which is clear. For it issued in the Judaism of the Return, which, for good and ill, was different from the past. What may have been Jeremiah's attitude to the men who initiated this movement is also debated. But again their attitude to him is clear; they first silenced and then imprisoned him. His message must have been integrally related to his time.

Much of the volume is occupied with detailed discussion of the authenticity of certain passages. The discussion will seem tedious to many. Yet the reason is that we have received the record of Jeremiah's life and words through the hands of the returned exiles. And these men inherited the attitude and the ideals of those who strongly opposed the prophet. They did not leave the records untouched. Duhm and Erbt were the first who adequately recognized this fact, which constitutes a grave difficulty in any study of Jeremiah. Duhm described those who transmitted the book as the men of the synagogue, and occasionally dismissed their accretions, calling them synagogue sermons. It is difficult to subscribe to this description, for the additions are not so much expansions of original oracles for hortatory purposes, as sincere efforts of a later generation to interpret material which the readers valued. Only the men held their own convictions so strongly that it appeared certain to them that a prophet must have shared them. They added what they did, not with any thought of distorting his message, but with the sincere desire to explain his language. Now any one who attempts to sift out the original from the later additions cannot expect to escape wholly from the danger which attends all such work, the danger of deciding authenticity by mere subjective impressions. But he ought to be prepared to show that there are other than subjective reasons which have guided him in each case. That must be the excuse for discussing at length certain vexed passages. It may be added that the several reconstructions of the original are cumulative in their effect, each reconstruction serving to support the other. And what helps to confirm them all is that then Jeremiah emerges with a consistent message and that there also appears a natural reason for the separate additions.

The volume is the outcome of many years' work. Several years ago I published in the *Expositor* studies on certain stages in the prophet's thought. While these have all been revised and rewritten before being incorporated in the book, they have been utilized; and it is just to acknowledge the courtesy of Messrs. Hodder and Stoughton, who have readily permitted them to be thus used.

Some readers may be puzzled by unfamiliar translations of

several passages from Jeremiah. These have been reproduced from a translation of the book of Jeremiah into colloquial English prepared for the National Adult School Union, and now appearing in a revised edition.

It remains only to acknowledge gratefully the help received from one of my students, Mr. Norman W. Porteous, M.A., who has revised the proofs, and prepared the index. The interest of all my students in my attempt to trace for them the great movement of Israel's life and religious thought has meant so much that I dedicate the book to them.

A. C. W.

New College,
Edinburgh.

CONTENTS

I

POLITICAL AND RELIGIOUS CONDITIONS IN JUDAH DURING THE REIGN OF JOSIAH

IT has been the singular fortune of Jeremiah that he has often been represented as a somewhat melancholy and even sentimental figure who watched with sad helplessness his nation's end. The fact that the Lamentations were mistakenly attributed to him undoubtedly helped to confirm this false impression, but cannot fully account for it. But, whatever its origin, this conception of the prophet must be dismissed, for there is no more constant or fearless fighter in the roll of Israel's heroes of the faith. He called himself one born to be at odds with and in opposition to the whole world; and, while he lamented the necessity, he never flinched from the task. Wherever his figure emerges into distinctness, it is militant. His opponents were the priests and prophets of Jerusalem, the successive kings of his time, the governing class in peace and war, and finally the little company which carried him into forced exile in Egypt. And the difference between the prophet and his contemporaries was of no academic kind, for it drove the men to take action in order to silence their antagonist. The religious authorities forbade him to exercise his functions in the temple so that he might be prevented from influencing the people. In the reign of Jehoiakim only the interference of the civil authorities delivered him from death at the hands of the priests. At a later period these civil rulers turned against him and became so convinced of the mischievous character of his power over the populace that they flung him into a cistern, where they would have left him to die.

Neither the universal character nor the violence of this opposition need surprise any candid student of the prophet. Jeremiah provoked it. Speaking at one of the great religious festivals in the capital, he accused priests and worshippers of turning their temple into a robbers' den. He denounced the nation's religion in bitter terms. 'How can you say, I am not defiled, you dromedary in heat, changing its mates, whose appetite cannot be restrained?' During the siege of Jerusalem he was confined for a period in one of the guard-courts; and the military leaders, who were responsible for the defence of the city, learned that the prophet was in the habit of declaring in the hearing of the soldiers that every man who remained in the capital should die by sword, famine, or pestilence, but that all who deserted to the besiegers should at least save their lives.

It is only the fact that men read these things in the Bible and so read them with muffled minds, which prevents them from recognizing how stinging, and above all how provocative, the language of Jeremiah was. No man who said these things and who meant what he said could expect anything except an opposition which passed into action. There are words which are acts: and many of the prophet's words are of that character.

These and similar words, which dealt alike with the political conditions and the outward religious institutions of Judah, were oracles uttered in the name of Yahweh, that is, they were considered by the prophet to be the outcome of his religious convictions. They must find their place in any estimate of Jeremiah and his message. But they are introduced here in order to point out how peculiarly necessary it is, in the case of this prophet, to attempt to see the political and religious condition of the nation at his time. Such an estimate is useful, and even necessary, in connexion with all the prophets. But, in the case of a man whose attitude was consistently one of opposition to that of his contemporaries, it is of special significance.

There were two leading factors which determined the political life of Judah, not only during Josiah's reign but for some time earlier. These were the relation of the nation to Assyria, and its relation to Northern Israel, which, since the capture of Samaria by Sargon in 721, had become a province of the Eastern Empire. Each of these factors was closely connected with the other, because anything the court at Jerusalem might hope to accomplish in Samaria depended on the power or the goodwill of Assyria. And both in turn had a direct and indirect influence on the religious attitude of the Southern kingdom.

From the period of Manasseh's accession till the beginning of Josiah's reign, Judah was subject to the empire of Assyria. It is not easy to determine how far Hezekiah's resistance to Sennacherib was successful, and especially it is far from clear that the check to the Assyrian advance on Egypt was so complete as it is represented in II Kings 19 : 35–7.[1] But it remains certain that, though Jerusalem could boast that the great conqueror had never entered her gates, the situation of the little kingdom was desperate. All Judah had been overrun; many of the inhabitants of the country-towns had been carried into captivity; the capital had been stripped of its wealth to provide the fine which Sennacherib exacted. No help could come from Egypt, which was conquered by Asarhaddon in 671. The only way by which Judah could maintain its existence was by speedy submission to the conqueror. Hence Manasseh appears among the Syrian princes who paid tribute to Asarhaddon, and sent a contingent to support his suzerain in Asshurbanipal's later campaigns against Tirhaka. Judah became a vassal state.

[1] Cf. on the subject, Sidney Smith, *Babylonian Historical Texts*, and Honor, *Sennacherib's Invasion of Palestine.*

The result of the prompt submission was that the internal affairs of the kingdom were not interfered with, except at one important point. The Assyrian Empire appears to have required from all subject states a certain recognition of the deity of the supreme power. Thus when Ahaz at a somewhat earlier date secured the support of the Assyrians against the league of Damascus and Israel, he sent from Damascus, where he had gone to arrange the terms of the submission, the pattern of an altar to his priest Urijah at Jerusalem. The new altar was set up in the temple in the place which the altar of Yahweh had previously occupied, and from this time Ahaz personally officiated there (II Kings 16: 10–16). This act was not due to any aesthetic admiration of new religious furniture. Nor was it meant to involve the cessation of Yahweh-worship in the royal chapel: the old altar of Yahweh continued with its attendant priest. It was part of the price which the Judean king paid for the support of Assyria. The subject king publicly acknowledged the religion of the Empire.

In the same way it is legitimate to infer that the religious reaction which appeared in Manasseh's reign was largely the outcome of the new conditions in which the kingdom was placed. There may have been a certain recoil from strict Yahwism due to disappointment with the results of Hezekiah's policy. But of the existence of such an influence in the national life there is no direct evidence, and the political factor is sufficient to account for the change of policy.

The kingdom could only be maintained on condition of submission to Assyria, and Assyria's terms involved the recognition of the god of the Empire. The Hebrew historian makes Manasseh personally responsible for the religious syncretism which was introduced during his reign (II Kings, chap. 21). Manasseh, indeed, became in the records of Judah what Jeroboam the son of Nebat was in those dealing with Israel, the typical bad king.

But there is no need to suppose that the change was made on his initiative. It may well have been the work of all the responsible leaders of the nation. Resistance to Assyria was hopeless: the cost which must be paid for Judah's continued existence was some religious syncretism. And the leading men at the capital, reluctantly or willingly, bowed their necks and paid the price. But the price was a heavy one, since the effect of the policy was gravely mischievous in the life of Judah. Manasseh was compelled to break with some of the best elements in the nation, the men who had learned through their prophets that Yahweh was nothing if He was not supreme and that the God of Israel demanded an undivided allegiance. In a period when men conceived religion to be primarily concerned, not with a man's individual relation to God, but with the divine relation to the nation, their religious attitude profoundly influenced their political thought. All the men who emphasized the distinctive character of their national faith, and who were conscious that their religion had made Israel's life a thing apart from all the rest of the world, instinctively aimed at separating their people in every form of its life from the environing heathenism. They instinctively revolted against all political action which threatened to assimilate Israel to the world. Hosea had hated the thought that Israel should become 'mixed among the nations'. And since the king was the anointed of Yahweh, and what he did was done in his capacity as the nation's representative, for the king to set up a heathen altar beside that of Yahweh in the temple was for all Israel to apostatize. The breach between the court and the religious leaders appears to have gone so far as to result in religious persecution. At least it is said that Manasseh shed innocent blood very much (II Kings 21 : 16). We are not told who these slain men were or what constituted their guilt. But the attitude of the Hebrew historian to all the kings of the period makes it a fair inference that the men whom the court put to death were persecuted because of their religious convictions. How far, again, the king's action was prompted by opposition to the religious ideals of these men, and how far it could justify itself as directed against public acts to which their view of religion drove them, it is impossible to say. They may have attempted some movement against the foreign cult. To give way to them in their just hatred of the foreign altar would have involved a break with Assyria. And it could be urged against such a policy that to break with Assyria must bring with it the very thing which the religious party desired to avoid, the disappearance of Israel with all its distinctive life from the world. The period was one of those when religion and politics are closely intermixed. And any one who has tried to draw the line between political repression and religious persecution in the age of Queen Elizabeth will hesitate to pronounce too hastily on the merits and demerits of the two parties under Manasseh.

A further effect of this policy was to bring a temper of indifference in the minds of ordinary men. Many began to lose their sense of national pride and national dignity. They were tempted to follow the customs and ape the habits of the great Empire. Zephaniah (1 : 8), about the same period, speaks of men in Jerusalem who were pleased to imitate Assyrian dress. All the elements in Judah which had felt the restraint of their religious distinctiveness only to resent it felt themselves free to do as they pleased. They did not confine themselves to a compelled recognition of the Eastern cult of their conquerors, but gave way to baser and lower superstitions which had been repressed by the official religion. As the women in Egypt said to Jeremiah (44 : 15–18), it was better with us when we offered cakes to the queen of heaven. When the State paid tribute for its existence by a certain recognition of deities in which it did not believe, it is not surprising to find women who made outward profit the final test of their religious fidelity. Certain utterances of Jeremiah win new force when they are set in relation to such a temper among the men of his time. Judah, he says (2 : 13), has forsaken Yahweh, the fountain of life-giving water, the source of everything that makes it a people, and has hewn out cisterns which cannot even retain their flat water. They are worshipping gods in which no one even pretends to believe. The only result of such conduct is to lose the strength and the help of their own religion. For a faith which exacts and receives no obedience can never afford any help; cf. especially chaps. 2 and 3.

The other leading factor in the political life of Judah was the desire on the part of its rulers to come into closer relation to, and even to claim some authority over, the remanent Israelite inhabitants of the old Northern kingdom. Here it is necessary to recognize that the conquest of 721 did not sweep the country bare of its original population. It is said in II Kings 17 : 6 that the king of Assyria took Samaria and carried Israel away into Assyria. But it is not to be supposed that the king took the time or the trouble to gather the people out of every hamlet from Dan to Benjamin. What is much more likely is that he seized the leading men of the nation, who were likely to give trouble to the Assyrians, and deported them, so that Israel disappeared as a political entity from the country. And that is what Sargon reports himself to have done. For in his account of his treatment of Northern Israel he declares that he carried away 27,280 captives. These, however, cannot have represented the entire population of the new province, since, when Menahem in II Kings 15 : 19 f. levied 50 shekels of silver from every man who was capable of paying that sum, the amount he handed over to Tiglath-Pileser implies 60,000 men sufficiently well-to-do to meet the assessment. It is true that the kingdom of Hoshea, in whose reign the captivity took place, was smaller in extent than that of Menahem, for Galilee had been in great part lost to Israel. Yet, on the other hand, the 60,000 were not inhabitants or even householders, but men capable of paying a capital levy of 50 shekels. Hence, even though the kingdom was reduced by one-third, it is hardly possible to suppose that 27,280 composed the entire population of a district which only a short time previously contained 40,000 heads of houses able to pay this assessment.

Again, Nebuchadrezzar, when he carried Judah into captivity, not only left the peasants in the country, but was careful to provide them with small holdings (II Kings 25 : 22 ff.; Jer. 39 : 10; 40 : 5). It is true that Nebuchadrezzar was a Babylonian, while Sargon was an Assyrian, so that it may be rash to conclude that both rulers followed the same method. But the policy of the two empires in the matter of deportations must have been guided by the same aim, viz. to break the obstinate resistance of the little nations and to assimilate them into the larger empire. To do that it was only necessary to remove the leaders who were likely to maintain the national temper. Obviously, however, the only effect of sweeping away the entire population would have been to ruin the economic basis of the new province. For, though the conquerors were careful to import settlers from the heart of their empire, these men, accustomed to grow grain on the wide flats irrigated by the Tigris or to herd sheep in the hills beyond Nineveh, would find it difficult for some time to accommodate themselves to the alien conditions of Ephraim. Certainly they could never have paid the tribute Assyria exacted from all its provinces. But further, if the deportation implied the transference of whole peoples, the king of Assyria would have done more than upset the life of the province he had won. He would have equally disturbed the economic basis of the district which he emptied in order to make room for the Israelites.

Sargon, in his inscription, describes his treatment of Northern Israel after its conquest: 'I changed the government of the country and set over it a viceroy of my own. The tribute of the former king I imposed upon them.' The great king had sufficient experience to know that a country is only able to pay tribute when there are men to till its fields and when the cultivators know the local conditions.[1]

Not only did the backbone of the population consist of the old Israelite farmers and crofters, but the men were at a later date permitted to renew the practice of their cult. The province became infested with wild beasts. Troubled by the plague, the newcomers concluded that the creatures were sent by the *numen loci*, who was angry because he did not receive his customary offerings of sacrifices and firstfruits. Ignorant themselves of the right means to propitiate Yahweh, they petitioned that a priest be sent them from among the exiles, who might continue in the country the משפט, the correct ritual of the god of the land. Their request was found reasonable, and a priest was sent who settled at Bethel. The time when this took place is stated in II Kings 17 : 25 to have been 'at the beginning of their dwelling there'. And this may be regarded as trustworthy, because wild beasts were more likely to increase and to become a nuisance after the country had been harried and its condition disturbed by the Assyrian campaign.

The historian describes the new situation of the community in II Kings 17 : 28–33. His account has been supplemented in a later section, vv. 34 ff. These verses are plainly an addition, since they open with a remark about what

[1] Cf. further the discussion in Thomson, *The Samaritans*, pp. 15 ff.

prevails 'unto this day' and since they contain a deliberate contradiction of what precedes. Verse 33 declares that the men feared Yahweh, while v. 34 definitely states that they did not. Evidently the conclusion of the chapter reveals the attitude of the Jerusalem community after the complete breach between the returned exiles and the Samaritans. The stricter party which came to control Judaism insisted that its rival in the North fell away from Yahwism from the period of the settlement after the conquest. What, on the other hand, the original verses reveal is a condition of religious confusion and syncretism.

Some of the old Israelite shrines were transformed into heathen sanctuaries (v. 29). In others, which remained in the hands of Yahweh-worshippers, the men made shift at restoring their cult by appointing priests from among themselves (v. 32). But at Bethel a priest of the old line restored the cult which had been practised there when Amos appeared at that royal sanctuary. It was a makeshift, but it served as a centre from which there might come a renewal of the national and religious life of the North. Now, since this man was sent to restore the true Yahweh ritual, 'the manner of the god of the land', he must have brought with him what would serve the purpose of his mission. To carry out true sacrifice, he must have sacred vessels, and these must have been as legitimate and regular as he was a legitimate priest. To teach the correct manner of worship, he must have had some law which he could lay upon the people. There was none better fitted for his purpose than the old Code of Deuteronomy which had originally been promulgated in and had guided the worship and life of old Israel.[1]

[1] Cf. my book, *The Code of Deuteronomy*. I have seen no cause for withdrawing from any of the conclusions reached in that volume. Since its publication in 1924 there has been some discussion of the terms employed to describe the sanctuary 'which Yahweh may choose in any of the tribes'.

Northern Israel thus appears, giving a certain undefined recognition to Yahweh. The native Israelites acknowledge in Him the God of their fathers, but the new settlers acknowledge His claim to some reverence even on their part, since He remains to them the God of the land. Yet they maintain alongside His altars the cults of their own deities, and, in spite of the efforts of the stricter Yahweh-worshippers, these foreign cults infect the minds and influence the practice of the native Israelites. At a somewhat later date Manasseh of Judah was required to send a contingent of troops to support the invasion of Egypt by Assyria. Since this was demanded from a subject kingdom, it is more than probable that Israel, which was even more directly under the power of the Empire than Judah, must have supplied troops for the same campaign. The descendants of these men, when they were settled in a frontier garrison at Elephantine, had no hesitation about building a separate temple dedicated to Yahweh. They had been accustomed to worship at their own national shrine in Bethel, and their code of Deuteronomy contained no demand of centralization. But the cult which they instituted in their new temple contained the same syncretistic elements which had also appeared in Northern Israel. The

But there has been no effort to meet the cumulative proof there advanced that the code ignores centralization except in 12 : 1–7, and that its constant theme is Yahwism versus Baalism, not central sanctuary versus local sanctuaries.

I take the occasion to add a note to p. 160 of the volume, because it comes into relation to what has been said above. I pointed out that Deut. 17: 3 was glossed at the conclusion. The verse runs: 'and he has gone and served strange gods and worshipped them and the sun or the moon or the whole host of heaven which I did not command.' The syntax of the clause which defines the heavenly bodies is hopeless. It is the bad syntax of the glossator. Probably the reference to this worship was added for the special need of the Israelites after the fall of Samaria. Living among men who practised these cults, they needed a peculiar warning against this form of heathenism.

type of religion which the papyri from Elephantine have brought to light was natural in a colony all the members of which were not of pure Hebrew descent, and some of whose members were actually pagan.

The new situation of Northern Israel could not fail to have an influence on the policy of the court at Jerusalem. The two kingdoms had been rivals during all their separate existence, and their nearness to one another had made their mutual jealousy more intense. But now it was impossible for Israel any longer to stand in rivalry to its sister people. Instead of jealousy came sympathy and the sense of common cause against the heathenism which had destroyed one people and could at any hour destroy the other. The native Israelites were inevitably drawn to seek support from their brethren of the same stock, and especially to look for help in maintaining their faith. Judah was equally drawn, by sympathy and by ambition, to extend its influence over the North and to make closer the bonds of race and blood. Accordingly, even Hezekiah is reported to have sent messengers throughout Ephraim and Manasseh, who summoned the people to make pilgrimage to Jerusalem and celebrate one of the national festivals at the temple (II Chron., chap. 30). The chapter is not wholly reliable, for the Chronicler's representation of all Hezekiah's activity is full of impossible details. But we may trust this story of a mission to the North to have a kernel of historical truth, because its attitude to Ephraim is entirely different from that of the exiles which has appeared in II Kings 17 : 34 ff. The representation in Kings makes all the men of Ephraim heathen from the time of the conquest: that in Chronicles recognizes Samaria to be desirous and capable of taking part in passover celebrations. We may also trust it the more, because it shows the beginning of the movement towards centralization of the Yahweh-worship at Jerusalem. For it is interesting to note that Hezekiah appears, inviting the Ephraimites to a passover celebration, but not summoning. There is no hint of a law which made it illegitimate for them to go elsewhere.

Manasseh seems to have gone farther, and to have exercised some civil authority over the Northern province. Kittel even counts it probable that he was appointed governor over united Israel. The Empire could trust one who had shown himself from his accession a submissive vassal, and who, in his loyalty to his suzerain, had broken with and sternly put down those intransigent elements in his capital which demanded a rebellion in the name of religious purity. If this were the case, however, Manasseh must have worked on different lines in the North from those followed by Hezekiah. While his predecessor appealed to the old Israelite stock on the ground of religion, he sought to found his power in Samaria and in Jerusalem on an amalgam of the two faiths. This suggestion of Manasseh having been appointed governor over Israel and Judah may in turn serve to explain the remarkable story of his exile to Nineveh. Kittel, again, suggests that this was due to suspicion of Manasseh on the part of the king of Assyria.[1] He points out that the Empire was about this period seriously troubled by movements which appeared in Syria. The Assyrian may have suspected Manasseh of being mixed up with these movements, and may either have summoned him to answer for his conduct or have counted it safer to remove him from the neighbourhood of temptation. He was detained at Nineveh under close supervision, either until he had cleared himself of the charge or until the troubles which had caused his detention died down. After this he was allowed to return to Jerusalem. If we might accept this interpretation of the course of events, it would supply an explanation of the story of Manasseh's repentance in the book of Chronicles. The Hebrew historian has not altered the essen-

[1] *Geschichte des Volkes Israel*, ii. 510 and 514, note 2.

tial facts, but has given his own interpretation of them. He was not interested in the political events which led to Manasseh's captivity and release. What interested him was to find a reason for the long reign of a king who stood in bad preeminence as a sinner. Yahweh suffered even him to continue because of his late repentance.

Toward the close of Manasseh's reign, however, a profound change was impending, not only over Judah and Israel, but over the Eastern world. The huge Assyrian Empire began to show signs of breaking up. The conquest of Egypt, which seemed to prove it invincible, hastened its collapse. The destruction of the hitherto unconquered and magnificent capital stung the vanquished people into a sense of nationhood. Egypt slowly drew itself together after a defeat which had seemed to prostrate it.

What helped its recovery was the emergence of serious danger to Assyria nearer home. The successive campaigns against Egypt and the need for maintaining a garrison in the Nile Valley had withdrawn the strength and the attention of the Empire from a peril which was threatening Nineveh itself. Egypt, at some time which cannot be exactly dated, passed from being a vassal into the position of an ally. Part of the troubles which arose in the Euphrates Valley may be traced also to the apparent success of Assyria. On its northeastern frontier the Empire had finally broken Urartu or Armenia, which had long been a thorn in its side. Yet, while Urartu had often seriously annoyed its southern neighbour, it had also formed a buffer between the Mesopotamian plains and the wild tribes on the north. Its disappearance left that frontier open, and the Scythians swarmed in by the route of the Caucasus. And though the tribes soon became allies of the Empire, it was significant that the danger arising from their invasion was averted, not by their conquest, but by admitting them to alliance. Nineveh was only too glad to secure their support, and did not consider that a loyalty which was based on advantage was only likely to endure until some one else offered better terms for disloyalty. The power which might offer such terms was already rising. The Medes had thrown off the Assyrian yoke and succeeded in maintaining their independence. In Babylonia a movement was on foot which was to result in the rise of the Neo-Chaldean Empire. Assyria could only make head against its enemies by the uncertain support of Scythia and Egypt.

In the later half of the seventh century a stir was abroad in the world. 'A spring breath passed through the nations. Peoples groaning under a century-long oppression breathed again when the Assyrian Empire began to creak in all its joints, and men felt the coming collapse. Psammetichus in Egypt, Samassu-milkin in Babylonia, Josiah in Judah, are all representatives of the same movement.' It is necessary here to examine more closely its influence on the political and religious life of Israel.

II

THE REFORM UNDER JOSIAH

NOWHERE was the movement for liberty likely to be stronger than in the little kingdom at Jerusalem, because Judah possessed the most distinctive life in the old world, and had resented most deeply foreign control. But the movement was also certain to take its own form there, because the distinctive life of Judah was so deeply based on and so closely connected with its religion. Independence was as dear to the Jew as to other men. Independence meant for him what it meant for all men, freedom to live his own life, but his own life was more intimately bound up with his distinctive faith. What makes this side of the movement in Judah bulk more largely in our view is the character of the sources from which all our knowledge of the period is drawn. These are not secular but religious documents. The historian naturally saw the entire movement from one particular angle, and he has selected and reported events with a view to their bearing on the religious life of his nation. It is necessary to remember that there was another side and that all these events had also a political bearing.

It is natural, accordingly, to find that the reign of Josiah saw a complete change in the political attitude of Judah, and equally natural that in the Hebrew records this appears as a religious movement for reform. The reform is described in II Kings 22 and 23, and when its terms are examined it becomes clear that it ran along two main lines. Josiah carried out a thorough purification of temple and city, destroying every emblem of the foreign cults and especially of the Assyrian cult. The leaders of the nation reversed the religious policy of Manasseh and decreed that Yahweh alone was to be acknowledged at the national shrine. But the act involved more than religion: it was tantamount to a repudiation of Assyria and a declaration of Judah's independence. As such, it was made possible through the weakness of the Empire. Nineveh had already begun its final struggle with its rivals in the East. Babylon, with the help of the Medes, was pressing it hard in the Tigris Valley. It could only maintain itself at home by help from distant Egypt and by the dubious aid of the Scythians: but it was now powerless to maintain its authority in Syria.[1] The policy of the court could not fail to be popular in Judah; all the different elements in Judah's life could combine to support it, though from very different motives. Religious men who hated Assyria because its dominion brought with it a departure from strict Yahwism, patriots who longed for the great days of national independence when Judah lived its own life, the common man who resented the Empire's grinding tribute, could combine in a national effort to throw off the foreign yoke. Religion and patriotism worked hand in hand.

The other side of the movement, however, was the momentous step which resulted in profoundly changing the character of Judaism, viz. the centralization of worship at the temple in Jerusalem. Because this side of Josiah's reform appeared to concern itself merely with questions of the methods of worship within Judah itself, and to have no obvious relation to the peculiar conditions of the kingdom at the time, some scholars have construed it too narrowly. Seeing in it no more than a religious reform, they relegate it to the post-exilic period when the men of the return, under the influence of their priests, were peculiarly interested in the best methods of reconstituting the temple-worship. In their judgement Josiah aimed at nothing more than the purification of the

[1] Cf. C. J. Gadd, *The Fall of Nineveh.*

temple from all emblems of the Assyrian cult.[1] Yet the movement for centralization, equally with the purification of the temple, had its political side and formed part of a large plan which the decrepitude of Assyria made possible. By drawing all worship to the temple at Jerusalem, the leaders of the nation were seeking to extend their influence over Northern Israel and to unite that province, now derelict, to Judah. The weakness of Assyria made it possible to renew efforts which had already been initiated by Hezekiah and Manasseh. That Josiah did exercise practically sovereign authority over Israel is clear from the account of his conduct there in II Kings 23 : 15–20. The historian, who is specially interested in the king's religious attitude, brings prominently forward the fact that he broke down the high places in Samaria and its vicinity. But any man who was able to do this, which like the corresponding purification of the temple implied the rejection of Assyrian power, must have been exercising full authority over the country. Josiah and his court had seized the opportunity of Assyria's weakness in order to make themselves masters of this district which the Empire was helpless to defend. But, unlike Manasseh, who held it under Assyrian suzerainty and therefore sought to blend the two elements of the population in a syncretistic worship, they appealed to the purely Israelite inhabitants and sought to make Yahwism the official religion.

Yet it is significant to notice that Josiah was not content to destroy the high places in Samaria. These, being more or less tainted with heathenism, were destroyed in connexion with the effort to make Yahwism supreme in the land. He went farther, for he also destroyed the altar at Bethel (v. 15). Now this can only have been the sanctuary at which the priest who returned from Assyria had settled. The altar was

[1] Cf. e.g. Hölscher, *Z. A. W.* 1922, and Oestreicher, *Das Deuteronomische Grundgesetz*. Cf. also in reply Welch, *Z. A. W.* 1925, pp. 250–4.

a Yahweh altar. The fact appears from the curious way in which the king's deed is reported. For the historian seeks to identify this shrine with the older place of worship built by Jeroboam the son of Nebat, and attempts to cast upon it the odium of having been no more than a high-place, and a high-place which owed its existence to that king of evil memory. And he justifies his hero, the reforming Josiah, by an appeal to an old prophecy about the shrine, as if the king's act in itself looked suspicious. Yet he cannot in his honesty hide the fact that the altar at Bethel and the high-place of Jeroboam were two things. And his appeal to the ancient prophecy only shows that there were devout men at that time who were shocked and startled by Josiah's deed in desecrating a Yahweh altar. The altar Josiah destroyed was the one which the returned priest had erected, and which had drawn to itself the reverence and the patriotic feeling of the Northern tribes. And his act in destroying it was in line with the centralization of the cult at the temple. No centre of national or religious life was to be left in the country except Jerusalem. Josiah was seizing his opportunity to reunite Judah and Israel and to restore the old undivided kingdom of David with its capital at Jerusalem. And, as David had brought the ark, the emblem of Ephraim, into his new capital and sought to make that both the political and religious centre of all Israel, so Josiah sought to centralize the worship and the government of the kingdom. Only he went a little farther than David had gone. The earlier king had not attempted to make Jerusalem the unique religious shrine: Josiah judged it possible to make this further advance.

The conditions of the time in both kingdoms made the change practicable, though centralization involved a far-reaching change in the religious habits of the people. Inside Judah every local shrine had been wrecked by Sennacherib, and their priests had been carried into captivity. The reign of Manasseh, who in the interests of his policy was damping down strict Yahwism, would not see these restored. So far as Judah was concerned, to centralize worship in Jerusalem was merely to make the temple *de jure* what it already was *de facto*, the only Yahweh shrine in the land. In Israel, again, the process of centralization had already begun: the altar at Bethel was the only centre where a legitimate priest was functioning. To transfer worship from Bethel to Jerusalem was merely to carry farther what had already begun. And the advantage of association with Judah may well have outweighed, in the minds of many patriotic Israelites, the practical inconvenience of giving up their own sanctuary.

Because the king's policy was no mere effort at better internal administration of Hebrew worship, but had larger political issues behind it, it had also political repercussions. For it serves to explain why Josiah came to his death at Megiddo. Nineveh, with the help of the Egyptians and Scythians, had been able to hold its own against the combined Medes and Babylonians, but when the Scythians went over to the enemy, the situation became hopeless. The capital fell in 612, and, though a king named Asshur-u-ballit rallied the broken army at Harran, that city was also captured in 610. The Assyrian Empire disappeared from history. Before the collapse came Pharaoh-Necho hurried a great army into Syria in order to support his ally.[1] When he found that he had arrived too late, he halted his army and tried to make his position in Syria secure before the inevitable battle against the Babylonians. What precisely happened to bring about Josiah's death at Megiddo it is not easy to say. The Chronicler (II Chron. 35 : 20 ff.) makes the Jewish king

[1] Here the Chronicle published by Mr. Gadd serves to correct the account in II Kings 23 : 29, according to which the Pharaoh was advancing against the Assyrians. Necho was in alliance with Nineveh and was hastening to its help.

attack the Egyptians and fall in a pitched battle; he even makes Necho seek to dissuade his adversary from interference. Yet it is difficult to believe that a petty king of Judah would attack without outside help the whole weight of the Egyptian army: and it is still more difficult to believe that Necho remonstrated with his enemy for the gratuitous attack. In my judgement there was no battle. Necho with his irresistible force was able to summon Josiah to explain his attitude, and, finding this unsatisfactory, he put him to death.[1]

In any case Necho found it necessary to clear Josiah out of his way. And the mere fact that Judah had denounced its allegiance to Assyria by the purification of the temple seems insufficient to account for this act. In the great stakes for which Egypt was playing, it made little difference though the city of Jerusalem had fallen away from Nineveh. Some larger cause is needed to explain Necho's action. And that can be found in Josiah's effort, and successful effort, to exercise control over Northern Israel. By this action on his part he had made himself master of all the hill-country of Ephraim. Now a power which held the heights above Esdraelon and above the coast-road was a dangerous enemy to an army which, in the event of defeat before the Babylonians, must stream home to Egypt along that route. Whether there was a battle at Megiddo or merely a military execution, the Egyptian was making sure of his line of retreat before advancing to Carchemish and to the fight for the mastery of Syria which must take place there. And he needed to make sure of his line of retreat, because Josiah had a dangerous hold of Northern Israel.

The two sides of Josiah's reform can be recognized as not

[1] For a full discussion of the situation cf. Gressmann, *Z. A. W.* 42, N. F. pp. 157 ff.; Welch, *Z. A. W.* 1925, pp. 255 ff.; Cannon, *Z. A. W.* 1926, pp. 63 ff.

only compatible with each other and suitable for the period and its conditions. It can also be seen that they formed together one large and consistent plan. The aim of the court was to seize the opportunity which the collapse of Assyria brought with it and to restore the independence of the kingdom. The removal of the heathen emblems in the city was the outward evidence that they had broken with the Empire. But the men also sought to restore the unity of all Israel under one political head and with one religious centre. The centralization of the cult at Jerusalem was part of this effort. On its political side the attempt completely failed. The death of Josiah at Megiddo put an end to all hopes of restoring the undivided and independent nation. Even without that catastrophe it may be doubted whether the hope could ever have been fulfilled. Babylon was taking over the world-empire from fallen Nineveh, and was scarcely likely to leave Jerusalem to deal as it pleased with a former province of that Empire. On its religious side, however, the effort to make Jerusalem the centre of worship for the whole country had a considerable success, even in the period of Josiah. That is proved in other ways than by the gathering of all Israel to the joint celebration of passover, on which the historian dwells with unction in his account of the king's reign.

For there is mention in Jer. 41 : 4 ff. of men from the districts of Ephraim coming on pilgrimage to Jerusalem even after the destruction of the city. If they continued to do this in spite of the ruin of the temple, it must have been because the practice dated much farther back. What makes their deed more significant is that these were ordinary peasants who came of their own free will. It was possible in Josiah's time to engineer a pilgrimage from north and south alike to the passover at Jerusalem. But there was no one to bring pressure to bear on these pilgrims. Again, Zechariah

(7 : 1–7) speaks of men from Bethel, who consulted the priests and prophets of Jerusalem on the subject of whether they should fast in the seventh month. The North was looking for guidance on uncertain questions to the authorities at the central sanctuary. From the time of Josiah's reform Jerusalem took a new position, not only in Judah, but also in Israel.[1]

But the aim of uniting the life and worship of the two kingdoms was not merely pursued by means of the centralization of the cult at the temple. At this period the sacred literature and traditions of the North were brought to Jerusalem and incorporated with those of Judah. The two sets of documents received equal authority within a united Judaism, and their combination was intended to serve the purpose of reunion. It is necessary to develop this position at some length, because it may appear to many startlingly novel. It is of course a familiar fact that the accounts of the origins of Israel, the two documents called J and E in Genesis, are derived from Judah and Israel or Ephraim respectively. But while some effort has been made to determine the date at which, little attention has been paid to the purpose for which, the two were combined into one whole. Yet the matter is of real significance and requires explanation. On the one hand, the combination has been carried out with great deliberation. So carefully has it been done that it is confessedly impossible to separate with entire certainty the different strands which have been woven together into the new texture. Accordingly, it is no sufficient explanation to say that the Northern document drifted into Judah after

[1] Oestreicher relegates centralization to the post-exilic period on the ground that it only became a practicable policy after the return. He has overlooked the conditions which show it to have been practicable; cf. p. 19 f. But he has also overlooked these facts which show it to have been actual.

the fall of Samaria, and came into the hands of some one who was sufficiently interested in the subject to unite it with his native traditions. The work has been carried out with deliberation to serve some special purpose. But, further, the character of the two sources must be recognized, when any effort is made to account for their combination into one document. This is not a case of two national histories written by private individuals, of which a new historian made use when he set himself to draft his own composition. Each document separately was authoritative, and had been produced to serve a public religious purpose. When they came to be combined, the resultant whole bore the same stamp and was intended to serve the same purpose. What each presented and what the combined account presents was the history of the origins of the Jewish people through the guidance of its God. And the united account presents, with deliberate insistence and with consummate art, the story of how Israel came to be a nation on the basis of its religion and how the controlling factor in all its life was its religion. Such a work was written, not by an interested historian, but by the acknowledged religious leaders of the people, to guide Israel's thought on its past. And the men who did the work had sufficient authority to make their new document take the place of the two which they combined. References in the Psalms and the historical books make it clear that there were other traditions about the early history of Israel besides those which have been preserved in the books of Genesis and Exodus. But the official account has driven these from the field.

Yet the E story of Israel's origin is only a small part of the literature which has had its source in Northern Israel. Thus there are psalms in the psalter which clearly derive from Ephraim. Peters claims that one of the minor psalters has been taken bodily over from the sanctuary at Dan, for the service of which it was originally written.[1] The claim stands in need of much more proof than has been supplied. Yet the suggestion about certain psalms having come from particular sanctuaries and of our psalter being composed of these separate collections opens up a fresh line of approach to the question of the minor psalters which appear in the larger book. The derivation, too, of a number of psalms from North Israelite sources may serve to throw light on the preference certain psalms show for the divine name Elohim. But, while Peters's suggestion must be regarded as unproved meantime, and while no single minor book can yet be proved to be of Northern origin, there can be little doubt that two psalms, 80 and 81, are Ephraimitic.[2] For the purpose of the present discussion the presence of two Northern psalms in the Psalter is sufficient. What makes the matter more important is that one of these, psalm 81, has been employed in connexion with a public festival. That implies that the official liturgies of the North have been drawn upon, and hymns which had their origin there have been incorporated into the official psalter of Judaism. Such a thing could not have come about by accident, nor can it be due to the fact that these Northern hymns fell into the hands of some man or men who counted them worthy of being preserved. It must have been deliberately done by those who were responsible for guiding the worship of the nation. And these men must have had a strong motive for taking this action.

Again, the books of Kings are a composite narrative down to the period of the fall of Samaria.

The historian not only includes sections which have been taken over from the Northern kingdom, such as the account of Ahab's reign and the stories of Elijah and Elisha: these

[1] *The Psalms as Liturgies*, p. 10.

[2] Cf. Gunkel, *Komm.* ad loc., and Welch, *Expository Times*, 1927.

were patently written where the events they relate happened. He also refers his readers for full information to the chronicles of the kings of Israel, and so shows that he knew of sources which were in existence and accessible to the men for whom he wrote. Here also Israelite material has been deliberately incorporated into the longer narrative of the history of the united kingdom. And this has been done by one who was no mere annalist, but by a man who was marshalling his material to serve a definite end. For the compiler did not pretend to include the whole of the records of either kingdom. He knew that there was much information which he had omitted, and, since some of his readers might be interested in subjects which he had lightly passed over, he referred them to accessible sources. He himself was writing a record for religious edification. He reveals this by the subjects on which he expands no less than by the subjects on which he sends his readers to other sources. He also shows it by his judgements on the character and conduct of the successive kings. And the standard he applies to them all makes clear his point of view. The men deserved credit or discredit, according as they helped forward or hindered the great reform of the centralization of worship. The story of the two kingdoms has been combined into one narrative in order to serve a religious purpose, even to serve an ecclesiastical propaganda.

Not only has a large amount of Israelite literature been amalgamated with that of Judah. Certain books of North-country provenance have been taken over bodily. With the exception of the section 1 : 1–2, 5, the book of Judges, since it only mentions the tribe of Judah in order to remark that it was ready to sell Samson to the Philistines, cannot have been written by a Judean. The books of Hosea and Amos must have been collected by the people to whom the oracles were addressed. And as prophetic books, histories, and liturgies have been taken over from Israel and made part of the sacred literature of Judaism, it is natural to suppose that the law-books were not differently treated. The suggestion which I made in 1924 that the code in Deuteronomy represents the law or use of a Northern shrine has confirmed itself through closer study of the material.[1]

The religious literature of the North has been combined with that of Judah, and, as the case of J and E proves, this has been done with deliberate care. It remains to seek a likely date for the amalgamation. It could not have been carried out earlier than 721, the year of Samaria's fall, for Israel would retain its own literature so long as it maintained its independent life, nor would Judah have any inclination to recognize the work of the rival kingdom. Nor were the returned exiles very likely to give countenance to material which derived from such a tainted source, even if it were easy to account for its survival through those troubled years. The religious guides of the Jerusalem community early quarrelled with their Northern neighbours, whom they denounced as heretics. It is inconceivable that these men admitted into the official Psalter hymns which had their origin from an Israelite sanctuary. The only date which remains open is the period from 721 to *circa* 610, the year of Megiddo. After Megiddo, conditions in Jerusalem became too disturbed and the minds of men too gravely concerned with the troubles of the time for such work to be pursued.

The amalgamation of the sacred literature of North and South must have been carried out by the men who were guiding affairs in Jerusalem between the accession of Hezekiah and the death of Josiah. Now this is precisely the period in which the Hebrew records state that the Judean kings were seeking to extend their influence over the Northern kingdom. In particular, these records ascribe to two of the

[1] Cf. *Code of Deuteronomy*, pp. 190 ff.

kings of that period, Hezekiah and Josiah, an effort to centralize worship at Jerusalem. The two movements were separate parts of one large plan. The incorporation of the sacred literature of Israel was deliberately carried out in order to win over Northern Israel to the surrender of their local shrine or shrines, and to make easier for them the recognition of the primacy of Jerusalem and its priesthood. There was to be again one nation with a single religious and political centre and one set of sacred books to guide its religious life.

Hitherto little attention has been given in Introductions to the Literature of the Old Testament to the date at which, and none at all has been given to the purpose for which, the reception of the Northern books was carried out. Yet the two questions hang intimately together. The matter is too large and too novel to be adequately dealt with here. But one or two illustrations may be given of the way in which the men who combined the Israelite and Judean documents left the marks of their work, and these betray the purpose which governed them in making the combination.

Skinner[1] remarked on the singular fact that, while J does not hesitate to speak of the patriarchs building altars in Palestine, it nowhere records that they offered sacrifice. Yet the same document does not hesitate to record a sacrifice by Noah and to provide him with clean beasts for the purpose. The Judean writer has the exclusive claims of the temple in view. On the sacred soil of Palestine no other place of sacrifice was legitimate. The man who combined the histories of Judah and Israel makes Jeroboam, who founded the sanctuaries of Bethel and Dan, the king who made Israel to sin. His standard, too, for the character of the successive kings of Judah is their conduct towards the high places. They were good or evil, according as they helped or hindered the movement toward centralization at Jerusalem. From the

[1] Commentary on Genesis, *I. C. C.*

time when Solomon built the temple, he calls the capital the place which Yahweh has chosen out of all the tribes of Israel (I Kings 8 : 16). When the schism of Jeroboam took place, he makes a prophet reserve one tribe to Rehoboam for the sake of Jerusalem, the city which Yahweh chose out of all the tribes of Israel (I Kings 11 : 32). It was only the political centre which was moved to Samaria: Jerusalem remained the unique shrine in all Israel. The same description of the temple as the shrine chosen out of all the tribes of Israel appears in the introductory section of the code of Deuteronomy (12 : 1–7), and is the only statement in the entire book which demands centralization of worship. This section, which has no connexion with what follows and which can be otherwise proved to be of later date, has been added by the men who edited the books of Kings.[1]

Finally there are three or four passages in Hosea which have generally been regarded as interpolations. These have been relegated to the post-exilic period, but in their present form are wholly unsuited to that date. In order to make them suitable to this late date they have been rewritten and forced into agreement. Here again the passages, read as they stand, agree best with the theory of the book having been edited to serve the centralization.[2]

The compilers who united the sacred literature of Israel and Judah were careful to countersign their work with the religious reform of their time. The possible date for such a task and the purpose which it served agree in setting it down to the time of Josiah. It was natural that the religious leaders of Israel, after the fall of their capital and kingdom, should bring the archives of their nation into safety in Jerusalem. It was equally natural that men who were seeking to

[1] Cf. for a full discussion of the question my *Code of Deuteronomy*, pp. 57 ff., followed by an article, *Z. A. W.* 1925, pp. 250 ff.

[2] Cf. for the full evidence my article 'Archiv für Orientforschung', 1927.

reunite the divided people should combine the literatures of its two branches into one.

If now the Code of Deuteronomy was originally the law of Northern Israel, which was brought for safety to Jerusalem, it becomes easier to understand the story of its discovery in the temple under Josiah. The account is and always has been difficult to explain. The idea of a wholesale fabrication by the priesthood of the capital must be given up. Apart altogether from its offensiveness to all moral feeling, an offensiveness which is not seriously lessened by appeal to the different standards of two widely separate periods, it cannot be said to fit the facts. A document which was composed or even compiled by priests to enforce the specific reform of centralization could never have borne the character of the book of Deuteronomy. For, however widely students may differ as to whether the Code (apart from 12 : 1–7) contains any reference to centralization, one thing is clear. It did not succeed in making that plain. And, on the other hand, it did succeed in making plain that the commanding interest of the legislators was to avoid contamination of their nation's religion by the practices of the surrounding Canaanites.[1] No body of men who wrote a law to enforce the principle of centralization could have produced the book of Deuteronomy which we possess to-day. Nor could they have used it as it stands, unless their adoption of it had been intended to serve another purpose.

Again, it has been suggested that Deuteronomy was a foundation deposit which came to light during the repairs Josiah effected on the temple. Yet the idea of burying a law which has nothing to say about the building of a temple, but which enters into full details on how a nation shall conduct war, worship, litigation, and marriage, seems a quaint

[1] Even Budde, in his long discussion, *Z.A.W.* 1926, pp. 177 ff., must recognize that this is the purpose which dominates the Code of Deuteronomy.

procedure in any nation. Israel had the practice of inscribing its laws on great stones and of reading them at its festivals—which seems a more rational habit. Nor does the appeal which has been made to the Assyrian and Babylonian custom of laying such deposits at the foundations of their temples help very much.

Mr. Driver of Oxford has courteously come to the assistance of one who is no Assyriologist by supplying the following statement, which defines the Assyrian practice in these matters.

'Almost through their history the Assyro-Babylonian practice was to put a brief inscription . . . containing the name of the god to whom the temple was built, followed by the king's name and style, variously short or full. They ran roughly as follows: To such and such a god, so and so, son of so and so, king or patesi, of such and such a town, district, or country this temple was built. There was hardly any change till Nabopolassar introduced the practice of putting in cylinders bearing often quite long inscriptions. These stated the god to whom the temple was built and gave the king's titles, &c., but they bore also a history of his building operations up to date (very rarely adding any events of secular interest), and closed with a brief prayer to the god in question for the protection of the king (and his family, &c.).'

And further, the law is said to have come to light during the course of repairs at the temple. 'Repairs' hardly suggests an operation which went so far as to lay bare the foundation. In Jerusalem, where men built of stone, it can never have been so easy and must rarely have been so necessary to go down to a foundation as it was in dealing with the brick structures of Mesopotamia.

If, however, a copy of the Code of Deuteronomy was brought to Jerusalem along with the other religious literature of the Northern kingdom, it was natural that it should be deposited in the temple. No immediate use was found for it, so that it fell aside and its very existence was forgotten until it came to light again at the time of the repairs. By this time some of the other documents from Samaria had been combined with those of Judah. When the code came to light, it too was adopted and acknowledged to form part of the Judean law. A code which insisted throughout on preserving the nation's allegiance to Yahweh alone could further the aims of the reform, so far as that was seeking to purify the capital and the country from all heathen emblems. But, just as the reformers have retouched the other documents by adding to the records of the history and to the book of Hosea evidence of their interest in the question of centralization, so, before issuing the Code of Deuteronomy, they countersigned it by the addition of the little section 12 : 1–7, the one section in the book which demands the unique sacredness of their temple.

The one problem which remains—and that remains on any interpretation of II Kings 22, though it is generally ignored—is the attitude taken by Huldah the prophetess. Why did she warn a king, who was busily engaged on the task of purifying the temple, with the need for doing this very thing? And why did she warn him that he might save himself by his obedience, but need not seek to save his people? It would be easy to frame theories on the subject, and impossible to prove any of them. For the remarkable feature of the following narrative is that Josiah proceeded to gather all Israel together from north and south to the first united passover celebration at Jerusalem. At the restored and purified temple, where Yahweh again reigned in His lonely majesty, and according to the peculiar rite of their national faith, a united people found its centre and sought to renew the kingdom of David. And the reformers did this, after Huldah had said in the divine name, 'my wrath is kindled against this place, and it shall not be quenched'.

III

JEREMIAH'S CALL AND COMMISSION

JEREMIAH was a member of a priestly family which possessed land at Anathoth, a Benjamite village some four miles north of Jerusalem. The place and circumstances of his birth gave him certain advantages in thinking about religion. Thus he belonged by sympathy as well as by descent to the Northern kingdom. In the condition and fate of that part of the nation he shows a constant and deep interest. A larger number of his oracles are concerned with, and even addressed to, his fellow-countrymen than has always been recognized. And when he speaks about them or to them, he does not think about the men as in exile: they are his neighbours, still settled in their own country. In his own way he was as profoundly interested in the remanent Israelites at Samaria as the courtiers of Josiah or the king himself.

Accordingly he is saturated in the thought and teaching of Hosea, the most spiritual of all the prophets and the fine flower of North Israelite piety. The resemblance appears not only in the use of language and figures: it extends to fundamental ideas on God and His relation to Israel. In the following chapter on Jeremiah's primary conceptions of religion it will be possible to point out how great was the debt which he owed to his predecessor.

Through being a member of a priestly family, the prophet was reared in the atmosphere of religious tradition. That again was a real advantage. Any man who undertakes to reform something is very much the better of knowing both the form and the purpose of the thing he proposes to reform. Ignorance is never less helpful than when it accompanies a reformer. But especially is this true in the case of religion. He who sets himself to interpret or re-interpret their faith to the people of his time will fulfil the difficult task more fruitfully if he knows the faith from the inside and does not merely judge it by its effects or from the outside. One recalls how the most efficient reformer the world has known was Luther, an Augustinian monk. Because he knew the greatness and sacredness of the matters with which he dealt, he was never content to reject, he always sought to renew. Accordingly he left a church, not a ruin.

Yet Jeremiah did not belong to the professional priesthood at Jerusalem. There, too, it is possible to recognize a certain advantage. He was free from the narrowness of vision and the timidity which are always apt to creep over an official caste. He had a wider outlook than the men who were working in association with the court at the question of Judah's religion. And what he did see for truth he could utter and obey with the singleness of mind which is more generally found among men who have not to weigh the effect of any change on their party.

Five years before the Josianic reform, the man with this training and outlook became a prophet. Whatever else that experience meant to him or brought with it, it implied at least that he believed himself to have entered into personal relation to Yahweh, the God of Israel. The divine will which expressed the divine character became the final norm which determined what should be the relation between Yahweh and Israel, between Yahweh and himself. Everything in the nation's life and religion must be referred to this standard. As he himself expressed it (6:27), he was set among the people to examine and test their conduct as a silver refiner deals with his material. He can and must do this, because he is a prophet appointed to the task by God. Yet his prophetic commission is no official privilege, which is once conferred and cannot be withdrawn. Only if he wholly surrenders himself to the divine guidance and makes clear the difference between good and evil, can he be like Yahweh's mouth-piece (15 : 19). He himself in his personal life must maintain the standards he is commanded to enforce. His right to speak for God rests on the intimacy of his knowledge of the divine will for men. It was his function to measure the actions of men and especially the laws which governed their conduct and their religion, not by their immediate and practical usefulness, not by whether they could appeal to patriotism and national honour, but by their agreement with the only enduring standard, the mind of Yahweh.

That divine mind was not something which had been revealed for the first time to him: it had been constantly revealed through all Israel's past for the guidance and help of the people. Jeremiah has, with a certain justice, been regarded as the most uncompromising individualist among the prophets. It would be more correct to say that he brings out, more clearly than his predecessors, the individualism which was latent in the prophetic attitude. But this individualism on his part merely involves that to him the relation to Yahweh is far too intimate to be adequately expressed under the forms of a national religion. God deals with souls which turn to Him. Yet this feature of his teaching does not imply any break with the long past of Yahweh's dealing with Israel or with that which other prophets have learned of His mind and will. Jeremiah not only represents a prophetic tradition: his constant use of Hosea's ideas is enough to prove his debt to the past. He shows himself conscious of it, for he does not hesitate to appeal to this tradition in support of his own position. Nowhere does this attitude appear more clearly than in chap. 28, where he was confronted by another prophet, Hananiah. Men in Jerusalem were debating whether it was wise to join a league which certain neighbour states were forming against Babylon. Hananiah was urging the king to join the league, and, appealing to a divine revelation, had declared that Yahweh had broken the yoke of the king of Babylon and that rebellion would bring success. This advice ran counter to Jeremiah's own conviction. But, since he could not claim to have a direct revelation on the subject, he did not venture to put forward his personal view. He questioned Hananiah's position on the general ground that the attitude it took was unlike that of all the older prophets. 'The earlier prophets who preceded you and me prophesied against many countries and great kingdoms about war, disaster, and pestilence: but, as for the prophet who foretells peace, when his message comes true, it will be recognized that he has really been sent by Yahweh.' Jeremiah is there claiming to be in the line of prophetic tradition, for he states that any oracle which breaks with this tradition stands in need of special confirmation.

Every reader, too, of the book of Jeremiah must have noted the frequency of the recurrent phrase: Yahweh sent all his servants the prophets, rising early and sending them. And while the sentence often belongs to additions to the original, the fact that it was glossed on Jeremiah proves the glossators to have recognized how well it suited his peculiar attitude of mind. Nor is this conviction surprising in the case of a prophet who derived from Northern Israel. For the law-book of his nation had already recognized that conditions might arise in which it would be difficult to determine whether a prophet's word could be accepted as a divine revelation. Deuteronomy had pronounced that the criterion by which a prophet must be judged was his agreement with the fundamental principles of the national faith, and had said that his task was to continue the traditions of Moses (Deut. 13 : 2–6; 18 : 15–22).

It is not difficult to see why the common element in prophecy must have risen before the minds of later prophets. The God who revealed Himself and His mind to Jeremiah was the same God who had made known His will to Hosea and Amos. And since His will was the expression of His character, it could not change. From the beginning He had spoken to Israel, and He was speaking now to Jeremiah. The message must be the same.

It is a fortunate circumstance that we possess so full an account of the prophet's call. The account may even be derived from Jeremiah himself, since the chapter is written throughout in the first person. If so, the curt directness of the language used deserves attention. Unlike Isaiah, the prophet has nothing to say about the date at which this supreme event in his life occurred, nor does he spare time to describe the circumstances in which he was placed. It is enough for him to say: the word of Yahweh came to me. And in this character of the bearer of a word which was not his own he found his justification and his encouragement. Thus, when the priests and prophets pronounced him worthy of death, because he had dared to prophesy against the temple, the only plea he entered was: Yahweh sent me to prophesy against this house and against this city all the words which you have heard. But, as for me, behold I am in your hand; do with me as is good and right in your eyes (26 : 12, 14). And when he was depressed by the unwearied hostility to which he was exposed, he rallied his fainting courage on the message: if thou surrender to me and I restore thee, thou shalt be my servant (15 : 19). His call was one to utter the word of Yahweh.

Since the prophet's call was to speak a divine word, his equipment for this task and the scope of his commission were equally furnished by Yahweh. God, who summoned his servant and who gave him his commission, formed him from the womb for nothing less, and appointed him to be a prophet to the nations (1 : 5). The greatness of the task is in close relation to the intimacy and thoroughness of the preparation given to the man who is to fulfil it. He who is to undertake a world-mission must be equipped with a quite peculiar care. But the wide scope of this commission, its abrupt announcement at the beginning of a career, and its supposed contrast with the view which earlier prophets took of their work as confined to Israel (cf. Amos 1 : 1), have led many to suspect and therefore to change the last words of the verse. Stade proposed to alter 'the nations' into 'my nation',[1] and thus to bring Jeremiah's commission into agreement with what he believed to have been the scope of Amos's work. He failed, however, to explain why Israel came to be described by a word which is elsewhere reserved for foreign nations.[2] Duhm[3] boldly but arbitrarily strikes out the word, calling it a late gloss, but in a fine comment full of insight makes a reader wonder what period and what conditions produced so worthy a glossator. Study of the numerous glosses which have been added elsewhere to the original text of the book does not increase a student's respect for these late scribes.

The Masoretic text gives no sign of having been tampered with, for none of the great versions departs from it. And when the verse in Amos, with which the wide scope of this commission is held to contrast, is examined, it becomes evident that the description of Amos as sent to prophesy concerning Israel is no part of his original oracles. It belongs to the later heading, which cannot be reckoned of equal authority

[1] Reading לְגוֹיִי for לְגוֹיִם

[2] There are two passages in which Israel is described as Yahweh's גוי, viz. Zeph. 2 : 9; Ps. 106 : 5. But in both cases the word is parallel to another, עם and נחלה, and has obviously been selected for the sake of variety in the parallel clauses.

[3] *Commentary on Jer.*, ad. loc.

with the rest of the book. And by the very irony of circumstance this apparent limitation set to the prophet's work is immediately followed by a series of oracles concerned with foreign nations.

At the forefront of Amos's message stands the doom pronounced against Damascus, Moab, Ammon. Evidently the prophet himself did not believe that he had no function to fulfil toward the world beyond Israel, since he pronounced judgement in Yahweh's name on all the peoples with whom his own nation came into contact, and yet did not judge them merely on the ground of their conduct to Israel. Nor is the reason for this far to seek, since to speak in Yahweh's name meant for Amos to speak in the name of the God of righteousness. Now righteousness is not a perquisite of Israel: it belongs to man, at once his glory and his judge. The earlier prophet's conception of the word of Yahweh which it was his to deliver was widening out the terms of his commission. What was thus latent in Amos because of the character of the God in whose name he spoke has become patent in his successor. The principle which was implicit in the older message has become explicit; and Jeremiah was merely bringing it to its clear issue, when he was conscious from the beginning that he had a mission to mankind. There was, said Amos, but one will which controlled the world and which determined the law for the conduct of all men: and that was the mind of Yahweh. He had made it known in the life of humanity, dimly perhaps but yet clearly enough to bring them in as guilty when Yahweh judged the world. Damascus, Edom, Moab, were thus condemned. But the divine mind which was only dimly made known to the other nations was clearly revealed to Israel through its prophets. Into this succession Jeremiah has been called.

That Jeremiah did not limit the task of his predecessors to Israel is clear from the attitude he took to the prophet

Hananiah. The larger conception of the prophetic function appears in his remark: there have been prophets before you and me, and they prophesied about many countries and great kingdoms (28 : 8). The difference between himself and his opponent turned round the content and character of the prophetic utterances, not round their scope. Jeremiah believed that his predecessors were able to recognize and did recognize that the truths they uttered and the principles they held were valid for all mankind. If the earlier men had been able to recognize this and had therefore spoken about the fate of alien peoples, to the later generation which had become more conscious of the unity of the world and of human destiny through the rise of the great empires, it might well have become clear that the laws which controlled that destiny were not parochial.

But Jeremiah was not content to say that he knew himself to be sent on a mission to mankind. He added that he was called even before his birth to the prophetic office. The two features in his call must have some connexion and must even be integrally related to each other. Duhm has another fine comment on the saying, in which he speaks of the singular and helpful simplicity life must present to any man who knew his aim from the beginning. He who is convinced that from his birth there is only one task for him is delivered at once from the mistaken false starts which waste the efforts of other men. Yet the comment merely proves that one false step in exegesis is bound to bring another after it. Duhm has cut out the reference to the nations and to the mission of Jeremiah to mankind. He must accordingly connect the fact of the prophet having been called from his birth with his hesitation in undertaking the task on account of his youth. That is, he must turn the passage upside down and make the encouragement introduce the hesitation which it was meant to remove. In reality, it is the greatness of the commission, the call to be a prophet to the world, which produces Jeremiah's dismay. How can he who is but a youth face this task?

What then is the connexion between the sense of being a prophet with a mission to humanity and the conviction of having been set apart to this task from birth? Surely this, that what qualifies him for his life-task is his naked humanity. A man's nationality is decided by his birth. He becomes qualified to speak to his own people through the fact that he shares its common life. He can speak to ideals which he understands, because they are also his. He can rebuke failures, which are also in his blood. But what he gains through sympathy marks also his limitation. He belongs to the people of which he thus forms a part. The prophet to the nations is set apart to his calling, before he has been born into any nation. He does not represent the will of God for Israel alone. To do that, it were an advantage to be chosen after he had become a Jew with a Jew's peculiar outlook. But he represents the will of God for mankind, and to do that it is sufficient that he should be a man. His qualification for his task corresponds with his message; and since his message is for humanity his qualification is equally wide.

Cornill[1] has pointed out that the same correspondence between function and qualification appears in two of the Servant-songs in Deutero-Isaiah. The servant of Isa. 42 : 6 describes his call and his commission: 'I Yahweh have called thee in righteousness and held thine hand, have formed (יצר) thee and given thee for a covenant of people, for a light of nations'. Even more definitely are the two ideas brought together in 49 : 5 f.: 'now saith Yahweh who formed (יצר) me from the womb to be his servant to bring Jacob again to him . . . yea he saith it is too light a thing for thee to be my servant to raise up the tribes of Jacob and to restore

[1] *Commentary on Jer.*

the preserved of Israel. I will also give thee for a light of nations that my salvation may reach to the ends of the earth.' Here also the commission is to all humanity, and the qualification for fulfilling it is purely human. When one recognizes how deeply Jeremiah's thought has influenced the attitude of Deutero-Isaiah, it is difficult to believe that the correspondence between the two passages is accidental. In each case the character of the call is brought into close connexion with, and answers to the scope of the commission; and both in turn depend upon and are related to the greatness of Yahweh who, through call and commission alike, is about to fulfil His mighty purpose for the world. As men's thought of their God grew, and as it was recognized that His purpose dealt with all the world, the prophets' sense of their function also grew. Their commission came to be one to all humanity, and their qualification for their task became broadly and ultimately human.

Because of the greatness of the task to which he was summoned, Jeremiah hesitated to undertake it. Isaiah had hesitated to take upon himself a similar duty when Yahweh called for service, but he held back on the very different ground that he was a man of unclean lips who dwelt among a people of unclean lips. Since, however, Jeremiah had learned that Yahweh had set him apart from his birth to a special task for which he did not volunteer, he dared not plead any unfitness of this character. For him to have entered such a plea would have been to doubt the divine wisdom which had thus selected him. What appalled him was the vastness of the task which was laid upon him. To him in his inexperience it seemed impossible that he should bring it to any worthy end. The reply to his protest contained no remission of the task to which he was being sent, but rather a renewed insistence on the very feature which had made him shrink from it. 'Say not, I am young, but unto all to whom

I send thee thou shalt go and all that I command thee thou shalt utter. Only have no fear before them, for I am with thee to deliver thee.' Those of whom the prophet is bidden to have no fear are the men to whom he has been sent, whose number and power might well have dismayed him. Jeremiah had pleaded in natural timidity that he in his youth and inexperience could not hope to fulfil this wide and tremendous commission. Yahweh inexorably reiterated His command. He must go to all to whom his God gave him a message, and he must utter this message in its entirety, keeping nothing back. Both the hesitation of the prophet and the renewal of the demand are best understood when the scope of the commission is recognized to be world-wide.

Thereupon Yahweh is said to have touched the prophet's lips in token that He has put His words into His servant's mouth. The connexion with what has preceded is not hard to see. It is no commission of his own on which Jeremiah is sent, nor is the message he is called to deliver one of his own creation. What he has to utter is that word of Yahweh which is operative of itself, since, when it goes forth from Him, it cannot return void but must accomplish all His will. From this hour the prophet is to utter this word. He has a commission which may well, to him who believes that it has been entrusted to him, bring fear lest he fail to fulfil it aright, but the assured possession of which removes all other fear. With this endowment also the prophet is clothed in an august and awful authority. He is not merely a man apart; he is one set in authority,[1] because he is the bearer of Yahweh's words, valuations, judgements.

How widely does this authority extend and to whom are these words of Yahweh to come? 'Over the nations and over the kingdoms to overturn and to build up.' Naturally Duhm

[1] The word used הפקדתיך is employed of Joseph in Egypt (Gen. 39 : 4), when Joseph was practically appointed viceroy under the Pharaoh.

with all who, like him, are unable to suppose that Jeremiah could conceive himself to be a prophet to the nations, strikes out the whole verse (v. 10), because it expresses the same idea in another form. The words to him embody a view of the functions of prophecy and of the word of Yahweh which is late and Messianic. It may not be unjust to suggest that Duhm really means late, because Messianic. It is taken for granted that Jeremiah could not utter anything which can be described as Messianic. But this quiet assumption of certain postulates is exactly what vitiates and makes arid a great deal of Old Testament criticism to-day. Fundamental to Duhm and to most students of Jeremiah is the *a priori* dictum that the prophecy owes its origin entirely to a threatened invasion of Palestine by the Scythians. Naturally, therefore, in their judgement the prophet can look for nothing wider than what an external and casual event like an invasion was capable of suggesting to any thoughtful mind. Every passage where Jeremiah appears with a larger outlook or with a bigger conception of the divine purpose becomes *ipso facto* suspect, and is by many rejected on no better ground. It has become necessary to plead for a scientific treatment of Scripture. Instead of approaching every oracle with the test of whether it conforms with a theory of how the oracles came to be and accepting only those which agree with this theory, oracles which in themselves are credible must be accepted and made the basis for a later theory as to whether they or any of them owed their origin to a Scythian invasion.

In reality this oracle substantially says no more than what is said of Jeremiah's activity in 6 : 27 ff., a passage the authenticity of which has not been questioned. There the prophet has it in charge to test the conduct of his own people with the knowledge that what he rejects in Israel's life Yahweh has already rejected. Yahweh is coming to judge His nation;

and the judgement is to proceed along the lines and according to the standards laid down by the prophet, to whom has been committed the divine valuation of Israel's good and evil. Here the judgement is not different in its character, it is only wider in its scope. Yahweh is coming to judge His world, and Jeremiah has it in charge to announce this coming. He can even announce the terms of the dread approach, for the judgement which is to result shall be after his word, which, since he has become a prophet, is nothing less than the word of Yahweh Himself.

Amos had already recognized that the nations as well as Israel were judged and condemned before Yahweh's tribunal, though they could not be called His people. In spite of the fact that they did not, like Israel, acknowledge Him for God, they could not lie beyond His control, because of what He was. His will of perfect justice was the one rule of human life and the one standard for human conduct. When He came for judgement, the nations were brought in guilty because in their conduct to one another they had failed to acknowledge anything higher than their own interests and desire for revenge. Israel was more guilty than the others, because it had had better opportunity to know the sureness and the sanctity of the divine will.

Jeremiah in his turn has seen two things. He has seen Yahweh, the God of perfect justice; and there is only one justice, which is not Israel's, nor Assyria's, but human. He has also seen the condition of the nation and the world in which he has been called to live and work. His function as a prophet is to set up anew the ignored but absolute standards. These standards are not of his own creation, nor have they been newly discovered by him. He is only standing in the succession of a line of prophets, to whom they have been revealed. The standards are Yahweh's, and therefore absolute and immutable. According to 6 : 27 ff. Jeremiah can determine finally on the worth, and therefore on the fate of his own people, because he brings to the judgement of its conduct the will of Yahweh whom nation and prophet alike acknowledge. But this will, being absolute, is beyond national limits; and therefore the scope of the prophet's commission is to the world, and he is called to declare it, not as man of Anathoth, nor as Jew, but as man. When the text of these oracles is interpreted as it stands, it becomes possible to recognize a consistent thread running through the account which they present of the prophet's call.

The call, however, has been made the preface to two following visions and brought into close relation to these. It is impossible to be sure that the visions immediately followed the call. But the fact that the whole chapter speaks of Jeremiah in the first person makes it at least possible that here we have to do with material which he himself wrote or dictated to Baruch. Should this be the case, the connexion between the account of the call and the visions is no accident of fortuitous juxtaposition. Their relation may be, not of date, but of substance. In this case it becomes natural to expect that the account of the call shall throw light on the visions, and that the visions may correct or support the view taken of the call.

The terms of the earlier vision, it must first be said, scarcely warrant the charming picture of the young prophet having seen in some wadi of Anathoth the fresh beauty of spring's first harbinger, the almond, and having drawn an oracle of hope from its appearance. For to recognize a flowering almond-bush and call it by its right name does not demand so great an effort of discernment that a prophet who had made it was likely to believe he heard Yahweh saying that he was right. It must have been possible to make a mistake about the name, or there is no point in the remark: 'thou hast seen right'. The twig was a dry twig, which could be easily mistaken for something other than it was. Besides, the idea of the spring bursting in early blossom across the wadies of Benjamin and revealing itself first in a flowering almond-bush does not agree well with the mission of the prophet to announce that Yahweh was bestirring Himself to send devastation out of the North. The one revealed the first stir of awaking life: the other was the promise of coming doom.

The twig was a dry twig, which seemed to promise nothing. But it is a *shāḳēdh*, an almond-branch, said the prophet. And I, said Yahweh, am *shōkēdh*, watching intently over the fulfilment of my word. The world was dry and apparently empty of any divine promise: but Yahweh was waking and about to fulfil His purpose among men.

What, then, was this word of Yahweh, and why did the prophet need the assurance that He was now intent on fulfilling it? It cannot merely be the general word of truth which God constantly commits to the lips and lives of all faithful men. In such an assurance there was nothing which specially met the case of a man who was newly invested with a special commission and who was in some hesitation over the magnitude of the task. Nor, if Jeremiah was merely one of the faithful servants of God, was there any need for Yahweh to set him apart from his birth and to give him peculiar authority by touching his lips. The word of the Lord, which He declared it was His intention to fulfil and about which He said that He was already on His way to fulfil it, must belong peculiarly to the prophets. It must be some specific word which it was a great part of their function to utter. And, as has already been noted, Jeremiah did believe that there was a common burden of prophecy, which it was his function to deliver and beyond which he did not always feel himself at liberty to go. He even declared that what had uniformly characterized all preceding prophets had been their expectation of judgement. In one of his pregnant sentences, A. B. Davidson has said that the Old Testament prophets are terribly one-idea'd men. They all believe that Yahweh acts. His great act was His self-revelation. He revealed Himself to the prophets before He revealed Himself to Israel and the world. With the knowledge these men received of the righteous God, they could not conceive of His purpose and its result as being indifferent. The immediate outcome of the divine emergence in this world of time must mean judgement, first on Israel, then on the world. Yahweh's word, since it embodied His mind, involved an initial disaster for all who had ignored its significance. Amos expressed the same thought by the mysterious 'it', which, he said, Yahweh should no longer keep back (Amos 1 : 3, 6, 9; cf. R.V. margin). Because of the prophet's prayer for Israel, Yahweh had refrained and given a longer opportunity for repentance (Amos 7 : 1–6). But at last He could hold back no longer, and must suffer His purpose to fulfil itself.

The reason, therefore, for Jeremiah in his first vision receiving the assurance that Yahweh was still watching over His word to fulfil it was that he needed such an assurance. He came in the succession of many prophets who had all announced the similar coming of God in judgement. And they were all dead: yet the judgement tarried. He had come, too, at a time when the world lay empty of promise like the almond-twig he was given to see. It was dry and sapless. It went about its accustomed ways. The last thing which occurred to it was that Yahweh was about to break in and make His purpose known. Yet He was waking, and was calling a prophet to declare the fact.

The modern world has not the same difficulty about the prophetic message which must have met many men in old Israel, or at least has it in a different form. Some Christian men have been able to separate the form of this message from its inward content. They have learned to recognize that under the form of the near coming of the Lord to judgement lay the great realities of the divine standards for what alone can endure, the sure ruin of everything which opposes them, the safe peace of such as commit themselves to their keeping. But it has taken a long time and much travail of spirit to make the distinction—and in certain quarters it has not yet been clearly made.

It was the weakness of the form of the prophets' message that, since each of them came to announce the near approach of judgement, men could turn upon them with the remark that they were always proclaiming the advent of something which never came.

There are sentences both in the prophets and in the psalter which show the presence in the community of men who complained that Yahweh after all did not intervene and indeed did nothing. The most natural explanation is that the men grew weary of expecting some interference for which they had been led to hope. And, since the words appear among the prophetic oracles, it is equally natural to conclude that it was the prophets who had led them to cherish these hopes and who seemed to have disappointed them. The meaning of the opening chapters of Ecclesiastes becomes clearer when its fundamental thought is set over against the expectation of the day of the Lord. What Koheleth reiterates is that nothing ever happens except the thing which has always been. The sun rises and sets in the patient and unchanging succession of day and night. The rivers run into the sea, but the sea never gets any higher: the waters find their way back to return in their accustomed channels to their starting-point. All things go on their unalterable way; and as for the expectation of the prophets that something which manifests more clearly the meaning of these things is at hand, it never appears. Koheleth is not speaking about laws of nature. He is thinking in terms of his own time. The world to him pursues its course, which has been its course from the beginning, and it never sees the changes which the prophet promises. What Koheleth said aloud at a much later period of Israel's thought was obvious enough to occur to the politicians of Manasseh's court and to the farmers of Judea. What has become of Amos's prophecy of judgement and Isaiah's promise of Immanuel? The world goes on much as it went in their time. It is as difficult as ever to make the olives grow and to steer the kingdom among the troubled waters of the world's politics. The vision of Jeremiah speaks directly to this situation. In spite of apparent failure Yahweh is watching over His world, and means to fulfil His ancient word. He does not sleep, He is even stirring; and Jeremiah has been called to become a prophet in order to take up the old prophetic word.

The exact terms of the second vision, that of the boiling cauldron, are more difficult to define, for the text varies in the versions, and the present Masoretic text gives no clear sense. Recourse must be had to emendation. In v. 14 it is said that 'evil shall be opened' from the North. But 'opening' as of a door is no natural description for the beginning of mischief, and the LXX has a different rendering. The generally accepted reading is 'shall be blown', since this word refers back to the description of the cauldron. It is a 'blown' or boiling cauldron; and its commotion is the symbol of the mischief brewing from the North.[1] The chief difficulty, however, is found in v. 14 b, where the cauldron is said to have its face from the direction of the North. Since the mischief comes from the North, the idea of the cauldron somehow facing away from that direction is pointless. It has accord-

[1] Cf. Rothstein, *B. H.*, תֻּפַּח instead of תִּפָּתַח. Volz reads נָפַחְתִּי 'I am blowing', which would be even better in the mouth of Yahweh and bring the verse into line with v. 15.

ingly been proposed to read with a slight change in the text that the face was turned toward the North.[1] Yet this rendering, while formally satisfactory, leaves the real crux of the phrase untouched. What is the face of a cauldron, and how can it be turned anywhere? Duhm is the only commentator who recognizes the difficulty, and he seeks to answer it by supposing that the pot was propped on three stones in the open air with an opening in the supports towards the North, through which fuel was introduced in order to stoke the fire. Unfortunately the open front of a fireplace is hardly the same thing as the face of a pot. One is driven to suspect that the corruption lies in the word which describes the pot as having a face at all, and to suggest that some word derived from the Hebrew verb to blow has been corrupted into 'its face'.[2] Then the vision runs: the word of the Lord came to me the second time to say, what seest thou? And I said, I see a boiling cauldron and the blower is from the direction of the North. Then the Lord said unto me: out of the North mischief is being blown against all the inhabitants of the world.

Whether the interpretation offered be accepted in all its details or not, the general sense of the vision is clear. Yahweh is about to intervene, and in particular means to cause evil to break out from the North. The precise sense of this direction out of which the mischief is to come—whether it must be understood to refer to the Scythians or the Babylonians or to any historic nation at all—must be left for more detailed and later discussion. Meantime it deserves to be noted that the mischief is coming with Yahweh's knowledge, and not without His will. Hence He can and does inform a prophet beforehand of its coming, and bids him warn men of its

[1] Reading מָפְּנִים צפונה or וּפָּנָיו מָפְּנֵי. Cf. how Ezek. 9 : 2 speaks of a gate turned northward.

[2] e.g. מַפּוּחַ which occurs Jer. 6 : 29.

expected arrival. A doom which comes according to Yahweh's purpose is already on its way. But further there is nothing in its initial announcement which compels us to conclude that this doom was confined in its effects to Israel. Since it includes Israel, it may specially interest a prophet whose primary mission is to his own people. But the terms in which it is described are applicable to a disaster which has a wider scope. In view of the terms of Jeremiah's call to be a prophet to the nations, of his qualification for this large function, of his commission and of the word he utters, the more natural sense is that a judgement is about to arrive which shall include the world.

Unfortunately the concluding verses have clearly received later additions. Thus vv. 15 f., as they stand, present a curious and confused picture. At the beginning the kingdoms of the North appear, setting up their thrones in front of Jerusalem and over against its walls. Peake[1] takes these thrones to be intended for judgement, and then, since the elders or the king sat in the gate to administer justice, he translates פֶּתַח 'in the gateway'. But כִּסֵּא, when left undefined, means merely a throne without any hint of judgement; and פתח means 'in front of', i.e. outside Jerusalem (cf. 19 : 2). Further, the judicial decision is here as elsewhere reserved to Yahweh: the nations cannot set up their thrones to usurp His function. This disposes of Peake's further suggestion that the thrones are to be set up after Jerusalem has been captured, as well as his half-hearted approval of Giesebrecht's proposal to omit the last two clauses of the verse, because they imply that the city has not yet been captured but that the siege is still in progress. The verses, then, do not describe a conquest carried out by the nations to be followed by a judgement and suitable penalty inflicted by these nations on the guilty captives. The oracle, rather, after

[1] *Century Bible*, ad loc.

having described how the thrones are set up before Jerusalem, proceeds to state that Yahweh will pronounce judgement on 'them'. Those who are thus judged are evidently the inhabitants of Jerusalem, for the rest of the verse contains a catalogue of that city's sins. The nations, therefore, are not present in order to judge the guilty capital. What then is their function? Either they are present to bear witness to the blackness of Judah's guilt and the justice of its condemnation by Yahweh, as Amos believed they might do with Israel (3 : 9, 13). In that case mischief does not come from the North, but directly from Yahweh: the nations are mere spectators. Or they are summoned in order to proceed to the siege of Jerusalem and carry out the penalty involved in Yahweh's condemnation, should the city fail to profit from the divine chastisement. In this case there are to be two acts of chastisement, one from Yahweh, the other from the nations, and the penalty which comes from man is to be the completion of the divine act!

But not only is the function of the nations left uncertain: it is equally indefinite who these nations were. All who find it necessary to suppose that Jeremiah's message arose from a definite historical situation are in perplexity over the verses. Thus Duhm points out that the representation cannot possibly refer to the Scythians since these always appear as one people. Nor does it agree with the Babylonians, since these also were a single people and did not come out of the North, though they might be described as coming by way of the North.

Is the representation historical at all? The whole conception is far more like the later idea of the nations being gathered before Jerusalem, sometimes to fight against the holy city, sometimes to be judged. Only the difference must be marked equally with the resemblance. In the later picture the nations are gathered to be judged, either through the world-war or the world-judgement, while Jerusalem is justified: here Jerusalem is to be judged, and the nations are gathered—for what purpose? Something of the same indefiniteness appears at Joel c. 4 and in the Sibylline Oracles III. 67 f. There also it is not made clear what is to be the fate of the nations or what is the precise reason for their being gathered. The only hint on the subject given by Joel is found in the name of the valley into which the nations are brought: it is the valley of Jehoshaphat, or the divine judgement. But how the judgement is to be carried out, or on whom, and what precisely is to be the fate of the nations, on these questions no hint is given. The verses in Jeremiah belong to a time when such ideas were current, so current that it was not felt necessary to explain their exact meaning. They are an added interpretation of the vision of the boiling cauldron. The fact that the interpolator was taking up current ideas of his own time made it natural for him not to feel the need to make clear their application to the prophecy. All that they contribute to our understanding of the vision is that, at the time when the verses were added, the early oracles of Jeremiah were interpreted in an apocalyptic, not a historical, sense.

In its original form the vision of the cauldron was as brief, enigmatic, and suggestive as that of the almond-twig. Remove the intruded matter, and at once the connexion is improved between 13 f. and 17 f. 'Mischief is being blown out of the north against all the inhabitants of the earth. Therefore gird up thy loins, arise, utter unto *them* all that I command thee.' The prophet is sent to announce and expound the coming doom.

The two visions stand in intimate relation. The first follows directly on Yahweh having put His word into the prophet's mouth, and insists that God is already rising up to bring His word to fulfilment. Jeremiah is not sent out into the world with the assurance that whatever he feels himself driven to utter is a word of the Lord. He is not asserting his claim to a limitless authority, as though all he spoke were *ipso facto* possessed of divine power. He is entering into the function of prophecy and taking up its perennial burden, that Yahweh is about to reveal Himself in and to His world. The divine word over which Yahweh watches to bring it to fulfilment is that which all the prophets asserted, which John the Baptist took up in turn, which the last prophet in the Apocalypse uttered: Maranatha. Hence the vision is early, belonging to the period of Jeremiah's call. It is not necessary to suppose that he had waited in vain for the divine word to fulfil itself, and needed support. Already, when he began his career, Amos and Hosea, Micah and Isaiah, had uttered their predictions of judgement; yet to most men all things seemed to continue in their old course. A new prophet who was to continue this succession needed and received an assurance of the certainty of that divine word which he was to utter.

The second vision merely continues and expounds the sense of this word. It is the old word: the day of the Lord is at hand. The cauldron is boiling in its place and the blower is at work. Mischief is coming on the wings of the northern wind on all the inhabitants of the earth; and this is by the will of Yahweh. He is about to bring in His day, which is now more clearly seen to be a day, not merely for Israel, but for the world which is His world and cannot escape out of His hands. Israel had stood in the forefront when Amos uttered that message first. Yet even Amos had included the nations in the act of Yahweh, because a judgement, the norm of which was righteousness, must concern all men. Now the world stands in the forefront, because Yahweh is more clearly recognized to be the God of the whole earth who executeth righteous judgement. But to both prophets Israel remains the primary theatre of the divine self-manifestation, because Israel has been more privileged than any other people.

In view of these things—the call to utter the divine word, the commission to exercise the divine test, the scope which includes all the world—what the prophet needs first and last is courage. Let him take courage and have no fear though the whole world be against him (v. 17). The command has received a later expansion, for v. 18 shows a turgid text, which contrasts strongly with the concise severity of what precedes. A fenced town and a pillar of iron and a wall of brass are sonorous phrases which are apt to recur. Probably the pillar of iron and the wall of brass have been inserted from 15 : 20, with the mistaken desire of heightening the effect, by some scribe who failed to notice that they were not very happy in this connexion, since nobody ever fights against an iron pillar. Again, the list of the kings of Judah, its priests, its princes, and its common people is suspicious, since it recurs in the edited reports of Jeremiah's speeches. Our account, as has been stated, seems to be derived from some autobiographical record before it was included in the larger book. Probably it then received these accretions, and the original text may have run: Lo, I have set thee a town on its defence against all the earth, or against all the peoples of the earth, and they shall fight against thee, but they shall not prevail, for I am with thee (cf. v. 8).

Jeremiah is the bearer of a word from Yahweh which concerns the world and which all men must sooner or later recognize in its tremendous consequences. He is qualified for the task through the fact that Yahweh has chosen him and set him apart to be the instrument of the divine purpose, a purpose which is beyond local and temporal conditions. He bears this, therefore, not because he is born of the children of Abraham, but because he is privileged to be in the secret of the Lord of the whole earth. Since he bears this word with such a commission, he need not and dare not fear any man, for the word, being of God, fulfils itself in the destiny of men.

IV

JEREMIAH AND THE ESSENTIALS OF RELIGION

IN a series of oracles Jeremiah has developed with force and precision his view of what constitutes the essence of true religion. It is not necessary to suppose that these were all spoken at the same time. More probably some collector, recognizing how closely they are related in subject, has grouped them together. He has, however, inserted among them a section (3 : 6–18) which, through its being dated, may show that it has been derived from another source, and which is best studied apart from the rest. The oracles are found in 3 : 1–5 and 3 : 19–4 : 2, and, when they are read together, they gain in clearness and in significance.

Another feature which appears in these utterances is that they are all addressed to the prophet's fellow-countrymen in North Israel. This may have influenced the collector in arranging them together, and may have been the reason which induced him to include 3 : 6–18, since that section has the same destination. But the fact warrants a further conclusion. We may confidently assign the material to the early period of Jeremiah's activity, before he was launched on the stormy currents of the political and religious life of Jerusalem. And the conclusion is supported by the extent to which these oracles are saturated with the fundamental ideas of Hosea. The younger man is reproducing for his own people of Israel the ideals which both they and he had first learned from his predecessor.

The first oracle (3 : 1–5) is a sharp indictment of the people's religious attitude: this is traced to a radical inability to recognize the character of the God it worships. Using Hosea's favourite figure of the relation of husband and wife to illustrate the relation between Yahweh and Israel, Jeremiah says: suppose a man has been compelled to divorce his wife, or[1] she has left him for another man, will he go back to her at a word? Is not that woman[2] defiled? But thou hast gone after many lovers, yet a return to Me is a thing of course. It is unfortunate that an explanation of the simple utterance has been sought in the precise regulations which determined the practice of divorce in early Israel (Deut. 24 : 1–4), or that it should be found necessary to discuss the legal conditions under which an Israelite was permitted to take back his divorced wife. The supposed reference to the marriage laws has brought with it the change of ' will he return to her ' into ' may she return to him ', since the legal difficulties lay in the restoration of the divorced woman to her husband.[3] Any change is seen to be unnecessary, when it is recognized that Jeremiah is not appealing to any law, but to the natural instincts of ordinary men. He is asking men whether in the intimate relations of life they ever act with the disregard to moral feeling which they unthinkingly practise in matters of religion. Will any one of them take back, without some evidence of change on her part, a woman who has been proved faithless to him? Such a thing is not done

[1] So, instead of 'and', with Volz, cf. 36 : 23; 43 : 3; 44 : 28. The prophet is envisaging two possible cases.

[2] Reading אשה for ארץ with the LXX. It might be possible to retain ארץ, applied in a figurative sense to a woman as ' land ' where seed is sown. The usage occurs in ancient literature: Plautus says about an adulterer ' fundum alienum arat '. But I can recall no analogous use in the Old Testament. If we retained ארץ in this figurative sense, the LXX reading אשה would be merely a case of a translation *ad sensum* for a community which would otherwise miss the point.

[3] An appeal to the LXX in support of the change is not justified, since the Greek is a doubtful rendering of the supposed Hebrew text.

anywhere. Thereupon he presses on the men to whom he speaks the bearing of this on their religious conduct. Yahweh never put Israel away: she went of her own choice. Nor had she confined herself to a single infidelity: her gods were as numerous as her whims. Let men but look round (v. 2) at the heights where the altars to strange gods stand: the land bears witness to their constant disloyalty. Yet they dream that it is an easy thing, which demands no moral effort or seriousness of purpose, to return to Yahweh.

Not only had their God been loyal to a disloyal nation. He had not failed to warn them of the sure outcome of this conduct on their part. The rains had been withheld from the polluted land, so that it refused its fruits (v. 3). But every warning had proved useless, since Israel had a whore's forehead[1] and despised correction.

Yet in all this Israel had had no desire to break off entirely its relation to Yahweh. Even in these circumstances[2] the people continue to call Yahweh 'my husband,[3] the friend of my youth' (v. 4). He remains to them the God of their fathers who brought them out of the land of Egypt; but this peculiar claim He has upon them seems quite compatible with a certain recognition of other gods. They do not see the need for giving Him their entire allegiance. It is true that He is austere and shows Himself angry at times, withholding the rains and sending drought; but He does not keep His anger long. There is accordingly no need for moral effort to avert

[1] There is no need for any emendation here. Generally אשה is omitted as a gloss on זוֹנָה; cf. *B. H.* But the expression is not uncommon; cf. Jos. 2 : 1 the house, Judges 11 : 1 the son, Ezek. 16 : 30 the work, of אשה זונה.

[2] That is the sense of מֵעַתָּה.

[3] There is no need to change אבי, as Rothstein proposes, into בַּעְלֵךְ. *Abū* is used in Babylonian for a husband (Barton, *Semitic Origins*, p. 68, n. 5), and the usage occurs in both north and south Semitic dialects (W. R. Smith, *Kinship and Marriage*, p. 117 f.).

an anger which passes as suddenly and unaccountably as it rose.

Jeremiah goes straight to that which is making his people unable to realize the need for any spiritual change—their radical incapacity to realize the unique character of God. Until men know that Yahweh has a character which sets Him apart in lonely dignity, they will see no reason why He should not take His place among the other objects of their devotion. As the God of their fathers He must always have a special claim on Israel, but this need not utterly exclude other gods. Holding His place among the rest, He may be angry, should He fail to receive what is due to Him; but His anger is lightly turned aside without any austere repentance. Again, until men recognize that Yahweh has a character, which is not only His own, but which is the expression of His nature and therefore immutable, they will fail to recognize that He can only come to men who are prepared to meet Him along the lines of His demand. His demand does not consist in something which He chooses and may on occasion forgo: it arises out of what He is and cannot but continue to be. To enter into relation to Him implies the acceptance of the conditions laid down in His nature. And this implies an allegiance absolute and unique like the character of Him to whom it is rendered. Religion to Jeremiah means submission to Yahweh on His own terms, and His terms are simply the expression of His nature.

In all this Jeremiah stands in the direct succession of Amos and Hosea. The two prophets seized the root-principle which underlay the Deuteronomic law of their time and gave it new spiritual content. The law had demanded that Israel must acknowledge no other god than Yahweh, and had proceeded to surround the nation's life with safeguards which might hold them back from any form of apostacy. Israel must have its own sanctuaries, its own priesthood, its own rituals, the outcome and the embodiment of its own faith. Everything which bore the taint of heathenism was abomination to Yahweh. Within the limits which are set to every legislation the law was admirably adapted for its immediate purpose, which was to drive into the minds of simple men that Israel was separate from other nations, because Yahweh was different from other gods. The law further declared that Israel owed everything to what its God had done for it, and insisted, in the parenetic sections which appear specially in the introduction to the code but which also characterize all the legislation, that the nation owed obedience and love to Him.

Here the law is in close relation to all Hosea's teaching. His leading principle is that Israel owed everything to a love which had brought it into being and without which it could not continue. The only worthy response to this free grace was a love which meant submission and loyalty. Amos had seen Yahweh's relation to the nation to be conditioned by righteousness, which demanded righteous conduct in return: Hosea saw the relation to be founded on a love which asked even more.

Because, however, Amos saw the relation of his people to its God to be primarily conditioned by His righteousness, he did not readily see how the relation, after it had once been broken, could be restored. All he was able to see was that the divine purpose which had chosen Israel for its own ends could not come to nothing. He had little to say about the conditions of repentance. Hosea, on the other hand, held the richer conception of a relation between God and people which had come into being through the divine love. The love which had made the relation possible and real could not rest without an effort after restoration, and could only be satisfied with reconciliation. Accordingly he has much to say about the nature of a right repentance. In 6 : 1–3 he quoted the terms of one of his people's penitential hymns. In it the people dwelt on how Yahweh had smitten and could heal, on how He might be angry for two days but should relent on the third without any need for contrition on their part. For His coming was as sure as any process of nature; it was like the return of the dawn or the arrival of the summer rains. Like these, it was unconditioned by moral demands. He came as the rain came, which falls on the just and the unjust alike. Therefore Hosea followed up the hymn with a summons to repentance, because it was his task to say that Yahweh's coming was unlike that of the rain, precisely because it must be morally conditioned. He could only come in benediction to men who had prepared themselves to receive Him by a sincere repentance which recognized what He was and what therefore He must always demand.

Jeremiah renews the demand of his predecessor to the same people. The conditions of Northern Israel, weakened by defeat and living among men of a different faith, have made it natural for them to give a certain place to other gods. They are counting it sufficient to recognize in Yahweh one on whom they have a special claim. When trouble comes, they take refuge in Him and can be sure that He will not leave them in the lurch. The prophet bids them begin unto the Lord with repentance. And repentance means submission to Yahweh's claim for their undivided obedience.

The three early prophets base their monotheism, not on the barren conception that Yahweh is one, but on the fruitful conviction that He is unique. He has a character which sets Him apart from everything else to which other men gave the title of god. Hence His relation to them is as unique as His nature. He cannot demand a little more or a little less from His worshippers. He claims everything. His jealousy is the proof of what He is. To admit the claim of another god is to deny the lonely and sufficient character of Yahweh. He does not demand His rights when He refuses to share His honour with another; He merely declares what He is.

All the prophets, also, show the singular uplift in human life which follows on accepting this supreme allegiance. They are conscious of how life is unified and steeled, when men have faced this ultimate claim. Yahweh's character conditions all His acts, and to know Him and to surrender to Him on His terms make all life simple and direct. Surrender to the will of Yahweh may seem a slight thing in itself. Since in reality it involves a tremendous claim on all the nature, it brings a resultant greatness.

Hence, while Jeremiah seems to close his first oracle with a declaration that there can be no return of the people to their God, he really states that there can be no return unless the people recognize who it is to whom they are to return. With the thoughts the men have about their God and their relation to Him, with their resultant thoughts of the way to find Him, they may find something but will never find Yahweh. Being what He is, the only way to Him is by repentance. Being what He is, He must have everything or nothing.

The prophet turns in his next oracle to speak about Yahweh Himself and His treatment of the people as contrasted with their treatment of Him: 'it was in my mind to treat Israel as a son' (3 : 19). Here again it is unfortunate that the explanation of the sentence has been sought in the incident related about the daughters of Zelophehad the son of Hepher in Num. 27 : 1–8.[1] There certain women whose father had left no male issue claimed to be put on the same footing as sons in a question about the inheritance of landed property. The interpretation requires us to suppose that the prophet in two addresses to the common people involved himself in the intricacies of Israelite law about the inheritance of real

[1] Cf. e.g. Peake, *Comm. Cent. B.* ad loc.

estate and the method of conducting divorce proceedings. It further involves that Jeremiah could make Israel's inheritance of Palestine from Yahweh parallel to the inheritance of land from a dead father. The prophet was thinking and speaking of something much simpler than any legal subtleties. And fortunately his language does not drive an interpreter into the law-courts in search of an explanation: 'to set among the sons' means nothing more recondite than to treat like a son.[1] Again, Jeremiah is following Hosea who spoke of how Yahweh called Israel His son out of Egypt (11 : 1). Having given Israel the status of a son by redeeming it from Egyptian bondage, He also gave the people its delightsome land. Yahweh did not confine His benefits to words, but, because of His love for the nation, He gave it a special dignity which made it marked and remarkable as His peculiar people. In return He expected Israel to make an equally vital response and, since He had acknowledged it for a son, to give Him the reverence due to a father. Instead of the due return the people betrayed Him as an unfaithful wife betrays her husband for the sake of a lover[2] (v. 20).

Jeremiah is urging the same theme as Hosea, with closer insistence on the past history of Israel. The nation owed everything to its God; its being and well-being alike were due to His constant and peculiar care. Without His intervention it would have been nothing, but He had also treated it before all the world as His son. Gratitude should have been sufficient to make evident His claim to its peculiar devotion. The men should have given all to One who grudged them nothing; but neither the recognition of what He is in Himself nor the knowledge of what He has revealed Himself to be in

[1] Cf. e.g. Ps. 118 : 7. יהוה לִי בְּעֹזְרָי Yahweh is to me among my helpers, means Yahweh is my aid.

[2] I retain מֵרֵעָהּ. Rothstein, following the versions, changes to בְּרעה, i.e. betrays her husband. But רע is used for lover at v. 1, not for husband.

all their past history has been sufficient to retain their allegiance to their God.

Is that then the end? Has all the travail of the past resulted only in futility? It might well seem so, but it is not so to the prophet. He has heard and seen something else besides the vulgar worship on the heights. 'Hark, on the lone heights I hear the wailing of the children of Israel, because they have gone wilfully astray and put Yahweh their God out of mind. Behold, we are still Thine,[1] for Thou art Yahweh our God. Surely the tumult[2] of the hills, the riot of the mountains has proved itself a lie; surely in Yahweh our God is help for Israel' (vv. 21–3).

To understand the prophet's meaning, it is necessary to think of him, a child of his own nation, bred on its soil, saturated with its genius and especially with its religion, proud of its traditions, disciplined by its history, conscious that all its past has moulded his nature and his outlook. He is sick at heart over the empty sensuous worship of his time, the riot on the mountains. He knows it all to be alien to the best which his nation has nurtured in him, and he cannot believe himself to be alone in his weariness and disgust. What he feels of nausea and revolt, because he feels it as a son of Israel through his national inheritance and training, cannot be unknown to many others besides himself. Because he fell back on all that was soundest in the tradition of the land which bred him, he knew that his revolt was not his own, but was shared by many who could not deny their national heritage.[3]

What Jeremiah hears is the soul of his people, misled,

[1] Probably, though not necessarily, read with Syr. הִנֵּה אֲנַחְנוּ לָךְ. The reading has the advantage that it recalls the familiar phrase: Israel Yahweh's people, Yahweh Israel's God.

[2] So read with Driver.

[3] Cf. Duhm's fine note in his *Comm.* ad loc.

bewildered, yet not wholly alienated from its God. Above all it betrays how much of a hold Yahweh retains upon its life, because it cannot be satisfied with the poor solace and strength which the coarse semi-pagan worship of its time can offer. The voice the prophet hears is the voice every prophet or preacher must hear if he is to continue delivering his message. He must believe that there are men who are capable of welcoming his word from the Lord, or he will cease to utter a word in which no one shows any interest but himself. Besides, while the prophet must be conscious that he is in the secret of the Lord, he must also be conscious that what he learns there is not his exclusive property. It must be communicable to other men, since it is given him for the sake of other men: it must therefore have its point of contact with and its appeal to their conscience. Indeed, because it is the word of the Lord and no imagination of his own, the more sure he is that it must be capable of becoming the possession of other men. And the more it has comforted and stayed up his own heart in untoward days, the more confident he will be that there are many who will exult to hear it, since it will speak also to their case.

It is possible, from descriptions in the early prophets and from hints in the historical books, to obtain an idea of what the riot on the mountains meant. We can piece together some picture of the crowds drawn by mixed motives who went on pilgrimage to the favourite shrines, of the singing, dancing, and feasting, of the mixture of fair and religious festival, the night scenes when the services of the day were past. And matters must have become worse in Jeremiah's time. Wars and corrupt government had wasted the country and had brought about the impoverishment and the coarsening of the peasantry who formed the backbone of Hebrew life. Through the transformation of North Israel into a satrapy and through the heavy blows inflicted and the crushing tribute imposed by the foreigner, the nation had lost its national self-confidence. As its religion had always been in close contact with its sense of national character, men, through losing sense of their national dignity, were losing hold of what gave the people its distinctive character, its specific religion. The nation was sinking back into one of the little Syrian principalities which cowered together before the colossus on the Euphrates or conspired together whenever there seemed a chance of casting off the hated yoke. One people among the many in a common fate of subjection, it began more and more to assimilate the spirit of that world in which it was submerged. Men, having lost confidence in themselves and in their national faith, turned to foreign superstitions which might cover their nakedness or deaden their misery. Cults and practices which in better days the virile faith in the God of their fathers had driven under ground, began to be welcomed. The old memories of their national past, when the faith in Yahweh had nerved the tribes to capture the land of their possession and had united them in the resolution to maintain it, ceased to appeal to the multitude. These were too austere to satisfy their jaded palates. Others found these memories, bringing their contrast with the present, too bitter to be cherished. They tried to make up for the inspiration of the past by plunging into the coarse superstitions which are apt to come to the surface in every period of national weakness and disillusionment.

Was Jeremiah wrong when he believed that the riot on the mountains was sometimes the louder because men were trying to make themselves believe in it? Was he a wholly false interpreter of his nation's character when he believed that these practices did not represent the true soul of his people and could not permanently content men? There were men in Israel who had drunk in like wine the sweet strong words of Amos's passion for righteousness and Hosea's demand for loyalty with its accompanying self-sacrifice, into whose blood had passed that new estimate of what gives life its worth and sacredness which made it impossible for Israel ever to abandon itself to pagan joy like the nations round it. Yahweh had His hand on them, whether they would or not. Such men were deeply conscious of the contrast between the scenes which now embodied their national faith and the stern bracing discipline of soul which their prophets had demanded in Yahweh's name. Verily in Yahweh our God is the salvation of Israel. All Israel's history from its beginning down to the present is the proof that the prophet read the temper of his people aright.

But to these broken men their estate seemed hopeless. The memory of Yahweh and of what faith in him could do was useless. All it served to produce was to poison their peace in the present and to bring vain remorse for the past. Their prevailing sense was one of moral impotence. 'Ever since we can remember, this false worship has eaten up the toil and devoured the vigour of our fathers; let us lie down in our shame' (vv. 24 f.). Their false relation to God and their failure to obey Him have destroyed in the people the power to return and to lay hold on that which is better. Their own sin and the sin of their fathers have served to ruin the capacity of holding fast the higher thing which yet they cannot help desiring. Let our dishonour cover us, for since the beginning we and our fathers have been at one in sinning against Yahweh.

It is unnecessary, though it is a common practice,[1] to remove any part of this plaintive confession and relegate it to that convenience of Old Testament criticism, the post-exilic period. It is true that this later period was gravely interested in the sins of the fathers, and referred to these with

[1] Volz, however, retains the section for Jeremiah.

great frequency. But one can hardly make the interest of the post-exilic generation in the sins of the fathers an adequate reason for pronouncing that nobody else at an earlier date could give a passing thought to the subject. And this ready method of disposing of the matter becomes not merely unnecessary but unjustifiable, when, as in this case, the subject is regarded from a totally different point of view. The men of the post-exilic time were generally, if not entirely, interested in the guilt of the past because it served to supply a reason for the punishment of the present.[1] Israel in its continued exile was being required to expiate the guilt of all its past. It could even be described as having received at Yahweh's hand the double for all its sins. But here the sins of the fathers are recognized as contributing to the moral weakness of their children—a very different situation. The post-exilic time was seeking some explanation for a difficult fact of human experience, and was sadly recognizing that no nation is permitted, in the awful providence of God, to make a clean break and begin anew as though it had no history. Partly in self-excuse, partly in explanation of the supposed delay in its God's mercy, it was acknowledging that the present inherits for good and ill the consequences of a forgotten past. Jeremiah was not seeking the explanation of anything. He was stating an actual reality. To him the evil in which men have been bred, the false thoughts of God and the slack habits in which they have been reared, have dulled the conscience of a nation and weakened the springs of its moral resilience. The false worship in Israel had eaten away the people's capacity to respond to every moral and spiritual appeal and its power to react to a new conviction. And it had eaten this away the more effectually because it did not begin its foul work with the present generation.

[1] Cf. Jer. 22 : 8, 9 (the verses are generally acknowledged to be secondary); Ezra 9 : 7; Neh. 9 : 26, 27; Ezek. 18 : 1–2, 20.

To such men, powerless to advance but unable to stand still, Jeremiah addresses his last oracle in the opening verses of chap. 4. Here, however, it is necessary to determine where the oracle ends, because the interpretation of 4 : 1 f. depends to some extent on the persons who are addressed. Hitherto the prophet has been addressing the house of Israel (3 : 20), the children of Israel (3 : 21), Israel (4 : 1), and has spoken of the salvation of Israel (3 : 23). He has also spoken of them and to them in the singular: they are to him a people. But with 4 : 3 f. he suddenly addresses the men of Judah and of Jerusalem, and therefore naturally speaks of them in the plural.[1] The original oracle ends with 4 : 2, and is addressed, like those which precede it, to Northern Israel. The question of the destination of the oracle has the greater significance, because the opinion that 4 : 1 was addressed to Judah has misled many scholars into a false interpretation of that verse. They have concluded that Jeremiah, when he spoke about return, must have been referring to a return from exile. And they have supposed that the prophet was making repentance a condition of restoration. What, on this interpretation, he said was: if thou desirest to return to Palestine, thou must first return to Me. This explanation has naturally served to make the verse suspect, since it seems to imply that the nation was already in exile. And it involves the prophet in the ambiguity of using the same word שוב in two distinct senses in a single verse without any hint that he meant two things by it.

Yet, if we take v. 2 as the conclusion of an oracle addressed to Northern Israel, v. 1 becomes capable of a perfectly straightforward explanation. In it שוב or return means what it has meant through the series of oracles, viz. repen-

[1] Volz omits v. 3 a on the ground that it is absent from four manuscripts of the LXX. But he fails to notice the difference between Israel and Judah, and cannot account for the sudden change of person.

tance, and the verse falls exactly into line with the rest of Jeremiah's thought. In 3 : 25 he is full of sympathy with weary and defeated men, who are profoundly conscious of their folly and guilt in having forsaken their allegiance to Yahweh, and who are as profoundly conscious that the only hope of new life for themselves and their nation is in their native faith. Yet they are defeated men who believe that they no longer possess the courage or the moral vigour to make a fresh start. The prophet with his heart yearning over them, yet with a clear sense of their dangerous estate, demands precisely this fresh effort.

They must not stand where they are, exposed to the dreary perils which attend the empty heart and disquieted conscience. 'If ye have it in mind to return, to Me ye may or must return.' The position of אֵלַי 'unto Me' in the sentence is emphatic, because the emphasis lies there, on Yahweh, who is at once the source of their self-disgust and the source of every new hope.[1]

Jeremiah is insisting on the possibility and the significance of a right repentance if men make it with singleness of purpose. He is conscious of the moral peril of a life which has become dissatisfied with its false worship, but which has not found content by turning to the higher. He is also urging men to recognize that Yahweh, who calls insistently for repentance, makes its issue sure. It is the flavour of the Yahweh faith, lingering in the nation's life and in these men's thought, which has made them unable to continue votaries of a baser worship. Let them, in leaving the false with disgust, close with the true, which has emptied the false of all content to them. To Yahweh they may, they must, they can return.

[1] Volz has recognized that there is no reference to the return from exile. But his otherwise excellent rendering 'wenn du dich bekehrst, Israel, sei mir willkommen' rather misses the demand, while it dwells on the promise.

'And, if ye remove your false gods out of my presence, do not then go wandering.' Probably, though not necessarily, we should follow the Septuagint, and, omitting ו before לא and joining מפני to לא, translate 'if ye remove your false gods, from My presence do not wander', i.e. do not remain with no god at all. The Greek text has a double advantage. It puts the emphasis on 'from My presence' as the previous clause put the emphasis on 'unto Me'. It also recalls Cain's description of himself as a wanderer נָד hidden from the divine presence מפניך (Gen. 4 : 14), and thus meets Driver's difficulty about using נוד in other than a physical sense.[1]

What Jeremiah warns men against is the weakness and danger involved in mere regret, with its barren pain and self-indulgence. The only wholesome repentance is that through which men come into a right relation to Yahweh. Life to a prophet does not come out of regrets, however sincere or tender these may be: it only comes from positive resolutions. The first and last condition of a true repentance consists in a return to God. In the very act lies a fresh spring of renewal and hope. To see God and to know Him merciful is to find the streams of a new life steal into the soul. Unto Him men must return.[2]

Although, however, the following verses with their demand to the men of Judah and Jerusalem to make clean work, breaking up the fallow ground and being careful not to sow among thorns, were not spoken at the same time nor addressed to the same hearers, they are genuine words of Jeremiah. And they contain part of his thought on the

[1] Apart from the above reference to Cain, the use of נוד in a moral sense seems to me guaranteed by Ps. 56 : 9.

[2] Verse 2, with its resemblance to Gen. 12 : 3 and 18 : 18, seems to me to be secondary. I acknowledge, however, that the argument based on resemblance between two passages is always dubious. A glossator may have added sentences borrowed from Genesis, but the writer in Genesis may have borrowed from Jeremiah.

meaning of repentance, though not the most significant part. Cornill judges otherwise. Believing 4 : 3 f. to reach the highest point in all the prophetic literature, he rejects v. 1, mainly on the ground that the demand it contains appears to him trivial in relation to the needs of the situation. So far as this judgement concerns the demand for repentance and return to God, the opinion of its triviality implies far too slight a sense of the positive character of Yahweh, as this was developed by Jeremiah and by his great teacher and forerunner, Hosea. To both these prophets Yahweh was the source of all life, physical and moral, in Israel. His relation to the people was always that of an active benefactor, bringing out of the riches of His grace fresh benefits. Hence Hosea could sum up the sin of the land in the charge that there was no 'knowledge of Yahweh' (cf. 4 : 1). To know Yahweh was to be in contact with One in whom were all the springs of right action. Hence, too, a right attitude to Him involved an active benevolence toward one's fellow-Israelites —a view which makes Hosea's ethics unique in the Old Testament, since with him alone do they become positive. Because the thought of God is not a barren intellectualism but rich in its positive content, to repent and thus be brought into living contact with Him is a profound and fruitful experience to Jeremiah.

Indeed it ought to be emphasized against Cornill that without this thought of God, vv. 3 f. by themselves become jejune and barren. Break up the fallow ground and do not sow among thorns. It is all very true, but what would the prophet have his people scatter broadcast over this lea? It is the weakness of all the moralists that they fail to supply this to their generation, and leave the ploughed furrows and the weeded garden without a crop. And it is the strength of the great prophets that they were more than moral reformers, and that they cleared no land except to plant it afresh. They were all religious men who had learned for themselves first and could declare afterwards that to be in right relation to God was to find a source of perennial, wholesome, joyous activity. The soul, according to Jeremiah, needs no more for its restoration and its stability than God. Only it must make clean work, and when it returns must return to Him with nothing kept back and whole-heartedly. Religion to him becomes a source of comfort, inspiration, and fresh hopefulness of heart when it means self-surrender. For the spirit, in surrendering to God, commits itself to One in whom is the secret of every renewal.

The series of oracles 3 : 1–5, 19–25; 4 : 1 f. form a connected whole, which deals with national reformation. Their early date is proved by the prophet's dependence on Hosea. All through, the thought of his great predecessor governs the attitude of the younger man. In the same way Isaiah began with the ideals and even in the terms of Amos. And they are addressed to Northern Israel, which can still be addressed as a people that has not wholly gone into exile. Hence the prophet's attitude and his profound sense of the need for renewal form an interesting illustration of the extent to which the better minds of all Israel were convinced, in the period of Josiah, of the necessity for some reform in the national religion. Men who had the true interests of their people at heart were troubled over the conditions which prevailed. They were conscious of the need for something being done to check the tendencies which were threatening to destroy all the distinctive elements in their people's faith. Especially were such men conscious of the peril which threatened the sister people of Northern Israel. Josiah and the men of Jerusalem were seeking to draw the bonds of religion more closely by bringing Israel into association with the purer and stronger life of the capital. Their method was to work through outward institutions of a common worship and of a common literature. Jeremiah was at work after a very different fashion. He began with repentance. Such a message was natural in a prophet, and such a method suited his function. He also develops all his thought positively, referring to nothing except the bastard mixture of heathenism and Yahwism which was sapping the life of his people. Hence it need occasion no surprise to find that he has nothing to say about the effort on Josiah's part.

Yet it deserves notice that he not only begins with repentance, but he ends there. And, in view of the fact that there was another reform-movement which did not think repentance sufficient, there is a significance in his silence. What a prophet does not ask may have meaning, especially when other men at the same time are making very clear demands.

V

JEREMIAH AND NATIONAL REFORM

IN seeking to discover the attitude of Jeremiah, who has demanded reform from his nation, to the actual measure of reform which was being carried out by Josiah, it is wiser to begin with his own utterances on the subject, if any such can be discovered. Mere general considerations should be kept severely in the background. Some students have counted it remarkable that there should be no mention of the prophet in the historical accounts which deal with the initiation of that reform and with the discovery of the book of the law in the temple. They express surprise that an otherwise unknown prophetess, Huldah, should appear in the role of adviser of king and court, and that the greatest prophetic figure of the period should be ignored. The only explanation which seems to them satisfactory is that Jeremiah was deliberately passed over because he was known to be in opposition to the movement. Yet the matter seems to be capable of an easier explanation. In Josiah's reign Jeremiah had not attained the prominence which later became his. Zedekiah, it is true, sent to consult him; but Jehoiakim treated him with scant respect, slitting his message into strips and tossing the fragments into a brazier. Zedekiah's captains paid him the compliment of being afraid of him and silencing the most dangerous voice in Jerusalem, but then he had made good his position. When Josiah initiated his reform, the young prophet had only begun his life-work some five years before, and was not likely to be consulted on a question of national policy. Add to this that he did not even belong to Jerusalem, but sprang from a somewhat inconspicuous village of Benjamin. When he came to the capital, he gave his impressions of the life there in terms which were not exactly calculated to commend him to its inhabitants and especially to its leaders (5 : 1–6). It was hardly to be expected that men who were planning a policy which involved the future of their state should turn for guidance to such a man.

Nor does it appear wise to attempt to determine the question by vague general considerations on the function of prophecy in old Israel. It is easy to lay down what ought to be the relation between one who speaks from direct revelation of the divine mind and men who are busy over practical reforms. But we do well to remind ourselves that prophecy in this period of Israel's history was not homogeneous. All the prophets did not give the same message or take the same attitude. Not only do we possess a series of oracles (23 : 9–33) in which Jeremiah gravely censures the temper and condemns the methods of the prophets of his time; but on two occasions he appears in direct opposition to men who were controlling the nation's policy and who were doing this in the name of Yahweh. Jeremiah's letter to the exiles in Babylon was written to counteract the influence of Zedekiah and Ahab, whom he denounced as false prophets (chap. 29). And chap. 28 reveals him and Hananiah giving diametrically opposite advice to King Zedekiah, yet both claimed to speak by divine authority. It must remain possible that one prophet approved while another disapproved the Josianic reform.

In these circumstances the humbler method remains the surer. We must attempt to find among Jeremiah's oracles any which give insight into his mind on the question. The first is found in 3 : 6–13, an oracle which has been interpolated among those which were examined in the previous chapter. The verses need not have been spoken at the same time as those among which they appear, and, as has been said, probably owe their insertion at this place to some collector. Yet it was a right insight which led to their being associated with their surroundings. For the oracle, like the others in chap. 3, is addressed to Northern Israel and is concerned with the conditions among that people. When it speaks of Israel, it speaks of it as a nation, using the second person singular in address. Again, if we may trust the opening verse, the oracle belongs also to the early period of the prophet's activity, for it is dated during the reign of Josiah. And finally it deals with the same subject, the conditions of national reform. Only, while the other oracles develop in positive terms what is needed for such a reform, and demand no more than a right repentance, these verses define what it must not be, and specially warn Israel against following the example of its sister-nation, Judah. The connexion between the oracles is close and integral, not accidental, as Skinner has called it.

Skinner dismisses the verses with the remark that 'if written by Jeremiah at all, it (the section) belongs to the post-Deuteronomic period of his ministry'.[1] By others they are denied to the prophet and therefore ignored. The reason for questioning their authenticity is their resemblance to the type of elaborate parallel between Samaria and Jerusalem which is said to have been introduced by Ezekiel. Of this a famous instance appears in Ezek. 23, where the two nations, under the titles of Oholah and Oholibah, are contrasted in a somewhat ponderous allegory. Yet it is always rash to pronounce in summary fashion on parallels which appear in different books and to decide that they must take their origin from the same writer. In this case it is peculiarly rash. For the chapter in Ezekiel, since it draws out the allegorical comparison to dreary length and enters into somewhat unsavoury details in connexion with it, bears all the marks of being the

[1] *Prophecy and Religion*, p. 80.

work of one who is following a model. The writer loses sight of his specific aim by following his allegory into wearisome and crowded detail. In comparison the oracle in Jeremiah is crisp and pungent. Above all, it has one point to make and subordinates the few details of its comparison in order to make this stand out clearly. The method of the allegory is, of all forms of literary composition, the most dangerous, because most liable to degenerate in the hands of an inferior literary artist. And the chapter of Ezekiel shows all the signs of being the work of such a writer who has caught at the method of a greater predecessor, but whom the dangerous method has mastered instead of him mastering it.

This may seem a subjective criterion. What has more force is to recognize that if the verses are denied to Jeremiah, it becomes necessary to find some period at which they could have been written, and even some reason for their having been carefully dated and assigned to this prophet. The time has gone past when it can be counted sufficient to pronounce a passage post-exilic and needless to make any further effort to account for its origin. In what period of the exile or after the exile was it possible to declare that Israel was better than Judah on the ground that Judah's reform had been falsely effected? Even if some one ventured to utter such a judgement on the sister nations, it remains necessary to find why the religious leaders in the time of Ezra–Nehemiah admitted it into the prophetic oracles, deliberately added a false date to it, thus connecting it with the Josianic reform-period, and pronounced it to belong to Jeremiah.

Accordingly Volz,[1] whether on these grounds or on others, has recognized the poverty of the proof which has been brought to deny the presence of Jeremianic material in the section 3 : 6–18. He has, however, raised another question in connexion with the verses. Hitherto it has been often

[1] *Kommentar zum A. T.* ad loc.

accepted[1] that the longer section (3 : 6–18), whether by Jeremiah or not, was not homogeneous, but must be divided into two oracles (6–13, 14–18). What led to this conclusion was that vv. 6–13 declare Israel to be better than its sister Judah, while v. 14 promises to Israel, by way of consolation or reward, that certain of its people should be brought to Zion. The same man, it was felt, could not have written these two sections, which betray a totally different opinion about Jerusalem. No one who declared Zion to have been the centre of a worse infection than any which has prevailed in Israel could have counted it a blessed thing for men in Israel to be brought to Zion, without adding something about the repentance or improvement of Judah. Volz, however, has rejected this division and redivides the verses. Grouping 6–15 and 18 b β, i.e. the clause 'in the land that I gave for an inheritance unto your fathers', he regards this as the Jeremianic original, while he considers vv. 16, 17, 18 a b α the later supplement. In view of the importance of the question for a true recognition of Jeremiah's position, it is necessary to test this position, and to point out that it is singularly unfortunate.

In Volz's judgement, then, the earlier verses 6–12 give a species of introduction to what follows and are in prose; vv. 13–15, 18 b β contain the oracle proper and are in verse. But already, in order to make the later verses read as poetry, he is obliged to change the reading in two of them, vv. 14 f. When he thus alters them, he does so without any support from the versions, nor can he appeal in favour of the change to any difficulty in the original text which is removed by the new reading. His sole reason for altering the text is that in his opinion the verses ought to be in poetic form and that at present they are not. This unscien-

[1] Cf. Peake, *Cent. B.* ad loc., who, however, seeks to retain v. 16 for Jeremiah, apparently on the ground that it is worthy of the prophet.

tific treatment of the text cannot be said to commend his conclusions.

Further, he appeals to the use of 'your fathers' in v. 18 b β, and concludes from the plural suffix that the clause was once closely connected with v. 14, where the plural is also employed. Unfortunately, however, he ignores that the plural appears also in the תרבו 'when ye be multiplied' of v. 16, so that his clause connects as closely with a verse he has excised as with the verse he retains. But he has also ignored that there is a broad distinction between vv. 6–13 and vv. 14–18, on the very ground that the former section always uses the singular, while the second section uniformly employs the plural. What makes this difference more significant is that there is a reason for the differing use. In vv. 6–13 the form of address is uniformly the second singular feminine, because there what is addressed is Israel personified as a woman. The speaker conceives the nation as existing in its national form. In vv. 14–18, on the other hand, the form of address is uniformly plural, for the simple reason that Israel is no longer thought of or addressed as a national unity. Instead we hear of a number of scattered individuals who are to be gathered 'one from a town and two from a family'. The different usage helps not merely to distinguish the different hands which have been at work on the section, but to mark their different attitude and point of view. When Jeremiah spoke to the men of Northern Israel in the other oracles of the chapter, he could and did still address them as a nation. They constituted the community for whose incorporation into the larger entity of Jewry Josiah, with the help of his court and priesthood, was eagerly planning. In that interest men were carrying out their reform at Jerusalem. What, on the other hand, the later annotator had in view was the diaspora, Israel scattered among the nations. He did not address himself to all these, but to the remnant among that diaspora, the one from a city and two from a family, who elected to return to Zion. These were promised a blessed return, but they came, not as a nation, but as individuals who cast in their lot with the returned exiles.[1]

The division into the two sections (6–13 and 14–18) must remain. And when it is retained it becomes possible to recognize why the Jeremianic oracle was expanded at this particular place. For it is no longer sufficient to cut out a phrase here or a section there and call these things later, without at least an effort to explain why the original was expanded. The cause of the expansion here was that the ambiguous word ' return ' gave an opportunity to soften the prophet's severe judgement on Judah.

The later generation naturally understood Jeremiah's summons to Israel in v. 12, שובה or return, of return from exile. To them the supreme proof of Yahweh's mercy consisted in their marvellous deliverance from Babylonia. To them also it was a blessed thing in itself to walk the streets of their recovered Zion and worship in its temple. What therefore they hoped and desired for their brother Israelites, scattered in diaspora, was that they should take the opportunity which

[1] Nor can Volz be said to be more happy in his detailed exegesis. Thus he includes in the original Jeremianic material v. 15 with its description of the רעים, shepherds or rulers, whom Yahweh is to institute. Joining this directly with v. 18 b β, he says they are to shepherd 'על the land which Yahweh gave your fathers'. In support of the original character of this saying and of his view that Jeremiah could speak of Yahweh raising up new rulers over the people He restores, he refers to 23 : 3 f. Unfortunately, when one turns to 23 : 3 f., one finds Volz himself compelled to acknowledge that the oracle raises 'starke Bedenken' strong suspicions about its Jeremianic origin. To lean on such a prop is like leaning on that Egyptian reed ' whereon if a man lean it will run into his hand '. And it only makes the situation worse to note that at 23 : 3 f. the shepherds are said, and naturally said, to shepherd על the people. That is what shepherds watch over, people or sheep. It is scarcely their function to watch over a land.

God had brought within their reach and become sharers in the new privileges of the community. Evidently, however, Jeremiah meant by שובה not return from exile, but repentance. Indeed, we should probably add with the Septuagint אלי and read 'return unto Me'. The reason for saying that this was evidently the prophet's meaning is that his exhortation to Israel to return is closely connected with the title he has given to the people. Israel to him is משובה, which means apostate, not exiled. Since Israel's guilt was summed up in its apostacy, what was first demanded from it was repentance, not a change of position, but a change of temper and heart. The oracle ends with a summons of the same character as that with which the series of oracles among which it has found its place end: 'O Israel, if it is in your mind to return, to me you must return' (4 : 1).

Again, it is specially incredible that Jeremiah could have believed or taught that a mere return to Zion should in itself be a blessed thing for Israel. Not only has he insisted that Judah was worse than Israel without adding any hint about the Southern nation mending its behaviour. But about the same period he was urging the men of Judah and Jerusalem to make clean work in their moral reformation (4 : 3 f.). And he was speaking, with the tone of one who has discovered its full horror, about the depravity of the inhabitants of the capital (5 : 1–6). It was impossible for a man to hold these opinions about the moral condition of the city and yet to say that Israel was to be blessed of Yahweh through being united to it. On the other hand, it was natural for the returned exiles to interpret the prophet's language in their own fashion, since they were proudly content with their restoration to the holy city and convinced that this restoration was in itself a proof of the divine grace.

Jeremiah's original message, then, said nothing about return from exile. To have demanded this from men who had not been carried away by their own choice and who were not free to return at their own pleasure would have been to mock them. Instead it spoke of what was and is within all men's power, a repentance for the evil past. And, since the prophet personified Israel and addressed it like an individual, he was evidently thinking of it as still constituting a national entity. He did not appeal to scattered fugitives among the nations of the world; he was still able to address the existing people which remained at Ephraim and which represented, though in weakened measure, the original kingdom. Hence he was commanded (v. 12) to go and proclaim his final message to the North, for this was the direction where the men whom it concerned were actually living. Duhm made merry over the absurdity of supposing that a prophet could utter a message which should reach the exiles in their distant new homes of Mesopotamia. He made this a chief reason for denying the oracle to Jeremiah, and referring it to that unfortunate post-exilic period, which is supposed to be capable of any absurdity about prophets or everybody else. The jest, and with it the argument, has rather lost its force, since it has come to be recognized how large a factor the remanent North Israelites were in the policy of the later kings of Judah.

In this oracle Jeremiah declares that Israel, apostate though it is, has put itself more in the right than back-sliding Judah. That in itself is a sufficiently remarkable verdict on the two sections of the people, though, in view of the fact that the prophet sprang from Benjamin and shows throughout a peculiar tenderness towards Ephraim, it might merely display the human side of the man. The most significant feature, however, is the reason given for pronouncing Judah to be worse than Israel. It is because the Southern people, warned by the fate which befel its neighbour in 721, carried out a reform, but a reform which was בשקר. The word used to describe this reform means something much stronger than the ' feignedly ' of A.V.: it implies falsity or treachery.[1] The word is a legal term, and Jeremiah uses it with some of its legal sense, for he continues that Judah through this reform has put itself more in the wrong before Yahweh than its sister-nation.

Yet it is a misreading of the writer to say that he saw 'any ground of hope for the restoration of Israel in the more aggravated guilt of Judah ',[2] and to conclude that the passage could not have been written by one who had Jeremiah's ' profound insight into the nature of religion '. As the following verse proves, his one hope for Israel rests in the possibility of its repentance, and for this change of heart he pleads. What he urges is that Judah through its false reform has persuaded itself that it needs no repentance. There is more hope for Israel, which has not thus persuaded itself that all is well between it and its God. And Jeremiah demands that it shall take a better way.

But to what reform does the prophet refer? Plainly it is one of a public and national character, for he speaks in terms of the two nations, personifying both and contrasting them on the ground of their character and conduct as peoples. And no other reform took place in Jeremiah's time which can be called national, except that which was carried out by Josiah. To this period also the oracle is referred in v. 6. Volz, who has accepted the oracle and counted it authentic, seems to be conscious of the conclusion to which his position is carrying him. At least he seeks to evade its consequences

[1] It is the word employed in the law to describe deliberate lying which does hurt to one's neighbour (Exod. 23 : 7), and about words which were intended to mislead (Exod. 5 : 9). Men who do שקר are men who practise wrong (Hos. 7 : 1; Jer. 6 : 13). A witness of שקר is one who bears injurious falsehood in his testimony, especially in courts (Exod. 20 : 16 ; Deut. 19 : 18. Cf. also p. 89 *infra*).

[2] Skinner, *Prophecy and Religion*, p. 83.

by remarking that several other efforts at reform were carried out by Jehoshaphat and Hezekiah, and that the passage may refer to any one of these or to their united effect. But all these are stated to have been the same in character as that under Josiah and to have been directed to the same ends. Apparently the earlier efforts were not so thorough-going or so successful as the last, but they were based on the same principles. Indeed, the success which attended Josiah's reform may well have been due to the fact that the work of his predecessors had prepared the minds of the people for the greater effort. It is more than difficult to believe that the prophet described the earlier reforms as having been wrought in falsity and as having served to make it harder for Judah to repent and return to Yahweh than Israel, and yet that he supported the Josianic reform which ran along the same lines.

One might seek to turn the edge of this severe judgement by supposing that Jeremiah was disappointed in the results which followed the Josianic reform. Accepting the view that his condemnation was directed against all such efforts, earlier and later, we might say that he condemned the new effort because it had failed to produce the effects which its promoters had desired and expected. But this fails to do justice to the strong and uncompromising character of the language or to its express terms. The reform in Judah is not condemned on the ground of its having been incomplete, or because it was content to aim at removing external and superficial abuses instead of dealing with the fundamental issues of the nation's heart and conscience. The reason is given for the prophet's condemnation. The movement has been bad in itself, since it was wrought in falsity or was false in principle. It has also been bad in its results, since its effect has been to make Judah worse and less capable of a right repentance than Israel.

Further, Josiah's reform was carried out in 621, and the

disaster at Megiddo cannot have been later than 608.[1] Now any man who could utterly condemn a great religious movement because in the brief period of a dozen years it had failed to effect all that its supporters expected from it, has forfeited the right to report on the condition of a nation. Especially has he forfeited this right, if he declares, on the basis of such a disappointment of his hopes, that the movement itself had been wrought in falsity and that its introduction had only resulted in making Judah worse than Israel. And, since there is no proof that its adoption produced these melancholy results in the nation, it would become necessary to ask whether the judgement was true in fact. Jeremiah, it should be noted, cherished no illusions about the conditions which prevailed in the Northern kingdom. The people were being seduced from allegiance to the God of their fathers and were worshipping other gods. They had gone up upon every high hill and under every green tree and were practising harlotry, which means idolatry. The prophet knew the deplorable effects of the worship on the bamoth. To him Israel was apostate and in desperate need of renewal of life. Speaking in the name of God, he urged the people to seek that which alone could produce a quickened life. But all this only makes it the more remarkable that he insists on the nation declining to take the way of recovery which Judah has chosen. Along that road it will merely become worse instead of better.

The only conclusion which does justice to the terms of the oracle is that here we have Jeremiah's verdict on the reform effort of the court and priesthood. Then it becomes

[1] Unfortunately the Chronicle discovered by Gadd contains no reference to Carchemish. Yet, since it has moved the date of the fall of Nineveh back, it seems probable that Carchemish and with it Megiddo should be set earlier. Baynes, however, retains the old date (*Israel amongst the Nations*, p. 98), and may have good reason for so doing.

unnecessary to suppose that the prophet had waited to measure the effect of the movement on the life of the nation. He had not needed to do this. For he judged the whole question by an entirely different standard, which was that of a prophet. According to Deut. 18 : 15, the law in which he had been reared, the task of the prophets in Israel was to continue the work of Moses and to guide the religious life of their people along the large and fruitful lines of his thought. Every movement, however flattering to the nation's pride or outwardly attractive, must be in agreement with this initial impulse. Otherwise it did not represent the mind of Yahweh for them.

It was the prophet's function to test each new development in the nation's worship or faith, and to pronounce whether it was a legitimate outcome of that which Israel received at the beginning. It would, of course, be premature to define here the reason which led Jeremiah thus to condemn the new movement of his time. In order to see why he counted the Josianic reform a departure from the prophetic ideals in religion, it will be necessary to study the rest of his religious message and to examine where and why he was in opposition to the prevailing conceptions and trend of his time. But meantime two things deserve to be emphasized. The first is that the Josianic reform meant a profound change in the worship of the nation. So great was the change that it marks a watershed in the history of the religion of the people. As such, it marked also a time when a prophet had a right to be heard and a duty to make his voice heard. And the second matter is that already it is possible to recognize one point of rupture. Few things determine men's attitude on religion more clearly than the statement of what they count essential to a right relation to God. Judah, by the Josianic reform, made the temple with its sacrifices and its ritual such an essential. To maintain the true religion with the people's access to Yahweh men must come to the one sanctuary and worship through a legitimate priesthood. To the prophet the only essentials for true religion were the repentant soul and a redeeming God. If Israel repented, it needed no more. Judah, in the Josianic reform, was demanding much more.

The recognition that Jeremiah was opposed in principle to the reform of his time serves to throw light on the remarkable utterance in 8 : 8 f. Unfortunately the oracle is entirely isolated, and no hint is supplied which might throw light on the period when it was spoken. The only suggestion of a possible date and reference to contemporary events must be gleaned from its contents, and these in their vague ambiguity have given rise to much discussion. But here the prophet appears, saying with some bitterness to the people or the priesthood : 'how can you say, we are wise men who possess Yahweh's torah or law? Yet it is clear that the lying pen of scribes has turned this into a lie.[1] Wise men are disappointed, full of dismay, tricked: what can their wisdom do for them, when they have rejected the word of Yahweh?' The first thing which is clear about this utterance is that it must refer to something other than the oral law which was delivered by the priests when occasion arose. Jeremiah is not, like Hosea, charging the priesthood with a faulty fulfilment of their duty through failure to give constant direction or through giving unworthy guidance to men who sought their decisions. The introduction of the scribes as the culprits and the special mention of the pen as the instrument of the falsification are enough to prove that reference is here made, not to a spoken, but to a written law. Skinner is able to write 'that Tôrā here means written law is so much the most natural view that we need hardly consider possible alternatives '.[2]

[1] The lying pen is עט שקר, 'into a lie' is לשקר; the recurrence of this word which also appeared in Jeremiah's condemnation of the reform in 3 : 10, is very marked; cf. p. 85, *supra*.

[2] *Prophecy and Religion*, p. 103.

But, further, there is a sharpness in the specific charge Jeremiah brings which argues that the prophet was speaking about some definite act which was, justly or unjustly, believed about and laid at the door of the priests. We are conscious of being in the presence of a real religious controversy where parties are sharply divided and where their difference concerns the question of what does or does not constitute the authoritative torah of Yahweh. The priests claim to possess this law, which is the norm for their nation's life. And Jeremiah definitely accuses certain scribes with having falsified this torah, not by the oral interpretation they put upon it, but by their false pen.

The oracle is undated, but it is difficult to find any period of Jeremiah's life to which it can be referred except the reign of Josiah. In the reigns of the later kings the questions which occupied men's minds were of a very different character. Jehoiakim was compelled by his attitude towards Babylonia to relax the stricter obligations of the law. The exigencies of his position prevented him from carrying forward the reform movement of his father. Zedekiah, again, was plunged into the burning question of continuing submission to Chaldea or aiming at independence. Jeremiah, during that reign, appears in connexion with matters of practical politics. But the early years of Josiah were concerned with reform, and in connexion with this the question of the law which governed and guided the reformers was of supreme importance. Men were driven back on principles. What was the divine law by which men were guiding themselves when they undertook to determine the forms of religion in the new state which was to comprise all Israel?

Hence Marti recognized that the oracle in Jeremiah must have some reference to the question of centralization which was before men's minds in the time of Josiah, and especially to the debate over whether there was any law of Yahweh to which those who introduced this novel principle could appeal. He, however, believed Deuteronomy to have been written or edited in the time of Josiah with the special purpose of introducing this change in Israel's religious practice. Whether written at that date or merely recast out of older material, it was the instrument employed by the court and the priesthood to make the temple the centre and the one legitimate centre for sacrifice. Since, however, it thus gave a new value to sacrifice and altar, making them essential in the national worship, Deuteronomy was highly offensive to the prophetic leaders, who had always revolted against the sacrificial system. What Jeremiah attacked in this oracle was the code of Deuteronomy in its new form after it had issued from the hands of its editors.[1]

I am still unable to find any reference to centralization in the body of the code of Deuteronomy. The only passage which clearly demands it is the little section with which the law proper begins, viz. 12 : 1–7. Now this section can be proved on independent grounds to be later than the similar legislation which immediately follows. And the terms in which the demand is there expressed, viz. that the people must resort to the sanctuary 'which Yahweh chooses out of all your tribes' to locate His name there, occur only in this passage of Deuteronomy and in several passages in the books of Kings and Chronicles. In the historical books the peculiar phrase is certainly original in Kings, from which it has been copied by the chronicler, and wherever it occurs in Kings it bears the marks of having been added by the editor of the records.[2]

[1] Cf. Marti, *Geschichte der Israelitischen Religion*, p. 166. The suggestion has been accepted by several Old Testament scholars. Volz refuses to see any reference to Deuteronomy in the verses of Jeremiah. His interpretation, however, involves so strained a sense of both scribes and torah that it affords no light.

[2] Cf. p. 29, *supra*, with the reference to an article in *Z. A. W.*, where I have given in full the reasons for these conclusions.

It is a natural inference that the peculiar description of the sanctuary which was added to the historical records in the interests of centralization was added also to Deuteronomy at the same time and for the same purpose. And the inference is strengthened, when it is noted that in Deuteronomy the section takes a later historical attitude on the treatment of the Canaanites. Deuteronomy, the Israelite law-book, was incorporated with the other religious literature of the North into that of Judah. But the little section, 12 : 1–7, was prefixed to it in order to bring the Northern law into line with the new aims of the leaders of Judah.

It is to this situation Jeremiah refers in his oracle. The original Code of Deuteronomy was not only one of the finest efforts ever made by any nation to bring the great commanding principles of a national religion into contact with the actual life of common men, it was also the law of Yahweh which had commanded his allegiance and worthily guided his thought in his youth. It was the law of Northern Israel to which he belonged.

The priesthood of Jerusalem have taken it over and acknowledged its validity for the whole nation. But in the process they have perverted it. The pen of the scribe has superinduced upon it, either as its only legitimate interpretation or as a novel and unwarranted addition to its regulations, something which has no authority. Jeremiah rejected this in the plainest terms, and called the men's act mere falsification. The change owed its presence to nothing more authoritative than the false pen of the scribes. And it was potent enough and far-reaching enough in its consequences to turn the law of Yahweh, into which it had crept, away from its original purpose.

In 3 : 6–13 Jeremiah rejected the Josianic reform because it was false in principle. In 8 : 8 f. he rejected it because of the falsity of the method in which it had been introduced.

It owed its introduction to no higher authority than the pen of certain scribes.

There is, however, a passage (11 : 1–8) which has frequently been interpreted to imply, not only that Jeremiah was in hearty agreement with the Josianic movement at least when it was first initiated, but that he became a kind of peripatetic evangelist in commending it to the capital and to the towns of Judah. The passage is somewhat clumsy in its expression, but it clearly contains two parallel sections (vv. 1–5 and vv. 6–8). In the former of these Yahweh pronounces a curse on all who do not listen to the words of *this* covenant. The covenant referred to is definitely stated to be that into which Israel entered immediately after the Exodus. To this message the prophet responds with Yea, Yahweh. In the second section Jeremiah receives a divine command to proclaim these words in the towns of Judah and the streets of Jerusalem. The words to be thus proclaimed are a command to the people to listen to the words of *this* covenant. And, in order to enforce the proclamation, it is added that the nation has never hitherto obeyed and has suffered for its conduct, since Yahweh has brought upon it the contents of *this* covenant.

It is possible that Volz is correct in regarding these two sections as parallel accounts which contain the same message. But that question may be ignored in connexion with the present discussion. What is of primary significance for the present purpose is to determine what covenant is here intended. Now since the document of II Kings 22 is called the book of the covenant, and since Josiah is said to have bound the people in a covenant at the time of the reform, it seemed to many a natural inference that the passage referred to this event in the national history. There was only one covenant before men's minds then, and, on the supposition that the passage was authentic, it seemed natural to conclude that

Jeremiah, in speaking of this covenant, could mean nothing else. Hence Erbt[1] not only thought it clear that the section referred to the introduction of the Josianic reform; he even believed that the use of the expression 'this covenant' proved its connexion with the solemn public act by which the reform was inaugurated. At the ritual which ratified the adoption of the reform by a covenant, whether at Jerusalem or at Anathoth, the young prophet was present and was profoundly stirred by the sight of a whole people taking part in a common act of repentance and renewal of its dedication to God. And there was borne in upon him in this great hour the conviction that the divine curse rested on any one who held aloof, and that he himself was summoned to rouse the conscience of his people and urge men to share in the common wave of renewed self-dedication.

The situation thus presented is very attractive, and psychologically quite possible. Unfortunately, however, it involves a radical revision of the text. Erbt was compelled to excise from the passage everything which identifies the covenant of which it speaks with the events at Sinai. Accordingly he omitted v. 4 in the earlier, and vv. 7, 8, with the exception of the last two Hebrew words, in the later section. He thus obtained for his original text the initial proclamation of Yahweh: 'cursed be he who does not listen to the words of this covenant', followed by the prophet's response, 'Yea, Yahweh'. After this came the command to proclaim these words, and to say: 'listen to the words of this covenant and obey them; but they did them not'. For the omission of v. 7 Erbt was able to appeal to the fact that the sentence is absent from the Septuagint, and he concluded that whoever introduced it there was responsible for the similar words in v. 4.

Erbt, however, failed to recognize that the shorter text of the Septuagint is in itself very unlikely to be the original.

[1] *Jeremia und seine Zeit*, pp. 138 ff.

For it retains the concluding words which definitely state that the people ignored the mission of the prophet. On the supposition that the passage contains nothing except the commission on which Jeremiah is supposed to have acted in commending the new movement of reform, how could this sentence have formed part? The two Hebrew words betray that something to which they refer and of which they form the conclusion has fallen out of the Septuagint. But, since the Masoretic text is the original in the second part of the section, the only reason Erbt can offer for suspecting v. 4 has disappeared. We are compelled to conclude that the covenant which the prophet was ordered to publish was that into which Israel entered with Yahweh at Sinai. It was commanded to Israel's forefathers at the time of the Exodus (vv. 4, 7), and its specific content was the rejection of all strange gods (v. 10). To recognize that the passage refers to the covenant at Sinai serves at once to explain why reference is made to the failure of the people to keep it. The prophet could not be commissioned to proclaim the terms of the new covenant under Josiah, and told in the same breath that the people had not obeyed what they were hearing for the first time. He was bidden renew the old demand, because Israel's constant disobedience had not destroyed its validity. The original claim, Yahweh Israel's God and Israel Yahweh's people, was as urgent and blessed as ever.

Recognizing that it is impossible to ignore the reference to the events at the Exodus, König is even able to assert that Jeremiah was here maintaining the supreme validity of the covenant at Sinai as against the position in Deuteronomy.[1] What lends a certain force to this view is that, while Deuteronomy recognizes the existence of the older covenant made at Horeb, it itself professes to be the product of a later covenant made on the plains of Moab. Hence its adoption

[1] *Geschichte der alttestamentlichen Religion*, p. 376 f.

might have seemed to threaten the superior value of the older rite. A scholar who, like König, believes the code of Deuteronomy to have been more or less the production of Josiah's time may well feel it natural that a prophet should enter some protest against a novel document which thrust or threatened to thrust the Mosaic original into a secondary position. Yet this reads into the section (11 : 1–8) a polemic which is not there. Whether the verses are original or secondary, their meaning is sufficiently clear. They claim for Jeremiah that he was called to deliver what was the burden of all prophecy from the beginning. All the prophets claim for themselves that they are in the Mosaic succession, and seek to recall their nation to the purity of its original faith. This section says no more about Jeremiah than that he exercised in Judah and Jerusalem the function of all his predecessors. If there is any polemic in the passage at all, it is against the supposition that Jeremiah was an innovator who broke with the prophetic tradition. Nor need it be surprising that he felt it necessary to make such a claim for himself or that some other made it for him. For we know that his message was questioned in his lifetime even more than that of his predecessors. Efforts were made to silence him and to shut him out of the temple. And it is specially noteworthy to recognize that he was in opposition, not merely to the priests, but to several of his fellow-prophets. It was natural that he should insist, or that others should insist on his behalf (for it is difficult to determine whether the oracle is authentic or secondary), that his word was the old word which formed the basis of Judah's religion, and that if he found slight acceptance, this had been the fate of other prophets. 'From the time when I brought your fathers out of Egypt down to the present day, I solemnly and persistently charged them to listen to my voice. But they did not listen or pay any heed.'

VI

THE FOE FROM THE NORTH

IN the second of his inaugural visions Jeremiah learned that mischief was about to arrive out of the North, and that this was coming through the action of Yahweh (1 : 14). The vision is set in close relation to the account of his call, so that it is clear that the prophet held this conviction from the beginning of his life-work. Evidently, then, he saw in the task of announcing the imminent arrival of such mischief a leading feature in his mission to his nation and to the world. Further, the two inaugural visions are integrally related to one another: the vision of an impending mischief from the North results from the prophet's previous conviction which assured him that Yahweh was intently watching over His word to bring it to its issue. The announcement of this coming calamity is bound up with and forms part of the fulfilment of the divine word.

Hence it is not surprising to discover, scattered through the book of Jeremiah, a number of oracles, some of which foretell trouble from this special quarter. In particular a series of such oracles is grouped at 4 : 15–31, and another series appears in chap. 25. These vary greatly in their view of the scope, the character, and the direction of the doom. Thus, to take first the question of the direction from which the catastrophe arrives, some of these plainly predict its arrival from the North (e.g. 4 : 5–8; 6 : 22–6; 25 : 9), while at other times the prophet describes the news as coming by way of Dan and Mount Ephraim, both of which places lay northward from Jerusalem e.g. (4 : 13–17; 8 : 14–17). Some of the oracles, however, ignore this feature, or even speak of disaster coming from the desert.

The character, again, of the doom varies more largely than the direction of its coming. A favourite description pictures it in terms of an invading and irresistible army. Then we read of cavalry and archers (4 : 27–31), of chariots like a storm-wind and horses swifter than panthers (4 : 13–17), of besieged towns (8 : 14–17). Once the enemy is personified; he is a lion from the North, a destroyer of nations (4 : 5–8). Yet, though invasion is a favourite figure in the description, it is no essential element in the picture, for the appointed doom can be called a blasting sirocco from the desert (4 : 9–12). This oracle breaks away from the northern direction as well as from the invader. In one case the effect is nothing less than chaos come again (4 : 23–6). The calamity there falls on more than men: it includes the mountains, the heavens, and the birds. Patently no human hand, invader or other, could produce what is there described. Only Yahweh Himself could bring the world back to the condition from which He alone had brought it in the beginning.

Finally, as the character and the direction of the resultant ruin are not uniform, neither is its scope. At one time it includes the world (4 : 27–31),[1] at another it seems to be confined to Judah (4 : 5–8).

Accordingly we find in Jeremiah the expectation of some catastrophe, vaguely defined as to its scope and its instrument. But it is an integral part of his prophetic message, for he receives the conviction of its coming shortly after his call, and he is commissioned to announce its imminent arrival. The ultimate source of this doom, too, by whatever means it is brought about, is Yahweh. Because He is bringing

[1] The uncertain meaning of הארץ which can be rendered 'the land' or 'the earth' makes it difficult to determine what is intended in every case. I have selected 4 : 27–31 because the connexion with the heavens makes the sense sure. About the oracle which precedes it, viz. 4 : 23–6, there can be no question.

it, He can reveal to the prophet its certainty and its nearness. And while it is to fall on Israel, and a prophet of Israel is deeply concerned in its effect on Israel, it is not confined to that nation. All the nations shall somehow be involved in it. It deserves note also that the matter falls rather into the background of the prophet's thought during the later years of his life. The message appears among his early visions, and the oracles which embody it appear near the beginning of his work.

What was Jeremiah expecting, and what moved him to form this expectation? Hitherto the question has been discussed in the light of a general theory as to what roused all the early prophets to active interference in the life of their nation. The men, it was supposed, were stirred to action by some threatening event in the political or historical conditions of their time. They were the stormy petrels of Israel's history which always appeared in a period of national crisis. They saw from afar the emergence of some power or some event which involved a threat to the existence of their people. Seeing it earlier and seeing its consequences more clearly than ordinary men, they sought to interpret its meaning for their contemporaries. Since they were able to proclaim this calamity to be the will of Yahweh, they prevented defeat and even exile from destroying the national faith, though these did destroy the national independence. Since they also declared these events to be the divine chastisement for sin, they succeeded in awaking a national conscience and effecting some needed reform. Thus Amos and Hosea saw on the distant horizon the threatening cloud of Assyria. Isaiah intervened when Israel and Damascus were attacking Judah. Jeremiah, it was concluded, must have been roused to activity by a similar cause. The difficulty in his case was to find any adequate cause in the events of Josiah's early reign. For neither the Hebrew nor the Assyrian records contained the hint of any troubles in Palestine in those years. Judah was a province of the Empire and still protected by it. Political troubles only appeared on the collapse of Nineveh.

But it was noted that Herodotus in one passage[1] reported the presence of a body of invading Scythians on the borders of Egypt during the reign of Psammetichus. This, it was said, was the event which had roused Jeremiah and made him a prophet. The Scythians broke into Asia by the route of the Caucasus: they were the mischief which arrived from the North. The direction of the doom was accounted for. Their coming was attended by the wreck of towns, the flight of the inhabitants, and the cessation of all ordered life: in such terms Jeremiah described the advent of what he dreaded. He spoke about men of a strange speech who came from afar: the Scythians hailed from Europe and spoke an Indo-European language. So thoroughly did the parallel commend itself that Duhm reduced the original elements of Jeremiah's prophecy to a series of Scythian songs.

There were difficulties in connexion with the theory. Thus Jeremiah spoke of a catastrophe which overwhelmed more than Judah, even other nations. A raid on Ashdod bought off by the Egyptian king seemed hardly adequate for such a description. But that was the natural exaggeration which was produced by the terrors of the invaded. Hebrew history, again, contained no hint of any ravages in Palestine during Josiah's reign. It was concluded that the Scythians divided their host into two, one part of which went by the old route of Esdraelon and Philistia while the other part advanced along the east of Jordan, so that Judah actually escaped. So we were supplied with useful knowledge of the Scythian language and of their line of march. Some of Jeremiah's description fitted the Scythians—their distant origin, their uncouth speech, their snorting chargers and swift movement. But other

[1] i. 103–6; cf. iv. 11.

elements were incongruous. Did such raiders possess the skill or the patience to besiege towns? Could a homogeneous people like the Scythians be called 'nations', as though many were banded together? For this there was the usual explanation. Jeremiah's original oracles were those which fitted the theory; the unsuitable sections or phrases were accretions or glosses. And as for the oracle which extended the catastrophe to the mountains and the very birds, that was apocalyptic.

A recent monograph by Wilke[1] has shed new light on the whole question. The discussion is long and thorough. Yet it is possible to present Wilke's argument to English readers in comparatively short compass. He has discussed the question along the two lines of the historical evidence and the exegetical proof. On the one hand, is there sufficient evidence to prove that the Scythians ever invaded Palestine at all? On the other hand, even if there were, is it a just interpretation of Jeremiah's oracles which has taken these to refer to the Scythians? The proof Wilke brings is cumulative, and neither side of it ought to be ignored.

The only evidence we possess as to the presence of the Scythians in or near Palestine is from the statement of Herodotus. According to this, they captured Ashdod, a well-known town of Philistia, and reached the borders of Egypt. They were there met by the Pharaoh Psammetichus who, by gifts and entreaties, succeeded in turning them back. While the main body were in retreat, a section of the band plundered a temple of Aphrodite in Ascalon. For this violation of her temple the goddess punished them by visiting them with a venereal disease which, adds the historian, has ever since been a recognized characteristic of the nation.

[1] *Das Skythenproblem im Jeremia Buch* in *Alttestamentliche Studien für Kittel*, 1913, pp. 222–54. On Wilke's explanation of the origin of Herodotus's story I am not competent to express an opinion. That is a question for specialists in history.

The story, it must be recognized, is not very credible in itself, and indeed bears all the marks of an aetiological legend. It is possible, however, that under its legendary form lies a trustworthy historical record. The difficulty remains of trying to fit the incident into the known facts of the period. Now Herodotus has given no date for the event. He does give twenty-eight years as the duration of the visits of the Scythians. But this, according to Assyrian historians, is impossible. What they count possible is that, while Herodotus was certainly mistaken in saying that the attacks lasted twenty-eight years, he may have meant that the invasion began twenty-eight years before the fall of Assyria. Since Nineveh fell in 612, the capture of Ashdod will fall in 640, i.e. in the period of Asshur-bani-pal, who conquered Egypt in 648. Whether that situation is credible in ancient history, it must be left to Assyrian historians to determine. It is hardly credible that Jeremiah, who was called to his life-work in 625, was roused by the memory of an invasion which had taken place fifteen years before.

Yet he may have been stirred by anticipation of a possible return. Remembering or learning the terror which attended the appearance of the Scythians on the borders of Egypt, and hearing that this powerful nation was reduced to the necessity of buying them off, he may have spoken to a court and people who were dreading this terrible return. But the Scythians of Herodotus were the Ashguza of the Babylonian and Assyrian documents, and Mr. Gadd's new Chronicle[1] has made it clear that these newcomers, after having forced their entry into the Mesopotamian valley, became the allies of Nineveh. It was indeed their help, along with that of the Egyptians, which maintained the Assyrian Empire against the attacks of Babylonia and Media. Not until they forsook Assyria did it succumb to its enemies. It is extraordinarily

[1] *The Fall of Nineveh*, 1923.

difficult to believe that any one in Palestine, which was at the time subject to Nineveh with which the Scythians were allied, could fear an invasion by this people. And it is equally difficult to understand why the Scythians should make an attack on Egypt at a time when Scythia and Egypt were united in seeking to maintain the tottering power of their common ally. The new information supplied by the Chronicle has tended to support Wilke's sceptical attitude to the story from Herodotus.

That question, however, involving as it does the uncertain relations between Assyria, the Scythians, and Egypt, must be left for final settlement to the historians. But, even if it could be proved that the Scythians advanced to the borders of Egypt, the second part of Wilke's monograph will retain its force. In this he has collected and carefully examined all the descriptions of the invader which have been hitherto appealed to, or which are capable of being appealed to, in order to prove that Jeremiah was referring to that people. And he has been able to point out that in every case these descriptions are employed by other prophets to whom the Scythians were unknown. He has then collated from the same chapters a number of descriptions about which it is possible to say that they are wholly unsuitable to the Scythians, so far as these are known to us, and which serve to prove that the prophet who used them could not have had this nation in his mind.

There is nothing said by Jeremiah about the foe from the North which could only have been uttered by one who was thinking about the Scythian hordes. There are also features in the description of the foe which do not agree with the characteristics of that nation which have come down to us. And all our historical evidence leads to the conclusion that it is difficult to believe in a Scythian invasion which overran Palestine in the period of Josiah. The conclusion seems to be inevitable that this invasion had nothing to do with Jeremiah's call to be a prophet or with his oracles after he was called. Accordingly Volz has followed Wilke in rejecting the identification of Jeremiah's foe from the North with the Scythians.[1]

But in that case what is to be said about the early oracles in chaps. 4 and 6 ? And in particular how can we explain that in the second vision after his call Jeremiah was warned of trouble coming from the North? If it was not the Scythians whom he expected, what was it? The questions do not distress Wilke. He cuts the knot by referring all these oracles to the time when Chaldea was threatening Palestine : to him Nebuchadrezzar was the lion rising from its lair, the destroyer of nations. Yet it is quite impossible, as Skinner and Volz have recognized, to relegate this expectation and all the material which deals with it to a late period in the prophet's life. He began his career under the impression that Yahweh was bringing trouble out of the North. Wilke's easy solution only brings with it fresh difficulties.

He has, however, recognized that, for all who, like himself, believe in the necessity for finding some historic invader to account for Jeremiah, it is a clear case of Scythian or Chaldean. And the new light he has thrown on the subject ought to make finally impossible one theory of the course of the prophet's thought, viz. that he began with a prediction of the Scythians and then transferred the oracles in which he had foretold their coming to the Chaldeans. Several students recognized, even before Wilke's monograph appeared, that

[1] *Kommentar*, p. 57 f. In reference to what has been called the exegetical side of Wilke's proof, I may be allowed to record my conviction of its finality. Having had occasion to work through the material before the publication of the monograph, I had collated the passages which were discussed and had reached Wilke's conclusions. The case is even stronger than it is there stated. Since, however, Wilke's proof seems sufficient, it is unnecessary to add anything extra.

the evidence for an actual Scythian incursion into Palestine was very slight. Accordingly they suggested that Jeremiah began his prophetic career with an expectation of a judgement which was to descend on Judah through these Northern invaders. When the predicted doom seemed to fail and the enemy did not appear, the prophet was naturally discredited in the eyes of his countrymen. That served to explain a supposed period of silence in his career. The catastrophe, however, was only delayed; it arrived during the reign of Zedekiah in the form of the Babylonians. Now it was noted that the prophet, after his first roll had been destroyed by Jehoiakim, issued a revised and enlarged edition of his oracles. It was supposed that he then took the opportunity to re-touch his original material and to adapt it to the new conditions in which Judah found itself. In particular he revised the predictions of the coming doom from the North so as to make the Babylonians instead of the Scythians its instrument.[1]

The theory was never put forward as more than a theory which might serve to explain a difficulty. But it was rather an unhappy suggestion, so that no one need regret its disappearance. For it had the painful effect of seeming to reduce Jeremiah to the level of those men who confidently predict the coming of judgement in 1940, and who, when 1940 comes and goes without any change on the world, shift their prediction forward by another score of years.

Indeed, it served to bring the prophet lower. For the modern men only profess to offer explanations of another man's prophecies, without claiming prophetic authority themselves. They can frankly acknowledge that they made a mistake in their interpretation of another's language. But Jeremiah must be supposed to have said in the name of God at the hour of his call that judgement was to come through the Scythians under Josiah, and then, after due correction

[1] Cf. e.g. Cornill, *Kommentar*, p. 86 f.

of his language, to have issued with the same authority a prediction that it was to arrive under Zedekiah.

The air has been cleared of this suggestion, and the issue might seem to be narrowed down to a choice between two positions. Either it becomes necessary with Wilke to refer all the oracles about the troubles from the North to the period of the Chaldean invasion. In that case it will be difficult to avoid the further consequences. The vision of mischief from the North and the oracles which deal with it cannot be separated from the period of the prophet's call. And we shall be driven along the road which Vernes and Horst have already taken.[1] Horst believes that the earliest authentic utterances of Jeremiah must be dated after the death of Josiah at the time when Babylonia began to be a menace to Judah. The beginning of the prophet's activity was thrust back to the time of the reform in order to serve a special purpose. Or, on the other hand, if we retain the connexion of the oracles with the date of the prophet's call we must with Skinner cling to the view that there was sufficient danger arising from the presence of the Scythians in Palestine to give rise to Jeremiah's fears with the resultant prophecy.[2]

It is clear that the course of critical inquiry into the origin of these features in Jeremiah's prophecy has led to an im-

[1] Cf. Horst's article, 'Die Anfänge des Propheten Jeremia', in *Z. A. W.* 1923, pp. 94–153.

[2] *Prophecy and Religion*, pp. 39 ff. It is a remarkable omission in all Skinner's discussion of the subject that he limits himself to the purely historical, as opposed to the exegetical, side of the question. He nowhere touches the matter raised by the second half of Wilke's monograph, viz. whether there is anything in Jeremiah which compels us to think that he must have had the Scythians in his mind, and whether there is not much which is wholly unsuitable to what is known about that people. Yet that is precisely the subject on which an Old Testament scholar has most claim to be heard.

passe. And what such a situation brings with it is the need to re-examine the whole line of approach to the subject which has resulted in this impasse. Now all the attempted explanations share one common presupposition which is taken for granted without question. Interpreters vary as to the particular nation which Jeremiah had in mind, some calling these the Chaldeans, others clinging to the Scythian invasion, a few attempting to combine both. They also differ about the political conditions of the world at the period when the prophet began his career, as they differ about the date of his call, because they are convinced of the necessity of bringing his call into relation to the nation which he is supposed to have had in mind and whose threatening attitude is conceived to have produced his call. But they are convinced, so convinced that it never occurs to them to discuss the question, that there must have been some political event, more or less near, more or less patent to the minds of thoughtful men at the time, which moved Jeremiah to become a prophet and to intervene in the national history. This preconceived idea of what summoned all the prophets into activity has determined the method of approach to the study of the book. And it has led to what can only be described as a kind of cul-de-sac with no way forward.[1] It is time to hark back and ask whether the mistake may not lie deeper than has yet been recognized. It lies in the mistaken idea that the prophets were roused to activity by outward events in the national history. The theory of their having needed some crisis in the world or in the fate of their own people to stir them to intervention does not correspond with

[1] Students of Isaiah will recognize that Fullerton, in his remarkable article on the present position of criticism on this prophet, 'Viewpoints in the Discussion of Isaiah's Hope for the Future', *Journal of Socy. of Bibl. Liter.* 1922, has pointed out the same deadlock. Yet he has done no more than signalize the deadlock: he has not ventured to suggest a new method of approach.

the facts of the case. Several of them, like Amos and Isaiah, were called to be prophets before Assyria had appeared on the horizon. Elijah denounced Ahab, when the house of Omri had succeeded in making Northern Israel a power which reached beyond the limits of its own territory. 'When Solomon had brought his kingdom to a peculiar pitch of outward security and inward organization, a prophet appeared, not to declare an imminent trouble from without nor to explain any impending catastrophe, but to appeal to elements within the nation and support Jeroboam against the king.'[1]

What all the prophets had to proclaim was a day of the Lord, in which Yahweh was about to manifest Himself and His purpose in judgement. At first the sphere of this self-manifestation in judgement was Israel, where Yahweh had made His nature and His purpose known. But already with Amos the scope of the divine action was widening to include other nations. In Jeremiah it has widened to take in the world. The prophet is not thinking in terms of a historic nation: he is thinking in terms of Yahweh and all the nations. The scope of the divine judgement corresponds with the scope of the prophet's commission.

Here it is instructive to note the position Volz has taken on the question. He acknowledges that Wilke has proved his case and that the oracles cannot refer to the Scythians. But he also recognizes that vision and oracles alike must belong to the early period of the prophet's call. He is further convinced that the account of the call is substantially correct and that there is no justification for the arbitrary changes in the text to which earlier students had recourse. The vision of trouble arising from the North and the oracles which depict this trouble must be integrally related to the call

[1] I have discussed the question at greater length in *Religion of Israel under the Kingdom*, pp. 48 ff.

and the commission. Jeremiah, therefore, could not be referring to the Chaldeans, who at that time were no menace to Judah. When, however, Volz seeks to explain what calamity was the occasion of the prophet's entry on his life-work, he takes refuge in what can only be called a half-way house, like that to which he has recourse after his admission that the oracle in 3 : 6–13 is authentic.[1] According to him, Jeremiah appeared with the conviction that judgement was coming on Judah and this judgement was connected with a convulsion in the world's history. 'Should any one however desire to refer the foe from the North to some other definite nation such as the Chaldeans, I count that also incorrect. Jeremiah intends to describe no definite enemy, capable of being politically distinguished. He has received from Yahweh the message that an invasion is bursting in from the North. He knows no more and desires to know no more.'[2]

But, though Jeremiah might thus be content to know no more, he could not prevent the men to whom he spoke from desiring and claiming to know more. After all, if the prophet appeared in a period of peace under Josiah when for a few years Judah was able to busy itself about its internal affairs, if he proclaimed that one of his primary functions was to announce a trouble coming from the North, if he continued by describing with extraordinary vividness the character and result of this trouble, it was inevitable that all who took his message seriously must have asked what he meant. And when in particular he called the leader of this invasion a lion from its lair, a destroyer of nations, he must have been prepared to say whether these phrases meant anything.

Volz's interpretation can only be termed a half-way house. He is prepared to surrender the reference of the oracles to one particular nation. It remains to ask whether they must be referred to any political event or to a nation at all.

[1] Cf. p. 85 f. *supra*.   [2] *Kommentar*, p. 58; cf. also p. xv.

If now we interpret the trouble which Yahweh is sending from the North in an eschatological sense, and see in it the proclamation of the coming judgement by God on a sinful world, it becomes possible to do justice to the position in which the vision appears. It follows immediately on Jeremiah having learned that he was a prophet to the nations. It is closely linked to the first vision, which assured him that Yahweh was watching over His word to bring it to its issue. It is followed by the announcement of a destroyer of nations. The doom is impending over the world. And the man who has to declare its imminence is commissioned for the world.

But it also enables us to do justice to all the features which appear in the oracles which follow, and to recognize that certain of these features are not novel to Jeremiah, but closely resemble similar descriptions which appear in the early prophets. Naturally all who believe that Jeremiah must have had some political event in view have laid stress on those oracles or sections of the oracles which describe the doom under the figure of an invasion of Judah. In the oracles which they regard as authentic they have slurred what gives a wider scope to the coming doom. And where this character was too patent to be ignored, they have questioned the authenticity of the passages.

It is not possible to examine here every particular passage in Jeremiah: that could only be done in a full commentary. But there are three oracles which bring out with peculiar clearness the large character and wide scope of the catastrophe which the prophet believed himself commissioned to announce. And it will serve the present purpose to examine these with closer attention.

The first is the little section (4 : 23–6) which contains a description of chaos come again. Yahweh, who made the world a cosmos, was about to reduce it to the condition from which He brought it. Duhm did not question the authenticity of the oracle and could not ignore its character. But he was content to remark that it gave an isolated feature of the prophet's expectation. But the feature it gave, however isolated, was one which was in utter disagreement with the idea of any historical invader. No nation could produce what Jeremiah declared he had seen. And the prophet ascribed it to Him who alone could effect it: the fertile earth was desert and all its towns were burned out through the act of Yahweh.

Volz, however, has rejected the passage for two leading reasons. Doom is denounced here against the mountains so that they reel and all the hills quiver. This, he says, meant the mountains which, according to Hebrew ideas, supported the solid earth, so that with their reeling the world fell to ruin. And he adds that this is a favourite apocalyptic conception, and therefore cannot be Jeremianic. The criticism might be passed so far as it concerns ההרים, the mountains. But Volz has failed to explain why in such a connexion הגבעות, the hills came to be associated with the mountains. And failing to notice the connexion he has not recognized that Jeremiah linked the two together as Isaiah 2 : 12 ff. had already done, and for the same reason. It was not because they supported the earth, but because they were among the high and lofty things which were to be levelled in the day of the Lord. Jeremiah was thinking along the lines of his predecessor. What makes the connexion here more significant is that the oracle in Isaiah is one in which that prophet most clearly revealed his expectation of a world-catastrophe.[1] Again, Volz draws attention to the disappearance of the birds of the sky (v. 25), and, quoting Apoc. Es. 5 : 6, considers this feature the sign of late apocalyptic ideas. But again he has ignored that an exactly similar feature had appeared in Hosea (4 : 3), a prophet with whose language and ideas Jeremiah, especially in his early oracles, shows himself

[1] Cf. my *Religion of Israel under the Kingdom*, p. 151 f., with note.

to be intimately acquainted. In both cases the later prophet was following his predecessors. And what Volz has termed a favourite apocalyptic idea has shown itself to be part of the prophetic conception of the day of the Lord.

The same conception of a universal calamity appears in the passage 4 : 27–31. Thus speaks Yahweh: the whole world shall become a waste. As has already been remarked, it is often difficult in these oracles to determine whether הארץ means the world or the land of Israel. Here, however, the contrast with the heavens makes the meaning unmistakable. Volz would again escape from the idea of a universal calamity here by the remark that this is the addition of a sympathetic reader who has inserted a phrase on the analogy of Jer. 14 : 2; Hos. 4 : 3; Mic. 3 : 6. Any one who will take the trouble to verify these references will find that they are quite different in their attitude. But even if the analogies or similarity were real, that cannot prove the sentence secondary. For Volz does not refuse 14 : 2 to Jeremiah. And if the prophet could say something in one place, this does not debar him from introducing the same idea in another. The other references are taken from prophets of an earlier date, with which it is surely possible that their successor was acquainted, especially when one of them is from Hosea, whom our prophet loves to quote. It becomes more than a little unnecessary to drag in an interpolator at all. Now the interesting and instructive feature about this oracle is that Jeremiah begins with the picture of a coming doom of a character which makes it impossible for any historic nation to carry it out. Yet he has continued with a vivid picture of towns taking flight and men climbing the rocks at the rumour of approaching cavalry and archers. The features which describe the judgement under the form of an invasion are merely a favourite form which Amos had already used to predict the impending calamity. But they did not exhaust its content, for both prophets expected a doom which was to include the world.

The third oracle which speaks in clear terms of a world-catastrophe is 25 : 1–29. The passage, however, has unmistakably been supplemented so that in its present form it is far from easy to detect its purpose. The verses must be examined with some care, with especial care in the direction of not allowing any bias to influence the decision of what formed the original. To begin from the conclusion, vv. 17–26 are certainly secondary. For they represent Jeremiah as having taken a cup from the hands of Yahweh and made all the nations to which he was sent drink from it, and these nations reach from Egypt to Elam, from Babylon to the Mediterranean coast. Such an interpretation of the picturesque figure in which (vv. 15 f.) Yahweh makes His prophet the medium of His just anger against the world could only have occurred to a somewhat dull literalist. To make the situation worse, the interpolator has thrust the description of the fulfilment of the divine charge between two sections which relate the instruction to the prophet. According to him, Jeremiah was ordered to take the cup from Yahweh's hand: he proceeded to deliver it to a long catalogue of nations: he then returned to hear the message which was to be given along with the cup to the kings who had already received it. The second verse of the intruded passage betrays the period of the interpolator, for he sends Jeremiah first to Jerusalem and the towns of Judah to turn them into a desolation and object of horror *as they now are*. Yet the oracle has been dated in the fourth year of Jehoiakim (v. 1), a time when the capital was still intact. Patently the description of this ruined land belongs to the period of the early exile, while Judah was lying desolate.

Again, vv. 11–14 are badly attested. Verse 14 does not appear in the LXX, and v. 11 b is only present in one manuscript which is not of the highest authority, and even there it appears in a different form from that in the Masoretic text. The promise of return has been added to the Greek in this place. That rouses the suspicion that vv. 12–14, which continue the subject of what is to happen after seventy years have run their course, are secondary. And that suspicion is confirmed when we read in v. 13 about all that is written in this book of Jeremiah's prophecies against all the nations. Whether the book here referred to was the collection of oracles against the nations in chaps. 46–51 or included the entire book of Jeremiah, only a late annotator was capable of putting this literary allusion into the mouth of Yahweh, and only a man who had before him the completed book could use it at all. Again we find ourselves in the period of the exile or of the early return, when men were searching their prophetic records for confirmation of their hopes. After removing the intruded clauses it becomes legitimate to notice that the LXX has preserved the original form of v. 11 a in its reading 'and all the earth shall be desolate'.[1] The sentence forms a natural conclusion to v. 9 f., where Yahweh brings the families of the North against this country and its inhabitants and against all the surrounding nations and devotes them to ruin. The clinching sentence follows: 'and all the earth shall be desolate'.

Further, the final clause in v. 9 is absent from the Septuagint, and in its present form cannot be parsed or construed. 'Behold, I am sending and taking all the families of the North, oracle of Yahweh, and to Nebuchadrezzar king of Babylon my servant' is impossible both in Hebrew and in English.

[1] I count it proved that LXX did not read the Hebrew הזאת which makes the words read 'this land', in v. 11 a, because in v. 13 it has *ἐκείνην*. The insertion of v. 13 in the section brought with it the addition of הזאת to the M.T. of v. 11 a, but the change was not made in the text which the LXX translators employed.

The same hand which has added the other references to the Babylonian conquest and captivity has been at work here. Writing carelessly, the annotator has been content to notice that Yahweh could send to Nebuchadrezzar, but has ignored the later verb.

The oracle has been revised after the destruction of Jerusalem by the Chaldeans. Hence it is impossible to give entire confidence to the opening verses which set down its date in the fourth year of Jehoiakim, which was the first year of Nebuchadrezzar. The section (1–8) contains a somewhat lengthy exordium of a type which is very familiar to every student of Jeremiah. And the mention of the exact date links itself with a suspicious exactness into the aim of those who revised the passage and referred it to the conquest and the exile. Jeremiah, the last prophet of Judah, was represented as having foreseen from the first year of the great king's reign the ruin which he was to bring on Jerusalem, and as having predicted the exact period during which this ruin was to last. That is the kind of proof of a prophet's truth which appealed to later annotators. It is impossible to trust the date with implicit confidence.

When, however, the accretions which have gathered round the original have been cleared away, there remains a brief oracle in which Jeremiah is told that Yahweh is about to bring all the families[1] from the North against Judah and the surrounding nations. The issue of their coming will be to turn the whole earth into a desolation. The prophet is then commissioned to take from the hand of Yahweh the cup of His fury against the nations. Should any of these refuse to drink, he must say that Yahweh is beginning to work hurt on the city that was specially dedicated to Him, and that therefore no other may remain immune. He is to announce a judgement which shall begin with the house of God, but

[1] Or, with the LXX, the whole family.

which extends to the world of men. And he is to announce a judgement on Judah, because it has identified itself with a world which is doomed.[1]

Now this oracle is, on the one side, in interesting and suggestive agreement with that of 4 : 23–6. In both cases the judgement, with its resultant ruin, is universal. Only the one describes its effect on the universe, the other is limited to its effect on the world of humanity. The whole earth is to suffer a change in the day of the Lord. That change extends even to the most stable things in this world, its hills and mountains. Naturally there it is Yahweh Himself and Yahweh alone who brings back His world to chaos. But, when the world of men is in the mind of the prophet, though the cup of wrath comes from the divine hand and is of the divine ordering, there is mention of an instrument by which all the ruin is brought about. Hence, on the other side, the oracle in chap. 25 is in suggestive connexion with the vision of the boiling cauldron. They hold in common and they bring into prominence that the mischief is to arrive from the North.[2] It will be necessary to consider the Northern direction later.

[1] It deserves at least passing notice that this passage has been connected with several fragments at the conclusion (25 : 30–8), oracles which are confessedly apocalyptic in their character. They were added here because they were similar in tone to the original oracle.

[2] The vivid picture of chaos come again and the no less vivid image of Yahweh delivering to the prophet the cup of fury against the nations leave on me the impression of both being the work of a young man. And a certain bitter intransigence in both oracles confirms the sense that we are here in contact with the vehement, but slightly crude, judgement of youth. After this fashion a man is apt to write and speak who, in the hour of his call, has come to a profound conviction of the reality of the ethical standards. To him the world lies under the power of the wicked. It is therefore ripe for judgement, and he, in his fire of youth and stern conviction, must declare a judgement from which nothing is excluded. But this is a mere subjective impression, and is not offered as though it held more.

Meantime, so far as Jeremiah predicted a ruin which was to involve the whole world, he uttered nothing new, but merely repeated in his own words what was present in all his forerunners. Isaiah began his teaching by announcing a doom which was to lay flat everything which was high and lofty: and among the lofty things which were to be levelled were the mountains and the hills (2 : 6–22). Hosea spoke of the Lord's controversy, the issue of which was to bring a mourning in which the birds of the heaven and the very fish of the sea should have their share (4 : 1–3). Amos expected a calamity from which men could not escape though they climbed into heaven or descended to Sheol (9 : 1–3). Only Yahweh Himself could produce the effects which His messengers were commissioned to announce. The scale on which these judgements were described was too vast for any human agent.

The men were sent to act as prophets to their own people. Accordingly they passed at once to consider how this calamity which they announced was to affect Israel. They were also preachers of righteousness and repentance, and they must insist on the attitude their hearers ought to take toward this revelation of their God's purpose. But the threat to Israel was uniformly set in the larger frame of a threat to all the nations. More than Israel was involved in it. The proof of this appears in the fact that the first of the series of prophets expressly stated it. Amos marshalled the nations round Israel which he selected as typical of his world, and declared that the time was ripe for their visitation.

What has prevented students of the Old Testament from doing justice to this fundamental element in the prophetic message has been the same cause which led to an impasse in the interpretation of Jeremiah. They have been bound by a theory, according to which the prophets were roused to action and governed in their outlook by some political event or some threat to the independence of their nation. Naturally men who began from such a casual and limited outlook could not have thought along the large lines which have been described. Yet all the prophets have told us where they began, and what moved or even compelled them in act and speech. They began from Yahweh, the God of Israel, from the thought of His character and His purpose. As the God of Israel, He was in His nature self-revealing, for He had made Himself known to Moses and in all the people's history. He had made Israel His people to serve Him and His will. His will was no arbitrary thing, since it was the expression of His nature, and that nature was righteousness.

But men who believe in a divine purpose are inevitably forced on to think of an end. The prophetic thought of the will of God which revealed itself to Israel could not fail to issue in an eschatology. It was involved in their fundamental conceptions. God's self-revelation was the expression of His will, and must issue in making that will valid. And since the divine purpose was the outcome of the divine character or its embodiment, it must issue in a righteous end. In the conditions of Israel and the world that end involved and could not but involve judgement. For righteousness could never be indifferent. A revelation of righteousness in such a world as that in which the prophets lived meant first a judgement on it. Again, if Yahweh was righteousness, His will involved more than Israel, and His end included all the nations. For there was and there could be only one righteousness. His judgement therefore, when it arrived, must light on the world to purge and to renew it.

The prophets did not begin from the Assyrians or Scythians or Babylonians in their threat to Israel's independence. Nor did they conclude from the emergence of an earthly empire which subdued all the other nations to the existence of a divine Emperor who was supreme over all other gods. The weakness of this position is that it fails to explain the norm which the prophets attribute to the divine government and why they all posit the same norm. A mere victory of Assyria over Israel supplies no norm except that Assyria was the stronger. Yet the prophets always predict a judgement on Israel, not because Israel was weak, but because it was sinful. The cause of the divine judgement was sin, its purpose was to punish and to remove sin. And all the prophets held the same view of what constituted the sin of Israel: they all agreed that the standard of the divine judgement was the failure of the people to live by the revealed will of Yahweh. Their conviction of the need and certainty of judgement sprang from certain standards of seemly order and worthy life which were held in common by them and their people. They did not therefore begin from a casual event in history, like the emergence of Assyria or the growing power of Babylonia. They began from Yahweh, whose character and whose standards they knew, and whose perfect will could not fail to bring about His end.

Jeremiah has entered into that great succession, but already he has entered with a difference. And the difference was due to the fact that he was not the first to entertain and to try to express these wide-reaching thoughts. Amos, when he posited Yahweh to be righteousness and saw His purpose about to reveal itself, had recognized that the judgement must include more than Israel. And he had found the reason for its falling on the other peoples in their conduct. Moab had burned the bones of the king of Edom into lime, and Ammon in its brutal border-wars had disembowelled pregnant women: they had sinned against no written torah, but against the decencies of civilized existence. Jeremiah did not find it necessary to give a reason why all men must be judged in the day of the Lord. He was content to say that mischief was afoot out of the North, and saw its issue to be that the whole world must become a desolation. In the same way he was conscious, when he received his call, that he was chosen to be a prophet to the nations. The universality of his commission corresponded with the universality of the judgement he was commanded to announce. That which was implicit in the attitude of Amos has become explicit in his successor. But, while it has grown clearer in the process, it has already lost some indefinable quality. What was a moral conviction in the earlier prophet is on the way to become, though it has not yet become, a theologumenon. In the thought of Deutero-Isaiah it has become a dogma, the initial nerve of which is disappearing. Among some of the later apocalyptists it becomes the source of a rank growth of speculation and new dogmas. Men fasten on little points in the great conceptions of the past. They try to determine precisely the date of the consummation: they lose themselves in pictures of its concomitant features. But is that process unknown to any student of church history, and especially of the history of doctrine? There are other large thoughts of God's ways with men, which had their birth in moral conviction or in religious insight, and which have become the prey of a barren intellectual process.

So far Jeremiah taught nothing new, but continued the old word, which had been the common burden of prophecy. Yet he introduced into it two novel features, one of which has had a long history. Thus he began his work with the conviction that Yahweh was bringing mischief, and that this was to arrive from the North. The direction from which the evil is to come might be passed over as insignificant, or even set down for a picturesque detail, if it appeared only in the inaugural vision. But it does not. It recurs continually, and indeed runs like a red thread through the whole of his book.[1]

[1] Cf. 1 : 13; 3 : 12, 18; 4 : 6; 6 : 1, 22; 10 : 22; 13 : 20; 16 : 15; 23 : 8; 25 : 9, 26; 31 : 8; 46 : 6, 10, 20, 24; 47 : 2; 50 : 3, 9, 41.

All the passages cited in the footnote cannot be regarded as genuine Jeremianic material. Several are taken from the oracles on the nations which are undoubtedly of later date. Yet even these possess in this connexion a certain evidential value. For later men, who copied the prophetic style, may well have introduced a feature which they recognized to be characteristic. And the presence of this feature in those particular oracles may well have led collectors to include them in the book of a prophet who was known to have employed the word.

But what does the expression mean? Nothing more than a statement of the direction from which the expected invader was to advance, say most interpreters. And all who saw in these invaders the Scythian hordes found in the word a confirmation, since the newcomers descended on Asia by way of the Caucasus. The supporters of the Chaldeans in the role of the enemy had more difficulty, since Babylon lay south-east of Judah. But they were able to explain that the line of the invading march necessarily ran by way of Carchemish with its ford, and that a prophet who thought of them only as invaders could naturally describe them in these terms. Yet it must be recognized that the repeated use of such a description for a people whom every man in Jeremiah's audience knew to live in the east must have seemed at least remarkable. And it became even unnatural in 4 : 5–8, since, when a lion was described as rising from its lair and advancing from the north, the obvious conclusion was that the lair, being the place from which it advanced, lay in the north. Besides, if Jeremiah was merely describing the direction of the invader's advance, why should he repeat this insignificant feature so constantly? Above all, why should he set it down in the opening vision after his call, as though the direction of the march deserved to be placed alongside the fact that Yahweh was bringing the mischief, that He commissioned a prophet to announce it, and that its issue was big with fate for the world? That mischief was coming specifically from the north must have had a larger meaning to the prophet than this, and it is of significance to ask what this may have been.

There are certain passages in the Old Testament where the North is mentioned and where it cannot be taken to mean a point of the compass. Instead the word is used with a peculiar significance which is not explained, as though it needed no interpretation.[1] The law prescribed that the burnt-offering and sin-offering must be slain northward before Yahweh: evidently Yahweh was connected with the North. The Psalter called Mount Zion the city of the great King on the sides of the North. In that it expressed an idea, and did not merely describe a geographical direction. A prophet could speak about the king of Babylon desiring to ascend into heaven to sit upon the mount of congregation in the uttermost parts of the North.[2] He may have borrowed from Babylonian mythology. A feature taken from that mythology was peculiarly appropriate in the description of the conduct of a Babylonian king. Yet, since the speaker was addressing his own people, he must have known that they would understand his meaning. And that implies that they too thought the North to be connected with deity. In the same way Jeremiah could use the word to describe the place from which Yahweh sent out a message, because Yahweh and the North were already associated in the minds of his hearers. And he could specially speak about mischief rising from that quarter, because Ebal, the mount of cursing, lay to the north of Gerizim. Hence the phrase, once the prophet had em-

[1] Lev. 1 : 11, cf. 6 : 18; II Kings 16 : 14; Ezek. 1 : 4 ff., 9 : 2; Ps. 48 : 3; Job. 26 : 7. There are a number of other passages where the same vague sense seems to obtain. But since these are capable, though with some violence, of being interpreted with the ordinary meaning, I have only cited the few cases where such an interpretation is impossible.

[2] Isa. 14 : 13; cf. Ezek. 28 : 14, 16.

ployed it, found easy entrance into men's minds and lodged itself in their thought. It had its connexion with ideas which were already there. From the time of Jeremiah, accordingly, it appears with greater frequency and always with the sinister meaning he had given it of a mysterious calamity. Thus in the theophany (Ezek. 1 : 4) Yahweh appears out of the North, and from the same quarter issue the seven messengers who are deputed to carry out judgement on the false worshippers in Jerusalem (9 : 2). It cannot be supposed that these messengers represent an invading army, or that the direction from which they come implies a line of march. Yet the direction is counted worthy of mention. In a lament over Egypt it is said that the princes of the North take their place beside Assyria and Elam, Meshech and Tubal (Ezek. 32 : 30). But, if the prophet is supposed to be there describing an actual historical campaign, it is hard to understand how he came to include Assyria after 612, when the Empire disappeared from history. The description appears in the prophecy about Gog from Magog, along with whose warriors from the north the Ethiopians and Libyans are mentioned (Ezek. 38 : 5, 15). Is then Gog an actual historical figure, and did Magog once lie in the north? One of the oracles against Babylon which has been included in the book of Jeremiah (50 : 3, 9) declares that the Persians out of the north are to attack the city. The king of the north, who probably stands for the Seleucid kingdom, appears in the prophecy of Daniel 11 : 6 ff. And finally the description is found in the figure of the northerner, הצפוני, in Joel 2 : 20. The mysterious character of that figure is apparent from the method in which he is expected to disappear. He shall be thrust, partly into a dry land, partly into the Western sea, partly into the East (2 : 20; cf. v. 2). How an actual physical invader could be disposed of precisely after this fashion has always been a crux.

In all these cases there is a curious insistence on the emergence of mischief from the north. This quarter of the world is uniformly associated with the sinister figures of coming calamity. It is possible to interpret the north in certain of these cases as meaning no more than a point of the compass, which gives the direction from which the enemy advanced. Thus Persia (Jer. 50 : 3, 9) may be said to lie north of Babylon, though it would be more natural to put it in the east. The centre of the Seleucid kingdom (Dan. 11 : 6 ff.) did lie north of Judah. But why did the successive prophets find it natural or necessary to dwell so constantly on the direction from which the enemy came? Why, when Ezekiel coupled Gog with the Libyans and Ethiopians (38 : 5, 15), did he say that the one body came from the north? If he was thinking in terms of geography, it was equally natural to say that Ethiopia and Libya lay in the south and west. Had this insistence on a certain point of the compass appeared in only one prophet, it might have been possible to set it down to his personal idiosyncrasy. He thought of the north in connexion with one great enemy, and he set it down in connexion with certain others, because he happened to think about it or even needed the words to fill out a line. But it appears in the writings of at least five men, who are separate in time, widely severed in locale, and who have not exactly the same purpose. It would rather appear that there was something at once mysterious and sinister in the phrase, which heightened the effect of their threatenings. And in particular the word appears in Joel in the bare form of 'the Northerner', as if this trait alone were enough to sum up the character of him who was there described.

The only satisfactory explanation appears to be that in these later oracles the geographical direction has become wholly indifferent, and that the phrase has now attached to it the idea of mysterious terror. It has become no longer a point of the compass, but the expression of an idea. Hence it can be added to Gog to mark the character of this great unknown, or it can be employed entirely by itself with no further explanation, as in Joel. The only question which remains real is whether Jeremiah used it from the beginning in this specific sense, or whether he began by employing it in connexion with the Scythians or the Chaldeans, who can be said to have reached Palestine by way of the north, and so developed the association of the north country with the horror and mystery of calamity.[1]

The second novel feature in Jeremiah's oracles on the coming doom is one which has had a profounder influence, as it has had a longer history. He created in his vivid imagination a central figure in the drama of the day of the Lord. The lion which rose from its lair, the destroyer of nations, became a great agent in the impending catastrophe. One part at least of the catastrophe consisted of this shape of mischief which Yahweh was to raise up from the North. Those who see in the Northern danger simply a forecast on Jeremiah's part of the Chaldean invasion naturally interpret this central agent to mean Nebuchadrezzar. The prophet was announcing to his people the advent of the great enemy who destroyed their capital and temple and who put an end to their national independence. And he bade them see in that which ruined their hopes, not a blind chance, but the judgement of God for their own sins and those of their fathers. The particular oracle in which this figure appears

[1] Duhm, *Kommentar*, p. 12, recognized this feature in the inaugural vision. 'Here, through the dark, mysterious suggestion of the quarter of the heaven, that quarter which contains everything terrible, destructive, horrible, an apocalyptic trait finds its way into the vision.' That to him is enough to confirm his suspicions about the originality of the whole chapter (cf. p. 2). For he takes it for granted that, when Jeremiah was speaking about the north, it must have been because he was thinking about the Scythians. Thus a theory about the determining cause for the prophecy is allowed to decide on the authenticity of the oracles.

(4 : 5–8) will then be dated later in the prophet's career than the time of his call. It may represent the impression produced upon his mind by the great victory at Carchemish, when Nebuchadrezzar defeated the army of Pharaoh Necho and made it clear that Syria, and with it Palestine, was to fall under the power of the Babylonians.

In my judgement the destroyer of nations was not a historical figure, any more than the North from which he came was a point of the compass. Both were expressions of an idea. The leonine destroyer of nations was the first faint hint of the conception which gave rise to the figure of Antichrist.

Such an explanation must of course stand or fall with what has already been said about the meaning of the North. All who are satisfied with the view that Jeremiah was predicting a historic invader will naturally be satisfied to see in the lion the leader of this invasion. The supporters of the opinion that the Chaldeans were the bearers of the coming trouble will even find here a certain confirmation.[1] But the more the difficulties connected with the historical interpretation of these oracles come to be recognized, the more natural will it become to seek another way out of the impasse into which it has brought all study of the prophecy. And then it cannot fail to be observed that, precisely as from the time of Jeremiah the North began to take on the character of the source of some mysterious calamity, so from the same period the figure of Antichrist began to bulk more largely before the imagination of the Hebrews. In particular, Jeremiah's immediate successor Ezekiel has seized and reproduces both. When that prophet spoke about the appearance of, and

[1] The theory in this connexion raises a new difficulty, viz. that Jeremiah spoke in no ambiguous terms, but very definitely and very clearly about the Chaldeans, and assigned to them a strictly limited function. But that question cannot be discussed here: it has been relegated to chap. x, on the political attitude of the prophet.

messengers from Yahweh which involved or presaged judgement, he spoke of them as coming from the direction of the North,[1] though the point of the compass had no real connexion with his expectation. And he described the destroyer of nations under the weird figure of Gog from Magog, who was to advance from the same quarter.

It has hitherto been generally accepted that Ezekiel intended by his mysterious Gog a purely apocalyptic, i.e. non-historical, figure.

Recently, however, Herrmann[2] has attempted to make even Gog a historic personage. The attempt cannot be called a success. History contains no reference to the danger of any such conqueror, in the period of the Babylonian captivity, coming down on Mesopotamia out of the North. As little can it supply any name belonging to this date which has even points of contact with the definite name Gog. Geography also refuses to yield a country named Magog, and both history and geography fail to show anywhere, except among certain tribes of Africa, a country and a king whose names are so oddly allied. Herrmann is reduced to saying that our ignorance of the time does not warrant the assertion that there may not have been some threatened devastation from the direction of Anatolia and that there may not have been a country called Magog, the king of which may have been Gog.

Even if it were allowed that all this is possible, which is not quite the same as probable, the difficulties of the explanation are not at an end. For it becomes necessary to ask why a Hebrew prophet in the exile should have been overawed by the prospect of an invader spreading ruin among the Babylonians, or, if he looked for the invader to enter Syria

[1] Cf. Ezek. 1 : 4 ff.; 9 : 2; 28 : 14, 16.

[2] In his *Ezechiel Studien*, and at more length in his *Commentary on Ezekiel*.

and capture the wasted Jerusalem, how he believed it possible to overrun a province of Babylon without first breaking the power of Babylon itself. And if Ezekiel dreaded the coming of such a conqueror, he took a singularly different attitude from all his contemporaries. For many of the oracles on Babylon in Jeremiah (chaps. 50 f.), which represent the hopes and fears of the exiles, show them to be eagerly on the watch for anything which might weaken the power of their hated conqueror. Deutero-Isaiah also was not appalled by the prospect of the coming of Cyrus: he saw in the fall of Babylon the hope of the liberation of Israel. All that Herrmann's discussion has done has been to bring to light more clearly and from another side the straits to which those are reduced who cling to the opinion that every prophet must have been roused to activity by a historical event or a political condition.

Hölscher[1] has found no difficulty in disposing of Herrmann's interpretation. But he has further proved in a very convincing way the dependence of Ezekiel, in his great figure of Gog, on the preceding oracles of Jeremiah. Yet this recognition on his part of the extent to which Ezekiel has borrowed from his predecessor both in language and in idea makes it the more surprising that he has not seen the inevitable consequence. For what follows from his conclusions is that Ezekiel did not interpret the oracles of Jeremiah about the invader from the north along historical lines. Before he could create such a gigantic figure as Gog out of the hints given by Jeremiah, he must have seen already in Jeremiah the prophecy of a devastation which was not local or historical, but universal and apocalyptic. In Ezekiel's language we see how it was natural for one Hebrew prophet to interpret another. Unless we are to suppose that there was a sudden break in all the prophetic tradition, which emerged at the time of the exile, we must also suppose that Ezekiel's inter-

[1] *Hesekiel, der Dichter und das Buch*, 1924, pp. 177–89.

pretation was perfectly legitimate and appeared natural to the men to whom he spoke. The new prophet continued Jeremiah's work, making use both of his ideas and of his language. And, so doing, he made all the prophetic expectation of the day of the Lord to have been on a scale which bursts through the historical conditions into a vaster judgement.[1]

How deeply the idea of Antichrist came to influence certain forms of later thought and how extravagant were some of the opinions to which it gave rise, it is not necessary to point out here. But one feature in connexion with it deserves emphasis and attention, because it serves to indicate that we are dealing here with its first appearance in its simplest form. In later thought, e.g. in the New Testament Apocalypse, all the forces of good are gathered up and personified in Messiah, while the forces which oppose the divine kingdom are united and personified in Antichrist. At times Antichrist developed into a power which is almost independent of God, and which at all times is able to disturb and even check the divine purpose with the world. Jeremiah remains faithful to the tradition of all the preceding prophets, or limited to their circle of ideas. They all subsume every hurtful power in the world under the government of Yahweh. They can only conceive

[1] Cornill has a long note on the subject in his *Commentary on Jeremiah*, pp. 83 ff. In this he insists that Ezekiel referred to Jeremiah's prophecies about doom, and, believing that they had not been fulfilled, proceeded to say that they were to be fulfilled now, i.e. in Ezekiel's own time. The later prophet then elaborated the figure of Gog, who was to be the agent for carrying out this doom. For the purpose for which Cornill uses this true remark it appears to me singularly inept. But the remarkable fact remains that, while Ezekiel believed that his predecessor's prediction was about to be fulfilled, he regarded it as about to be fulfilled, not by a historical figure, but by Gog, whom Cornill also counts non-historical. This implies of course that Ezekiel found it natural to interpret Jeremiah's prophecy of doom along what are generally called apocalyptic lines.

evil to exist because of His permission. Shall there be evil in the city, Amos can say, and Yahweh has not caused it? For they are all convinced that Yahweh is the supreme Lord of the world. There is nothing present which can finally escape His control or which can operate without His knowledge. The supreme question to them all was the question of how this divine control was to assert itself and reveal itself to be the ultimate reality in this universe. Believing that this control was to appear through an act of God in judgement, they made everything which brought that judgement merely the divine instrument. Jeremiah's figure out of the North was roused and sent by Yahweh. But the later men were moving away to the wider question of how there could be evil at all in God's world. And to them, approaching the matter from a new angle, Antichrist occasionally escaped from this limitation and became almost a power of evil co-eternal with good.

There is nothing resembling this in Jeremiah and Ezekiel. The mischief which comes from the north in Jeremiah is coming according to the will of God. Its leader is roused to his task by Yahweh Himself. The seven who go forth from the North in Ezekiel to carry out judgement are Yahweh's messengers. Gog issues into the world through the divine will, and fulfils merely his appointed and limited task. Antichrist remains the instrument of the divine work of judgement on the world, but he is no more.

Antichrist has developed on a parallel course to Satan. Satan begins in Job as one of Yahweh's messengers, who does no more and no less than what he is permitted or commissioned to do. Hence he bears no specific name. He is simply the Satan, or the opposer. His title is still lost in his function. His task is to test or try or oppose those to whom he is sent. But, since his work is all of one kind, he comes to be identified with it. And since that work is one which a later generation hesitated to ascribe to God or had difficulty in regarding to be divine, he came to have almost an independent position. He ceased to be the opposer, the messenger to whom one duty was committed, and became Satan, a malign power whose only business it was to impede the work and misinterpret the service of the saints.

VII

THE TEMPLE ADDRESS

AFTER the death of Josiah at Megiddo, Pharaoh Necho deposed Jehoahaz, whom 'the people of the land' had made king in place of his father, and appointed a nominee of his own in the person of another son. At the same time the Egyptian took the curious and inexplicable step of changing the name of his vassal to Jehoiakim, i.e. he substituted the divine name Yahweh for that of El in the name of the new king. We may be sure that the act was deliberately intended to have some meaning, but what that intention was eludes us. This must have taken place about 607, and was part of Necho's plan for settling Palestine in his rear before he advanced to the decisive struggle against the combined force which had destroyed the Assyrian Empire. Unfortunately the exact date of Carchemish, the battle which made the Neo-Babylonian or Chaldean kingdom the dominant power in Asia, is still uncertain. But evidently Jehoiakim remained the vassal of Egypt for one or two years, since II Kings 23 : 35 relates that he raised the tribute demanded by his suzerain. Jeremiah's oracle (22 : 13–17) in which he denounced the king may be referred to the same period. There Jehoiakim is condemned for building a great palace in Jerusalem and employing forced labour for its erection. Such an undertaking implied peace in the kingdom and a certain measure of prosperity in the country. We may, however, be confident that at the beginning of his reign the new ruler made no change in the religious settlement of his father. Egypt does not appear to have demanded from vassal-states the public recognition of its gods to the extent to which the Assyrian Empire had done. And the change in the king's name, whatever else it may mean, proves that his appointment to the throne did not require any departure on his part from strict Yahwism.[1]

Carchemish altered the entire situation and determined for some time the fate of Asia. Not only was Egypt driven back into Africa, so that it retained no further control over Syria and Palestine (cf. II Kings 24 : 7). But the Neo-Babylonian Empire which passed into the hands of the competent Nebuchadrezzar was by him consolidated, and became the dominant factor in all the East. It was inevitable that Judah should, sooner or later, become a province of the Empire. The precise year when this took place is uncertain. Yet it need not have followed immediately after Carchemish. For Nebuchadrezzar learned at the Euphrates news of the death of his father, Nabopolassar, and was apparently compelled to leave the scene of his victory in order to hurry back to Babylon, where he took the hand of Bel and was invested with his royal authority. Other and more urgent needs may well have detained him at the capital and prevented an immediate settlement of affairs in Syria. He must confirm his hold on his new authority, and especially must settle accounts with the allies, Scythians and Medes, by whose help Babylon had pulled down Assyria. Even when the little kingdom of Judah was incorporated into the new Empire, there is no suggestion of a war or conquest: in his days Nebuchadrezzar king of Babylon came up and Jehoiakim became his servant three years (II Kings 24 : 1). The terms of the Hebrew record suggest that resistance on the part of Judah was felt to be hopeless. Besides, the same records always refer to the

[1] Baynes, *Israel amongst the Nations*, p. 100, thinks there was a religious reaction under Jehoiakim. The only indubitable proof he can bring, however, is the king's treatment of the two prophets, Urijah and Jeremiah. But this rests on the opinion that Jeremiah was persecuted because he was a supporter of Josiah's reform.

deportation under Jehoiachin, the son of Jehoiakim, as the beginning of the captivity of the Southern kingdom, from which it is a just inference that Jerusalem under the earlier king escaped all conquest by a prompt submission.

The book of Kings, however, adds that after the three years of submission Jehoiakim rebelled against Babylon (24 : 1). It then continues with the statement that the Lord sent against Judah bands of the Chaldeans and bands of the Syrians and bands of the Moabites and bands of the children of Ammon (24 : 2). In its connexion this seems to imply that these troubles befel Jehoiakim in the later years of his reign, and were the outcome of his rebellion against Babylon. The incident, also, of Jeremiah's meeting with the Rechabites (Jer. chap. 35) is dated (v. 1) in the reign of this king; and these sectaries state that invading Chaldeans and Syrians have compelled them to forsake their ancestral customs (v. 11)—they even declare that Nebuchadrezzar himself had invaded the country. Apparently, therefore, the Babylonian king had his hand in the troubles, though it is not necessary to accept literally the remark about his being actually present. Why he did not interfere more directly and decisively it is impossible to say. But he may have had his hands full with more important matters, and may have been content with fomenting opposition against the rebel Judean which would keep him in check until he could be more effectually dealt with. Only in the reign of Jehoiachin was he free to march in person into Syria, and among other tasks to capture Jerusalem and reduce Judah (II Kings 24 : 10–17).

Politically, therefore, the reign of Jehoiakim, which lasted for eleven years, was troubled. But religiously Judah suffered no interference from without. The Josianic reform was able to continue among the people, to confirm itself and to reveal its consequences for the national religion. Hence we find that, while Jehoiakim is condemned, he is condemned in the vague phrase that he did evil in the sight of the Lord, as all his fathers had done (23 : 37). No specific charge is laid against him; and in particular there is no mention of his having encouraged the worship on the high-places. The ideal of the one central sanctuary had so commended itself to the leading men of Jerusalem that no one thought of departing from it. Indeed, the historian did not find anything in Jehoiakim's conduct which could account for the troubles which came upon him in his later years. He was fain to seek a reason, not in anything the present could show, but in the evil past. Surely at the commandment of the Lord came this upon Judah,...for the sins of Manasseh (24 : 3 f.). The writer of this verdict on the king and his period evidently had some difficulty in finding anything in the actions of the court which could account for the gloomy end of the reign. The impression that the outward religious life of the nation went on in its familiar course is confirmed when the two appearances of Jeremiah during this period are examined. On one occasion he appeared at the temple when the people from the country towns as well as from Jerusalem were gathered at a festival (chap. 26). On the other he sent Baruch to the same place to read a message addressed to a community which was publicly assembled at a fast (chap. 36). From this it would appear that Jehoiakim at least threw no difficulties in the way of the priests carrying out their religious duties. And clearly the temple was now the natural centre to which all Judah resorted: there is no hint of worship on the high-places.

Both these oracles were intended to be solemn and public indictments, challenges to the national conscience. And they were recognized to be such, for the leaders of the nation, in one case the priests, in the other the councillors and Jehoiakim himself, took prompt and decisive action in reply to them. In using the temple for this purpose and in taking advantage of the fact that the men at such a festival were in a mood to listen to a divine message, Jeremiah only followed prophetic practice. Amos appeared among the worshippers at a festival in Bethel. And the practice did not die out, for on the last day, the great day of the feast, Jesus stood and cried saying, If any man thirst let him come unto me and drink.[1]

The first of these, the temple address, has been preserved and handed down in two forms. In chap. 7 a collector, who was specially interested in the prophet's oracles, has retained the words Jeremiah spoke and combined them with other material. Rightly feeling, however, how much the place where this oracle was delivered lent force to its contents, he has fitted it with a short introduction in vv. 1, 2. The address ends with v. 15: what follows is addressed to the prophet himself, not spoken by him to the people. In chap. 26, again, an editor, who was interested in the life and experiences of Jeremiah, has not reported the words so fully. He has merely included in his account so much of the oracle as might serve to explain the anger of the priests, the tolerance of certain laymen, and the effect which the incident had on the fortunes of the prophet. But he also dated his account, setting it in the beginning of the reign of Jehoiakim. The oracle was therefore delivered during the period of the reign which fell before the troubles with Babylon disturbed the peace of the kingdom. That date is confirmed by certain features which appear in the story. Thus the occasion was a festival at which worshippers from the country round about Jerusalem were present in the capital. And the men who intervened for the protection of the prophet were elders from the country, who protested that after all he was saying nothing worse than Micah had already uttered. The men recalled, better than the inhabitants of Jerusalem, the lan-

[1] St. John 7 : 37.

guage of one who like themselves was no native of the capital. They may even have come from the maritime plain of which Micah is said to have been a native. Judah was at peace when men from that district were able to come up on a festival day to the temple. Later in the king's reign the marauding bands which were let loose on the country must have disturbed attendance at the feasts.

Though the address has thus come down in two forms, it has not been preserved in its original content in either, but has been slightly retouched in order to accommodate it to the ideas of the men through whose hands it has been received. It is necessary to sift out the original from the later accretions, and in order to do this without following mere subjective impressions as to what Jeremiah was likely to say, it is useful to recognize two general features in the prophet's utterance.

Thus the primary purpose of the address was to utter a strong polemic against the temple and the worship there. Anything which Jeremiah may have added about the future fate of the people was subsidiary to this leading aim. Banishment or conquest, if he foretold either event, was not mentioned for itself, but was only introduced as the means by which Yahweh was to bring about the doom which He had pronounced against the temple. Both reports of the address take the same attitude on this subject. The writer of chap. 7 recognized it, since, while he included the address among other oracles, he prefixed to it alone a statement of the scene in which it was delivered. It was spoken in the temple to a company gathered from all Judah at one of the religious festivals. In the same way an evangelist[1] noted that Jesus uttered certain trenchant words against the temple on one of the high days of its solemn feasts. The place where the words were uttered gave extra significance to what was said. The editor of chap. 26, again, brings out the same feature by

[1] St. Mark 13 : 1 ff.

his remark that it was the priests who were the first to resent the prophet's utterance and most eager to take prompt action. Had he concerned himself chiefly with the fate of the nation and the state, there would not have been the same reason for the priesthood to take umbrage at his words, nor would the laymen have been likely to support him in opposition to their clerical leaders.[1] Further, the comparison, which appears in both accounts, between the well-known fate of the sanctuary at Shiloh and the impending fate of the temple at Jerusalem has only point on this basis. The one became the leading sanctuary when Israel first constituted itself after the conquest: the other was the commanding shrine now that Judah was all that remained to the people. The doom of the national place of worship was the theme of the address.

The other general feature of the address is that the destruction which Jeremiah predicted was not contingent but absolute. It did not depend on any change in the conduct of the people, but was Yahweh's fixed will. Here matters are not so clear, for it was precisely in relation to this attitude of the prophet that both accounts were watered down. Yet chap. 26 betrays the real situation with sufficient clearness. It is true that the editor in his brief synopsis of the address (vv. 3–6) makes Jeremiah threaten Jerusalem with the doom of Shiloh except the people repent, and thus makes the threat contingent on the presence or absence of national repentance. But immediately after the priests show where the real sting lay through their question (v. 9): 'why hast thou prophesied in Yahweh's name saying, This house shall be like Shiloh and this city desolate without inhabitants?'

[1] It gives additional force to this conclusion to notice that in the similar case of chap. 36, where Jeremiah spoke about the fate of the kingdom, it was the councillors of state and the king who took action against him: the priests did not appear at all. Cf. p. 154, *infra*.

It might be possible to conclude that the men, already incensed against the prophet and glad to get an occasion against him, did not hesitate to give this turn to his words. Men whose minds are heated in debate do these things. But when the prophet replied to them in vv. 12–14 he made no complaint about his language having been twisted, nor did he seek to soften the harshness of the words they had put into his mouth. He simply appealed to the fact that what he had said had been uttered by him in his prophetic capacity. For the priests, therefore, to put him to death because of his faithfulness in delivering a divine message was to bring the divine wrath more swiftly on themselves and on their city. When Jeremiah thus fell back on his inability as prophet to say anything different from what he had spoken, he showed himself to be conscious that the message he had delivered was of a character to need some such guarantee of its being divinely commissioned. His oracle must therefore have been more than contingent, since in that case it had been merely a specially solemn summons to repentance. If it had contained no more, there would have been no special need for urging that it came from Yahweh, since all the prophets called men to repent. Accordingly, when the leaders and the people delivered Jeremiah from the enraged priests, they said nothing about these men having misrepresented his language. Instead they took their stand on the liberty of prophesying, for they recalled how Micah said nothing worse than this when he foretold that Zion should be ploughed as a field and the mountain of the house become as the high places of a forest. The unconditional doom pronounced by the later prophet recalled to their memory the similar unconditional doom pronounced by his predecessor. Hence it becomes natural to conclude that v. 13, which breaks the connexion in which it stands with a suggestion that Yahweh may yet repent of the doom He has sent the prophet to pronounce, has been added by the same hand which interpolated vv. 3–6. Both are due to the editor.

When we turn to chap. 7, the same ambiguity about the prophet's intention appears. Thus in vv. 12–14 Jeremiah announced in set terms that Yahweh meant to do to Jerusalem what He had already done to Shiloh, and invited his hearers to go to the site of the older sanctuary and see the completeness of the ruin which had befallen it. But in vv. 5–7 he is represented as having made the ruin contingent on the repentance of the people. The two attitudes are not compatible, and the only question is to see whether the section offers any means by which it may become possible to decide on the original. Duhm has already cast suspicion on vv. 5–7 on the ground that they contain nothing but pious commonplace. Personally I have never felt that we are justified in denying to Jeremiah or any other prophet the right, or even the duty, of uttering commonplace, so long as it was really pious. Indeed, it may be no small part of a prophet's function to recall men to great religious truths, which have become to them so commonplace that they have forgotten how true they are. Besides, Duhm has overlooked what the editor of the chapter had already recognized, that place and circumstances often bring fresh light and force to what would elsewhere and in other circumstances be justly called commonplace. It is a more serious objection to the verses that they have misunderstood Jeremiah's language. For they interpret 'this place' in the sense of the land, whereas the word is plainly in v. 12, probably in v. 3, used of the sanctuary.[1] The editor, who inserted vv. 5–7 and so turned the edge of Jeremiah's polemic against the temple by making it an attack on the nation, is probably also responsible for the

[1] It was easier for this to be done, because מקום has this double sense. It is a favourite word in Deuteronomy for a sanctuary, but it is also frequently employed more generally.

pointing of the clause in v. 3 which makes it read 'that I may cause you to dwell in this place'. Ehrlich for other reasons has suggested that the real sense there is, 'amend your ways and your deeds that I may dwell with you in this place', i.e. the temple.[1] When, however, the words were taken to mean 'that I may cause you to dwell in this place', it was obvious that the people could not live in the temple, but in the land. 'Place' could only be understood of the place where the people did live, and room was made for a familiar exhortation to the effect that Judah's possession of its land depended on its loyalty to its God. But, when Jeremiah in v. 4 continued 'put no trust in lies saying, here is the temple of Yahweh, the temple of Yahweh, the temple of Yahweh', he showed clearly what place he intended in v. 3. It was the sacred place, the divine dwelling. And, with the elision of vv. 5–7, the connexion between v. 4 and v. 8 becomes clearer and more pungent. See, you are putting trust in false and profitless talk. Will a man steal and murder, commit adultery and perjury, sacrifice to Baal and wander after strange gods, and then come and stand before me in this house which is my peculiar property, and say, we have been saved to do such vile deeds? Has my house[2] become a robbers' den in your eyes? Lo, I too count it such. Then follows what Yahweh will do with the temple.

Freed thus from later accretions, the oracle gains in directness of aim and singleness of purpose. All Jeremiah has to say is directed against the temple and against the false place it has come to hold in his people's estimation. Its sanctity has come to rank so high that it is believed to cover deeds

[1] The suggested reading involves no alteration in the Masoretic text, but merely in the pointing: וְאֶשְׁכְּנָה אִתְּכֶם instead of וַאֲשַׁכְּנָה אֶתְכֶם; cf. *Randglossen zur Hebr. Bibel*, iv, ad loc. The two words then contain a common expression in Deuteronomy for the divine presence at a sanctuary.

[2] So with the Septuagint.

which show their perpetrators to have no real conception of the character of Him who is believed to dwell there. And the prophet gathers up what he has to say on the situation in a couple of sentences which may be freed from the weak secondary phrases about 'rising early and speaking' and 'being called by my name'. 'Go to my holy place in Shiloh where I set my name in the beginning, and see what I did to it on account of the wickedness of my people Israel. I will do to this house in which you put your trust as I did to Shiloh.' [1]

As soon as we have seen good critical reasons for rejecting these accretions from chaps. 7 and 26, it becomes legitimate to recognize what led to their insertion. All Jeremiah's oracles have come down through the hands of the returned exiles. And these men were unwilling to believe, probably were sincerely unable to believe, that a prophet could pronounce an oracle of irrevocable doom against their beloved temple.

The temple address, which defines Jeremiah's attitude to the temple, must be considered along with another passage (7 : 21–3), which gives his view of the sacrificial system. This little oracle is entirely isolated. The verses which follow deal clearly with a different subject, since the doings of the fathers are not connected with the sacrifices. Besides, the oracle of vv. 24–6 cannot even be ascribed to the prophet, for it

[1] It is peculiarly difficult to be confident about v. 15, 'I will cast you out from my presence, as I cast out your brethren, the entire seed of Ephraim'. Erbt, e.g. has no hesitation in counting it secondary and rejecting it. But the phrase 'the entire seed of Ephraim' speaks strongly for its originality here. Jeremiah was always interested in Northern Israel, and came of priestly stock with an adequate knowledge of priestly tradition. Hence he might well be thinking in the words, seed of Ephraim, not merely of Northern Israel, but of the special connexion of Shiloh with Ephraim, Joshua's tribe. The two temples shall come to ruin, and Judah shall share the fate of its neighbour. But the rejection of Judah is subordinate to the doom on its sanctuary.

directly contradicts the idea of the innocence of the wilderness period, an idea which Jeremiah (2 : 2) shared with Hosea. The oracle on the sacrificial system may originally have formed part of the temple address. The omission of all reference to it in chap. 26 could be easily accounted for. The editor of that chapter, who was mainly interested in the life and experiences of the prophet, required only to quote so much of the address as was needed to explain his narrative. The polemic against the temple was sufficient to account for the irritation of the priests, and obviously led on to the measures taken by the laymen to rescue the prophet through appeal to the similar language of Micah.

However this may be, the two oracles are intimately related, since they deal with the same subject. Whether Jeremiah uttered the verses which deal with the sacrifices at the same time as those which refer to the temple or uttered them on a different occasion, he declared that the sacrificial system formed no essential part of the revelation made to Moses, and he also announced in the divine name that Yahweh was about to destroy the temple, the religious centre where these sacrifices were offered. What such an announcement in the name of Yahweh means is that the interests of true religion would be better served if the whole system should disappear.

Now the noteworthy thing in this attitude is its uncompromising character. Thus the prophet repudiated the sacrificial system of his nation in principle. He did not accuse the people and the priesthood of having laid undue emphasis on the cult in comparison with the weightier matters of the law, or of having, in exaggerated devotion to ritual, neglected justice and the love of God. He denied the existence in Judah of any ceremonial laws which had the right to lay claim to the authority of Moses. We need not complicate the question by asking whether the prophet was correct in this representation of the original character of the Mosaic revelation. Obviously, of course, he contradicted the fundamental position of the Jewish law on sacrifice, since all the leading codes in the Old Testament claimed to have been delivered by Yahweh to Moses and therefore to have divine authority. Nor need we ask how he explained the origin of the cult or how he supposed it to have made its way into the nation's life. Jeremiah may have been entirely incorrect in his conviction that the original Mosaic revelation had nothing to say about a sacrificial system. The question of the accuracy of his judgement about the past and its religious usages cannot alter the fact that this was his conviction. As a result, he was prepared, not only to see temple and sacrifices disappear without a pang of regret, but to see in their disappearance something which would be then in the interests of true religion. For he could and did say that nothing less than this was the divine will.

It is at once the uncompromising character of this judgement on the sacrificial system and the terms in which it is expressed which give Jeremiah's statement its peculiar note. Every Old Testament student knows that all the prophets were more than a little dubious about the national cult, and very critical of the position it held in the minds of their contemporaries. From the beginning they had no hesitation in declaring that obedience was better than sacrifice. But it is far from clear that the men were not seeking to purify the cult from its grosser elements, or to define its relative significance in men's lives. Thus Hosea, to whom religion consisted of entire dependence on Yahweh and gratitude to Him, really supplied a rationale for a cult. Tithes, sacrifice, and firstlings could be construed as the expression of men's gratitude for an unfailing grace. He gave an ethical and spiritual basis to gifts which were once brought from a very different motive. Men brought their tithes to Yahweh, not because

He needed them or even claimed them, but because they needed to bring them. And Yahweh, who did not demand them for Himself, did not retain them: they were devoted to the poor. The principles of the prophet could find a place and a wholesome place for sacrifice and offering. But to reinterpret the cult or to define its relative place in the estimation of the true worshipper is one thing: to say that the system had no place in the original worship of the nation is another. Men who hold one or other of these attitudes do not differ in degree: they differ in principle. Jeremiah rejected the cult as such. Evidently, too, he was stating his view in the form of a polemic. Indeed, one cannot escape from the suspicion that the prophet was being driven by his polemic into an extreme statement of his position. As is usual in such a case, the polemic received a sharper edge, because he knew himself to be a protesting voice against a movement which was capturing his hearers. The movement against which he protested was one which made the existing cult essential, and so made it unalterable.

It is only, however, when the condemnation of the sacrificial system is set beside the doom against the temple that the full significance of Jeremiah's position can be recognized. Exactly as the prophet attacked the principle of a divinely ordained ceremonial law, he rejected the principle of the peculiar sanctity of the temple. The two belonged together in his mind, and constituted a double evidence of the failure of the nation to grasp the meaning of true religion. Here, again, it is clear that Jeremiah must have gone beyond what any of his predecessors had said about the temple. The laymen's appeal to the immunity of Micah is enough to prove this. To them there seemed nothing novel or nothing unprecedented in such an utterance on the part of a prophet. The priests were either clearer in their vision of what was involved, or had advanced to an opinion about the sanctity of the temple which the priests of Micah's time had not held. They could not tolerate now what had once been freely uttered. It was this attitude which had forced Jeremiah into opposition. In the place his nation gave to temple and cult these two were becoming a hindrance, instead of a help, to true religion. In order that men might learn the simple essentials of their faith, Yahweh must remove what had been erected into a means of hiding His grave and simple demands. The prophet has been driven into a polemic, not against the misuse, but against the use of certain accessories of religion, because the people were in danger of believing that their religion could not exist without them.

Some years before Jeremiah delivered this address, the Josianic reform had been carried into effect. Jehoiakim, as has been pointed out, had continued the policy of his father in religious matters, so that the reform was beginning to make its way into the habits of the people. Now the undoubted aim and the inevitable result of the movement were to give the temple a new sacredness in the minds of all Israel. It had also given the sacrifices which were offered there a new value as a means of access to Yahweh. The address could not fail to have some relation to this significant event in the nation's religious life. Jeremiah must have been thinking of the aims and results of the reform when he went up to the temple at one of the leading festivals and spoke in these terms of sweeping condemnation. The only question which remains open is whether his utterances are consistent with the idea that he began by supporting the reform, though he later changed his attitude, or whether they imply that he was opposed to it from the beginning. If, now, Jeremiah had once supported the Josianic reform, the main effect and aim of which had been to give the sacrificial worship a higher place, it is difficult to see why his first great public address should be directed against the temple and the worship there. A man who was disappointed in the spiritual results of such a movement might well denounce the people for having failed to recognize its true scope, or the priests for not having kept its higher issues before men's minds. He might even acknowledge that he himself, in his youthful enthusiasm, had expected too much from an improvement in the machinery of worship. But Jeremiah came forward to say that in the interests of true religion Yahweh meant to destroy the temple, and about the same time he declared that laws about sacrifice formed no integral part of the Mosaic religion. These things are hard to explain on the lips of a man who had supported a movement, the main purpose of which was to determine the true place of sacrifice and to define its character.

It may, however, be said with some justice that all this rests on the supposition that the two oracles were uttered in the early years of Jehoiakim's reign, and that it is impossible to place implicit confidence in the dates which are attached to events in Jeremiah's life. The address may have been delivered at the later period when Judah had become subject to Babylon. And, since the Chaldean Empire may have followed the example of the Assyrian in requiring from its subject-states some recognition of the Imperial gods, there may have been a return to the policy of Manasseh, and heathen emblems may have reappeared in the temple. In such circumstances Jeremiah might have been moved to strong censure of what appeared to him to be national apostacy. And what might have stirred him most profoundly was to see men profaning the very shrine which they had but recently cleansed in a great movement of national reform. Yet the terms of the address will not admit of such an explanation. For it is directed, not against a desecration, but against a false valuation of the temple and its worship. It opens by saying that men are trusting in lying words, and these lying words are 'the temple of Yahweh, the temple of Yahweh, the temple of Yahweh are these'. Men who say such things are plainly in danger of making too much, not too little, of their national sanctuary. It continues by charging them with ignoring the claims of the moral law and counting it possible to meet Yahweh in His appointed place with these sins unrepented and unatoned. The worship of foreign gods is mentioned there, but it is the worship of Baal and of other illegitimate deities (7 : 9). And even when false worship is introduced, it is subsumed under the heavier charge of their moral failure. The fault laid at the door of the worshippers is that they set the temple worship in place of true devotion, and are helped to ignore their sins by their diligence in ritual observance.

What makes all this more significant is to notice that the prophet says nothing about any invader through whose act the temple was to be destroyed. The fact would be negligible if it were not that Jeremiah spoke so differently to Zedekiah. Then he declared that the Chaldeans should come and capture the city and burn down the temple. Here, however, he confines himself to the announcement that Yahweh shall bring down temple and city as He once destroyed Shiloh, and shall deal with Judah as He dealt with Ephraim. He thrusts into the foreground the religious significance of this doom. The impending ruin is not to be the outcome of political conditions or the result of a mere shifting of power among the nations. The temple is to go, and its sacrifices are to be discontinued in the interests of true religion. Yahweh is to bring about this thing.

If, however, Jeremiah regarded the centralization of worship in Jerusalem as no real reform, but a false step in religion, both features in the oracle receive instant explanation and new force. It was precisely the new position given to the temple by Josiah and his supporters, by which it was made essential to religion, which was leading the people to feel themselves secure in its possession. They were saying with a new accent in the confidence which the words inspired: 'the temple of Yahweh are these'. The whole reform, also, had turned round the right methods and place of sacrifice. Its inevitable result had been to throw into the background the glaring social evils in the body politic and the sins of every man's private life. Men compounded for neglect of the moral demands of their religion, and even for laxity in a certain acknowledgement of heathenism, by a zealous interest in the new programme of reform. They felt themselves to be faithful adherents of their ancestral faith by flinging themselves into the new movement with all that it represented. Instead of making them better men, it covered their moral failures with the cloak of an outward zeal.

Jeremiah had warned his fellow-countrymen in Northern Israel that the national reform had only made Judah worse instead of better, and had told them how every true reform must begin with the simplicities of repentance and a new obedience. He now came up to the temple-court at Jerusalem during the celebration of a Yahweh festival. And he came with a harsher message. For the city had committed itself to the new regulations of court and priesthood. There was little likelihood of a prophet from Anathoth being able to turn them back on the way they had chosen. Jeremiah could only declare that they thus ran counter to the divine purpose with Israel and that Yahweh Himself, in the interest of true religion, would destroy the temple which they were making essential to His worship.

By taking this public action Jeremiah had boldly challenged the policy of the leaders of his nation, and in particular of the priesthood. And it deserves notice that he was not alone in his attitude of opposition. For another prophet, Urijah of Kirjath-jearim, appeared prophesying in the same terms (26 : 20–4). Evidently the conduct of the authorities at Jerusalem did not commend itself to all religious minds even in Judah. Other prophets besides Jeremiah found in their policy something which ran counter to the prophetic ideals of religion. Jeremiah voiced in the capital and at a festival the dissatisfaction of a larger body of opinion. Hence it is not surprising to learn that both men met with vigorous opposition. And it is wholly unjust to suppose that this opposition rose from factious intrigue or narrow self-interest on the part of the priests. The men honestly believed in their reform policy, and counted it a necessary means of purifying the nation's faith. If they were the first to take action against men who opposed it, they did no more than was to be expected from them. For they realized, more clearly than ordinary men could, that the question did not turn round trivial points but involved principles. In the same way the priests and scribes, to whom was committed the charge of Israel's religion, tested the opinions of the young prophet of Galilee. And as soon as they had realized the aims and convictions of Jesus of Nazareth, they declared that this would never do. If this teaching was to be accepted, the traditional attitude to temple and sacrifice was gone. It needed the long hard insistence of St. Paul to drive into the minds of the early converts that Christianity stood for something which could not be bound to circumcision and temple ritual. But when he succeeded in making that clear, he said no more than what the religious leaders of his people had recognized from the beginning. The clash between prophet and priest in Jeremiah's time was one of principle. Naturally the men who took up the quarrel were those who had best reason to see how deep the opposition ran.

So serious did the danger appear to the priests that they appealed to the secular authority to silence the prophets. Urijah was compelled to escape into Egypt, but was brought back thence and executed.[1] Jeremiah was only saved from a like fate by the interference of Ahikam. But, though the priests were not able to put him to death, they were able to silence the dangerous voice by forbidding him to enter the temple. At a later date, an official among the Babylonian exiles appears writing to Zephaniah, the leading priest in Jerusalem, to remind him that one of his functions was to restrain and even to put in irons unruly prophets who disturbed men's minds by unseemly appearances in the temple (29 : 24–9). Accordingly he takes the priest severely to task for not restraining Jeremiah. Evidently the temple priesthood had been given or had arrogated some authority over those who testified too rudely at public worship. The need for such discipline should not surprise any one who recognizes that men of a very different type from Jeremiah or George Fox have exercised great liberty in testifying. The priests had authority to forbid the prophet free access to the temple, for we find him compelled a little later to send his second message by the hand of Baruch and to have it read to the worshippers. He himself, it is said, was prevented from going into the temple (36 : 5).

What the exact contents of this second message were it is extremely difficult to determine (chap. 36). It was read by Baruch in one of the temple side-chambers on the occasion of a public fast, and it led to a breach between Jeremiah and Jehoiakim as absolute as that between the prophet and the priesthood. Many students, basing on the description of the

[1] The fact that Urijah was 'extradited' from Egypt serves to support the statement of the text that these events happened at the beginning of the reign of Jehoiakim. It was only while that king was a nominee and subordinate of Necho that he could appeal to the Egyptian court for such action in his interests. Further, since the court was so ready to take action at the instance of the priests, it is evident that the two authorities were on excellent terms, and that there was no departure from the Josianic reform during this period of Jehoiakim's reign.

letter in vv. 2 f., have been able to see in it what may be called the first edition of Jeremiah's oracles, since it is said to have contained 'all the messages which I have uttered to you about Israel, Judah, and all the nations from the time when I began to speak to you in the lifetime of Josiah down to the present day'. When this was destroyed by Jehoiakim, a new and enlarged edition was prepared, for 'Baruch[1] took another scroll and wrote on it to Jeremiah's dictation all the contents of the book which Jehoiakim king of Judah had burned: there were also added many passages of a similar character' (v. 32). And those who accept this view have even insisted that all study of the complicated question of the composition of the book of Jeremiah must start from the presupposition of such a book which derived directly from the prophet. Yet it must be recognized that, even if a book of this character ever existed, there is no proof that it survived to be made part of a later collection.

Further, it is clear that chap. 36 presents two views of the contents of Jeremiah's scroll. Verse 2 states that it contained all the prophet's oracles from the time of his entry on his mission until the present day. Now Jeremiah was called in the thirteenth year of Josiah, 624: the year which saw the preparation of the scroll was the fourth year of Jehoiakim, 603. The scroll therefore contained everything which he had spoken about Israel, Judah, and the nations during a public career of twenty-one years. Such a record must have formed a somewhat lengthy document. Yet it was read aloud in the course of one afternoon no less than three times: before Micaiah (v. 11), before the court officials (v. 15), and before the king (v. 21). It was also of such a character that Micaiah could sum up all the words he had heard to the officials (v. 13), and these in turn could report its gist to Jehoiakim (v. 20). Even if it could be believed that men hastily read the record

[1] Reading after the LXX.

of twenty-one years' work three times in one afternoon, it is hard to suppose that after this hurried reading they could so readily sum up the contents of messages which had dealt with Israel, Judah, and all the nations.

There is a patent difference in chap. 36 as to the length of the scroll. And there is also divergence of view about its contents and their character. For v. 29 declares that Jehoiakim had taken offence at it because it stated that the king of Babylon should come and ruin Judah, destroying out of it man and beast. Yet the scroll contained oracles about Israel, Judah, and all the nations. If it should be said that the king ignored the other messages and fastened on the one which was peculiarly offensive to him in the situation in which he found himself, the difficulty is not cleared up. The king is described as having slit up the scroll page by page from the time he heard its first words. The offensive oracle must then have stood at the beginning of the whole, and must have been of so definite a tenor as to close Jehoiakim's mind against everything which followed. Did Jeremiah's early oracles contain anything which unmistakably referred to a ruin wrought by Babylon? Even those who believe that the passages which refer to the lion from the North and to the coming invader spoke of the Chaldeans must credit the king of Judah with a remarkable power of solving what has exercised the minds of many interpreters of the prophet. He was able to detect in those vague and baffling utterances a prophecy which threatened his throne.

It would appear to be equally impossible to reject the story and to reach a certain conclusion about its original form. The account itself is inimitable, and ranks among the finest passages of Hebrew descriptive narrative. The man who wrote it knew the pre-exilic capital, the customs of the palace, and the habits of the officials. He knew how the climate of Jerusalem determined the room where the king sat at certain seasons of the year. He knew the attitude the court officials took to their master. His picture of the men after they have read the paper, agreeing in their agitation that 'we must really report all this business to the king' (v. 16), and yet turning to ask Baruch a futile question about how he came to write it, is drawn from the life. And over against flurried officialdom he has set down the calm, almost stolid, attitude of the secretary with his report that 'he' went on dictating while I wrote.[1] Even the vague 'he' which has led some Baruch-like commentators to suspect the text is eloquent. Neither the troubled officials nor the secretary needed to ask or to explain who 'he' was. There was only one man in Jerusalem who was capable of issuing such a message. And behind Baruch and the courtiers he introduces Jehoiakim, imperturbably confident that all a king needs in order to get rid of prophets and oracles of Yahweh is a penknife and a pan of charcoal. A student of much in the book of Jeremiah, when he returns to this chapter, can only say: 'O, si sic omnia'.

It is only possible to suggest a conclusion, and to underline its uncertainty. If we might accept the statement of v. 29 that the scroll was a brief message, which contained a prophecy about the coming ruin through the king of Babylon, it would serve to explain one remarkable feature in the incident. It differs from the temple address in this, that the priests do not appear at all. As soon as Baruch has read out his commission, a secretary of state took action. And his action was to report the matter to the officials. The courtiers at once decided that the business could not be kept from the ears of the king, though they showed no great eagerness to undertake the task. They seemed to be aware that the only result would be what in fact it was. And they, or at least

[1] With the LXX omit בדיו with ink. Baruch was not quite so matter-of-fact as the M.T. has made him.

some of them, were not in agreement with what their king was sure to do. For three of them did their best to dissuade Jehoiakim from burning the scroll. Its contents, therefore, were not concerned with the temple or with its worship, otherwise the priests instead of the courtiers must have taken action. The message had some political bearing and referred to a line of policy which the king proposed to take, but with which all his advisers were not in sympathy.

It is impossible, in our limited knowledge of the events of the period, to say whether Jehoiakim contemplated any change of policy in his fourth year which was of sufficient gravity to call for interference on the part of the prophet. It is more hopeless to speculate on the subject, because we do not even know whether any such change was made. Jehoiakim may have been compelled to surrender his plan because of the opposition of some of his leading courtiers who found courage to protest against the destruction of Jeremiah's scroll. What is of greater interest is to find the prophet suddenly intervening in the political life of his time, as Isaiah had done before him, and to notice one feature which is common to them both. When the one meant his hearers to understand that he was speaking about the king of Assyria or the king of Damascus, he made the matter perfectly plain. And when the other threatened Judah with an invasion from Babylon, Jehoiakim could not mistake his meaning.

It may be added that the conduct of Jeremiah in re-writing the scroll, whatever the scroll may have contained, need not imply the issue of a new, revised and enlarged, edition of the oracles. I venture to see in this no more than an expressive description of the prophet's attitude after his message had been rejected. When Ahaz evaded Isaiah's offer of a sign from Yahweh in connexion with the coming of Immanuel, the prophet replied that the Lord Himself would give the king a sign (Isa. 7 : 10–14). The divine purpose stood, whether a king listened or refused. And so a penknife, though Jehoiakim wielded it, could not undo what God was bringing on Judah. It could not even undo the scroll which a prophet had written. He merely took fresh parchment and re-wrote it, adding a little more.

VIII

JEREMIAH AND THE EXILES

IN spite of his rebellion against Babylon, Jehoiakim died in peace. The storm, however, which he had raised burst on his luckless son, Jehoiachin, who after a reign of no more than three months was forced to surrender to a besieging Chaldean army (II Kings 24 : 8–12). The young king—he was a lad of eighteen—with a number of the prominent men in the capital and nation was deported to Babylonia, and along with these captives Nebuchadrezzar carried away most of the temple vessels (vv. 13–17). It is an evidence of the new importance which attached to the sacred accessories to worship that the people were more concerned about the fate of these vessels than about the plight of the exiles. This was the first deportation in 596, and while the number of the exiled is variously estimated in II Kings 24 : 14, 16 and Jer. 52 : 28, it is clear that they were relatively few in comparison with those who were carried away with Zedekiah. The men are also stated to have been the leaders in the life of the capital, but nothing is said about their religious attitude. Thus, while the prominent priests are mentioned in connexion with Zedekiah's captivity (II Kings 25 : 18), there is no reference to priests among the earlier exiles. And since we do not know the causes which led to Jehoiakim's rebellion, and have no reason to conclude that religion was concerned in it, it is likely that the Babylonian selected men who had been identified with the rising or were likely to foment new troubles.

But this captivity raised at once a religious question which was of vital importance for all the future of Judaism. The little community which lived together in Babylonia presented a novel phenomenon. They were not merged in the population of their new country, but were evidently permitted to live apart. For they retained their identity and even a certain measure of their old organized life, since there is mention of elders among them and of prophets continuing to function (chap. 29). They were also not merely desirous but able to maintain some connexion with the central community at Jerusalem, for letters and messengers passed and repassed. Yet these men must have found themselves, religiously speaking, in an entirely anomalous position, on which, and on their true way of meeting which, their faith could give no guidance. Were they able to maintain any real relation to Yahweh in this foreign land? And if they were able, by what means was this relation to be maintained? Their faith could give no answer to these grave questions, for the simple reason that the question had never before arisen. Yahwism had hitherto been practised in the holy land of Palestine. And the ordinary means of maintaining men's relation to their God had there been within their reach. They could always find a sanctuary where Israel's festivals were celebrated and true sacrifice was offered. But all this was cut off from the exiles at a stroke. Loisy has put the situation with much force.[1] 'From the point of view of antiquity nothing could be more abnormal than the religious position of the believing exiles who were the guardians of Yahwism. The principles and teaching of the prophets did not allow them to serve the gods of Chaldea; on the other hand, Judaic tradition, strengthened yet more by the Deuteronomic reformation, fixed Yahweh in Zion.' Whether Judaic tradition ever localized its God at Zion may be doubtful. But it is not doubtful that the centralization of the cult made Zion essential for the worship of Yahweh. Men could not enter into full relation to the God of the covenant

[1] *Religion of Israel*, p. 194.

except by sacrifice and festival, and this worship could only be offered at the temple in Jerusalem. The exiles, through the mere force of circumstance, were being robbed not only of their fatherland, but of their God.

All among them who took the position which appears in a saying of David to Saul (II Sam. 26 : 19): 'they have driven me out this day that I should have no share in the inheritance of Yahweh, saying Go, serve other gods', must have dumbly resigned themselves to the inevitable. But it is an interesting proof of how the better minds in Israel, even if they ever accepted it,[1] had outgrown the conception of their God as a local deity that the exile community evidently did not so resign themselves. Instead of calmly acquiescing in this apparent outcome of their exile, they were perturbed by it and, according to chap. 29, turned for guidance in this perplexity to their prophets. And these prophets in Babylonia and Jeremiah in Jerusalem had no hesitation in giving their judgement on the situation. Incidentally the condition of matters which is thus revealed throws another interesting light on the function which the prophets were expected to fulfil in the life of the nation. The priests might be relied on to guide the minds of worshippers in all ordinary circumstances. But, when a new situation emerged which demanded a decision in the light, not of the practice of the past, but of the principles of the Mosaic faith, it was to the prophets men turned for direction.[2]

While the situation of the exiles thus raised the gravest questions among themselves, it also raised similar questions in Jerusalem. How was the central community to think about, and what attitude was it to take to, its exiled brethren?

[1] There are such things in Hebrew literature as picturesque exaggerations. To make these vivid phrases into theological dogmas may argue a want of imagination.

[2] Cf. the task of prophecy in Deut. 18 : 15–22, and p. 88, *supra*.

Were these men to be recognized as forming a real part of Judaism? The question was vital at any time and in any circumstances, but it won a new importance in the minds of men who had centralized worship in the temple and so made a share in this worship dependent on the possibility of access to Jerusalem.

Because Jeremiah was a prophet, i.e. because his business was to guide the thought of his people in new and difficult conditions in the light of his fundamental convictions as to Yahweh's relation to Israel, he has given his judgement on both questions. In chap. 24 we have his verdict on the relative value of the exiles and the remanent population of Jerusalem: in chap. 29 we find a letter which he wrote for the guidance of the exiles themselves.[1]

In connexion with the first of these, the vision of the two baskets of figs, it is necessary to emphasize that the prophet was pronouncing on a question of religion. That was the reason for his seeing the baskets set before the temple. Cornill struck out in v. 1 the clause 'set before the temple of the Lord', because he believed the figs were designed there for offerings and found it impossible to suppose that any worshipper brought uneatable gifts to the temple. Ehrlich[2] went farther, and since he also supposed the baskets of figs to be firstfruits, rejected the entire parable and pronounced it unauthentic. Yet we have scarcely the right to pronounce that the baskets must have been actually seen by the prophet at the time when he uttered his oracle. The connexion of the fig-baskets with the temple may be merely a part of the allegory. Still less have we the right to pronounce that, even if he did see them, he must have supposed them to be in-

1 Volz (*Komm.* ad chap. 24) would add to the messages about exile the passage 13 : 1–11. As I cannot accept the authenticity of this passage, I must ignore it.

2 *Randglossen zur Hebräischen Bibel*, ad loc.

tended for firstfruits. Besides, to make either the peccant clause or the entire allegory a later insertion does not do anything to help the supposed difficulty. It merely implies that some post-exilic annotator invented a gratuitous libel on the religious habits of his contemporaries and foisted this on Jeremiah. The temple was introduced into the allegory because it was relevant. The question in debate turned round religion, and in particular it was the relation to the temple and its worship of the two bodies of men represented by the figs which interested the prophet.

For the contrast Jeremiah instituted between the exiles and the men of Jerusalem was concerned with the fate Yahweh had allotted to these two sections of Judaism, not with their moral condition. The one company was in exile, the other was still in the holy land. Volz may be taken as the latest representative of a prevailing view which ignores or slurs this cardinal feature of the oracle. He writes truly 'the centre-point of the contrast lies, not in their character, but in their fate'.[1] But he continues: 'Yet the moral factor is always silently presupposed by the prophets. When Jeremiah compared the two sections of Judaism, he must have the impression of the exilic community as more pleasing to Yahweh. In it were priests like Ezekiel, officials from the good time of Josiah (cf. 36 : 25), capable workmen, men of serious mind who, after they had accommodated themselves to their condition, built up a spiritual home in a foreign land. On the other hand, the conscienceless self-seeking mob in Jerusalem appeared to be a lost mass, a basket full of abominable figs.'[2] Then the situation which chap. 24 reveals will be something like the following. The Chaldeans had naturally

[1] *Kommentar*, p. 245.

[2] Incidentally it must be said that this verdict on the exiles stands in violent contrast with the judgement expressed in 13 : 1–11, which Volz accepts as authentic.

selected and carried into exile the leading men in Judah, its more educated classes and its skilled workmen. What was left behind was the undisciplined mob which, in the pride of its new position, was pluming itself on its privileged liberty and new-found authority. The men were boasting that they were better than their old leaders and dearer to Yahweh, for they saw in the misfortunes of their fellows a proof of the divine judgement. The situation is psychologically possible. Men who had suddenly reached a novel position of dignity might readily seek to buttress their authority by belittling their predecessors, and might point to the verdict of facts in which they saw the finger of God. The captivity was an evidence of the divine anger on the exiles, and their own escape from being included in it a sign of His favour. A prophet might well take up his parable against this insolent self-righteousness, which used its crude interpretation of the divine will as a basis for harsh judgement on other men's misfortunes. We should not be surprised to find Jeremiah pronouncing men who were capable of such an attitude worthless before God and man. And the denunciation of a like fate upon them and their city (vv. 8 ff.) would be quite in accord with prophetic teaching.

But this interpretation, while it may serve to explain the terms in which Jeremiah speaks of the men in Jerusalem, will not explain the language he uses about the exiles. He says with emphasis that Yahweh has caused them to be carried away into Babylonia. Yet this is supposed to be the fact on which his hearers based their verdict on their brethren. Was Jeremiah going out of his way to support them in their view of the situation? He continues that Yahweh has a regard for the men in the new condition into which He has brought them, that He will give them a heart to know Him so that they shall continue to be His people and He shall continue to be their God. He adds that all this is sure on the one condition that they turn to Yahweh with their whole heart. This is the deliberate verdict of the prophet on the men of the captivity. And in it he says nothing about their moral character or social standing. Indeed, he expressly asserts that everything he holds out before them depends on their maintaining a right heart toward Yahweh, and so leaves it to be concluded that they may well need the reminder. And this verdict was spoken to the men at Jerusalem, evidently because they needed to hear that the fate which had befallen their brethren, while it had come from Yahweh, did not involve exclusion from the grace of their God. It was possible for them, if they repented, to find the favour of Yahweh in Babylon.

It will be observed that Volz speaks of the exiles 'building up a spiritual home in a foreign land'. But that is precisely the question which the new conditions in which the men found themselves were forcing on them. Could they build up a spiritual home in a foreign land, and what was the character of the spiritual home which Judaism could build in any other land than Palestine? The kernel of the whole difficulty was their fate. Hence Jeremiah goes directly to this central point in what he says about the exiles. They had not gone of their own will to Babylon. Yahweh had brought them there, and He had not forgotten them in the new world of difficulty into which He had brought them.

It is especially necessary to avoid an inference which might easily be drawn from Volz's description of the two bodies of men, exiles and remanent Judeans, and which has occasionally been drawn from similar descriptions. According to this, the best elements of the nation, socially and intellectually, had been deported into Babylon. What was left was composed of the lower classes of the community. Even if this were the case—and it will be noted that the statement greatly exaggerates the importance of the early deportation under

Jehoiachin—it does not imply that the exiles constituted the best religious and moral elements of the nation. The conqueror did not select his victims out of any other consideration than that of weakening Jerusalem's resistance. He chose the men who were most likely to be troublesome to him, men who through birth or capacity were capable of rising to leadership. Now Jeremiah believed that these men were under the special regard of Yahweh. They were the good figs, and the people of Jerusalem were bad figs. To suppose that he based his verdict on the higher social position or the better culture of the exiles is nothing more nor less than to accuse the prophet of snobbery.

In their thought about themselves and their brethren in exile the men of the capital were not influenced by arrogance and undue self-confidence. They were controlled by something far more dangerous and ultimately more disastrous, a false conception of their common religion. They themselves were secure, because they sat under the shadow of the temple. In leaving them there, Yahweh had proved anew His favour. They were the elect of the nation, since they were suffered to continue in the holy land and in the holy city. They could by their sacrifices maintain their relation to Yahweh, and He would maintain them and their city. As for the exiles, their fate had been decided by the same divine act which had declared in favour of the men of Jerusalem. Through being driven out from the holy land they were cut off from the sure mercies of God. The Josianic reform was revealing its inevitable implications. By making the temple the one centre of worship, and its sacrifices the one covenanted means of approach to their God, men had made Yahweh a local deity. He could not be rightly worshipped by men who were unable to seek His face at the temple. The reform had given a new basis for the old crude verdict: thou hast cast me out from the inheritance of the Lord, saying, go serve other gods.

Read in this light, all Jeremiah's utterances win new meaning and force. He seizes with the boldness of a man of strong conviction and clear insight the central position of the men to whom he speaks. The exile was the expression of the divine verdict. Yes, said Jeremiah, Yahweh sent them out of this place into the land of the Chaldeans—for good. So long as they, like the men of the capital, depended on the temple, they could not learn the full meaning of their God's grace. They have the opportunity in their new land to learn that Yahweh does still regard them. And that He does still have a mind toward them, so that they can continue to be His people and He can remain their God, the prophet repeats with emphasis. All they need in order to realize it is to turn to Him with their whole heart. The God of their fathers can be found and worshipped in the new land, because He has brought them into it.

Not only does the verdict on the exiles win meaning along these lines, but the judgement on the men at Jerusalem gains new force. What is denounced upon them is that they shall follow their brethren into captivity. On the ordinary interpretation this becomes no more than a barren punishment of men who were filled with insolent self-righteousness and harsh judgements on the unfortunate. A barren punishment, because it means no more than penalty. To Jeremiah a punishment which comes from Yahweh means more than penalty. The exile could be made more than penalty to men in Babylon. The destruction of Jerusalem which Jeremiah announces can be more than the wreck of men's hopes. It can be the liberation of their souls, if they see in it the wreck of false hopes. They too are to learn, or at least to have the opportunity of learning, that city and temple are not essential to their true life, and that in any land to which Yahweh sends them in turn they may find Him.

Chap. 24 is undated, and its contents might have been

spoken in Jerusalem at any time after the first captivity. Chap. 29, which contains a letter from Jeremiah to the exiles, is also undated but may belong to a later period, for it shows the exile community not only settled in their new country but profoundly stirred over questions which had arisen there. The questions were primarily religious in character, since they were raised by two prophets who had issued certain decisions in Babylon and since Jeremiah, another prophet, felt it necessary to intervene. Yet they also involved the political attitude of the little community, for the Babylonian authorities took action against the two prophets, and they would scarcely have interfered unless the advice of these men had concerned more than domestic religious differences. Besides, Jeremiah declared that the fate of the two men at the hands of the Babylonians was to be so terrible that the exiles should use their names as a curse: Yahweh make thee like Ahab and Zedekiah. Duhm has rightly insisted, not only that some horrible end must have befallen these two, but that their punishment at the instance of the local authority is better attested historically than the letter from Jeremiah. For, unless their fate had been a well-known fact, the Jewish community would not have preserved a record which declared that all this doom had been pronounced beforehand by one of their great prophets.

Why, then, were the two prophets burned to death by the Babylonian government? The form of punishment, which was rare in Israel, evidently impressed the exiles profoundly, and may have been selected for this end. Jeremiah is stated to have given two reasons (v. 23). According to him the men had debauched their neighbours' wives and had spoken falsely in the name of Yahweh. The first charge would be enough to explain their doom, had that come from the hands of their fellow-Jews, for the adulterer was punished with death in Israel (Deut. 22 : 22), and burning was denounced against certain sexual offences (Gen. 38 : 24; Lev. 20 : 14; 21 : 9). But it is wholly unlikely that the Babylonians were so deeply interested in the sexual morality of their captives as to make adultery the ground for a public and peculiarly terrible example in the case of two prominent Jewish leaders. The onus of the charge cannot have lain there, but must lie in something the men had done in their religious capacity. They as prophets had misled the exiles. At first sight this might seem to involve a greater perplexity, since the Babylonians were as unlikely to interfere in the religion as in the morals of their captives. But it is necessary to ask whether Jeremiah did not attach a definite meaning to the charge of false prophecy. Now he is found to characterize as false prophets certain men in Jerusalem who were advising Zedekiah to rebel against Nebuchadrezzar (27 : 14). He would naturally find the same falsity in similar prophets among the exiles, if these were teaching in Yahweh's name that their co-religionists must expect a speedy deliverance at the hands of their God and must take every means to ensure their deliverance from exile. A prophecy of this character would account both for the terms in which Jeremiah denounced Ahab and Zedekiah and for the prompt and severe action of the civil power which could only see the men to be fomenting sedition.

Because the situation thus regarded is natural and probable, there is no ground for pronouncing the charges of adultery and false prophecy secondary elements in the chapter. Jeremiah, writing to Jews, did not give the reasons which prompted the Babylonians. He regarded the whole matter from a different angle. To him the punishment meted out to the two prophets was due, not to the jealous watchfulness of a civil power, but to the anger of Yahweh. And if he could be informed of the character of the men's utterances, he could also be informed of their private morals.

When the incident is examined from the side which

historically is best authenticated, it reveals a movement among the exiles for resistance to the Babylonian government which was based on their religion since it was fomented by two prophets. Then it becomes easier to find a reason for the chapter having been placed after chaps. 27 f. In chap. 28 Hananiah, leading certain prophets of his school, urged king Zedekiah in Jerusalem into rebellion against Babylon and promised in Yahweh's name all success. The movement was not confined to Judah, for according to 27 : 2 f. Jeremiah warned the messengers of the kings of Moab, Edom, Ammon, and Phoenicia, as well as his own king, against the scheme. The projected league came to nothing, whether because Judah refused to join or because Nebuchadrezzar was too well-informed and too quick for the plotters. But it is possible that the great king required Zedekiah, in person or by deputy, to send an explanation of his conduct. The Elasah and Gemariah of 29 : 3 may have been these deputies sent from Jerusalem to satisfy the Babylonians. The suggestion would serve to explain how Jeremiah was able to send his letter to the exiles. The journey was too costly and difficult to be readily undertaken by a man in his position. But it was an easy matter to transmit the letter by the mediation of a royal embassy. And nothing is more natural than to suppose that envoys whose business it was to improve the relations between the court at Jerusalem and its suzerain power should have carried a letter, the purpose of which was to counteract an agitation against Babylon in the exile community. The editor, then, who combined chap. 29 with the preceding two, and who dated the troubles in Jerusalem early in Zedekiah's reign (cf. 27 : 1 and 28 : 1), has set these inter-related events in the period before Jeremiah's influence at the court became nil.

In our uncertain knowledge of the historical situation, and particularly in our ignorance of the influences at work in Zedekiah's court, all this cannot be called more than an attractive hypothesis. But, even if it should be ignored, the letter to the exiles was integrally related to Jeremiah's denunciation of their two prophets. Letter and threat had the same purpose of quieting the minds of the Jews in Babylon and counteracting the influence of men who were leading them to identify their religion with certain political aims which filled their hearts with vague and delusive hopes.

Jeremiah's letter, however, has not reached us in its original form, but has been re-touched and added to. No modern student accepts its terms as they stand, but there is serious difference of opinion on the question of the extent to which the revision has been carried. In view of the importance of the matter at issue, it is necessary to present a somewhat full discussion.

Thus vv. 16–20, or at least vv. 16–19, have long been recognized as an addition. The section is absent from the Septuagint, except in its Lucianic text.[1] It speaks of the king and men of Jerusalem becoming an execration among all the nations whither I have driven them (v. 18), and so betrays the post-exilic attitude of the writer. Verse 17, too, contains a reference to the parable of the fig-baskets in chap. 24. Since that parable was spoken in Jerusalem, Jeremiah could not refer casually to its contents in a message to men who had never heard it. When the intrusive matter is removed, the connexion between v. 15 and v. 21 becomes clear. 'But you have said: Yahweh has raised up prophets for us in Babylon',

[1] The evidence of the Lucianic text always needs to be weighed, since that text is full of conflate readings. In this case it is peculiarly suspect, because it has inserted the section before, instead of after, v. 15. Now when a verse or verses which do not appear in one text occupy a different position in two other texts which contain them, the probability of the verses being secondary is great. The copyists or editor have sought to find a place for the passage, but have differed in their judgement of the appropriate position in which it should stand. When the Lucianic text inserted vv. 16–20 before v. 15, it showed real judgement, since it refused to break the close connexion between v. 15 and v. 21.

and therefore we need no guidance from Jerusalem. 'Thus speaks Yahweh Tsebaoth God of Israel about Ahab ben Kolaiah and Zedekiah ben Maaseiah who prophesy lies to you in my name.' Then follows the doom. Jeremiah, having written his own letter of advice, turned to the situation produced by the Babylonian prophets, whose followers might resent the intrusion of a prophet from far-off Jerusalem in their concerns. And, instead of turning aside to a somewhat stereotyped denunciation of Jerusalem which had no real significance for the exiles, i.e. vv. 16–20, he denounced these men as misleading the people.

In the earlier part of the letter, vv. 1–3 form a historical introduction and are clearly editorial. Doubt, however, has been thrown on the authenticity of v. 4 because of the description of the men whom Jeremiah addressed: thus speaks Yahweh God of Israel to all the exiles or the whole *golah* whom I caused to be exiled from Jerusalem to Babylon. Duhm hesitates to pronounce, but Erbt has made the sentence end at 'golah' and declared the relative clause to be an addition which served to bring out that Jeremiah was writing to the early body of exiles under Jehoiachin. But if that was the intention of the glossator, he was singularly helpless in conveying his meaning, for that is what the clause does not say. What the words do say is that the captivity was the act of Yahweh. Jeremiah said the same thing in v. 7: work for the good of the country[1] to which I have brought you as exiles. And he set it in the forefront of his message, because it was what the men most needed to recognize. The situation in which the exiles were placed had led men at Jerusalem to call them bad figs, and was leading men in Babylon to despair over, or to rebellion against, their condition. Jeremiah has to say that there was no need for either despair or rebellion. The exiles were not at the mercy of

[1] Reading הארץ with LXX instead of M.T. העיר the city.

circumstance: they were in the hands of God, who had brought them to Babylon.

Therefore Jeremiah continued that it was the task of the exiles to see in their present political fortune an expression of the will of God for them. To accept this heartily should bring contentment and strength. The exiles must not merely live in their new country, building houses, planting gardens, rearing families and homes. They must pray for it, because in its well-being stood their own. Life in its new conditions could be more than tolerable, it could be made useful and even happy. But, if it was to become this, their religion must not be interpreted simply as a constant means of resenting and reacting against untoward conditions. To Jeremiah religion was no mere political irritant or social ferment. It had its own content and brought men into its own high and serene world. When men lived by it, it supplied its own secret and ineffable strength and high courage.

Within these verses, 5–7, text and meaning are clear and straightforward.[1] But the situation is very different when we turn to vv. 8–11. Here the first thing which is apparent to the student is that it contains three sentences which all begin with כִּי or for,[2] and which give three separate reasons

[1] The one exception is v. 6, where the LXX omits the clause 'and let them, i.e. your daughters, bear children'. That lends a certain force to Duhm's remark on the passage. He notes the LXX omission, and, finding the verse a little turgid, thinks the clause was added by those who came to set a period of seventy years to the exile. The grandchildren represented the second generation. But while the letter is written in rhetorical prose, I do not believe it was originally in poetic form. And it is only a conviction that we have to do with a poem, of the exact forms of which we know all the laws, which produces the impression of turgidity. What Jeremiah was insisting on was that Jewish families could and should be reared in Babylon, and, to emphasize this, he may well have used the familiar idea about children's children.

[2] Verse 9 begins in the same way, but its 'for' connects with the preceding verse: vv. 8, 9 form one Hebrew sentence.

why the exiles should follow Jeremiah's preceding counsel. They must do what he has advised, because the prophets to whom they have hitherto listened were false prophets, because their exile was to end after seventy years, because Yahweh had not forgotten them but purposed their good. In itself that confused arrangement rouses suspicion. And when we turn to vv. 8 f., the command to ignore the advice of their own prophets, the suspicion as to its originality is strengthened by its form. It begins with the formal opening: thus speaks Yahweh Tsebaoth, and closes with the equally formal conclusion: oracle of Yahweh. The two phrases are common signs in the book to mark the beginning and the end of an independent message. But, further, the contents of the oracle are out of place here, since they anticipate the subject of v. 15. There Jeremiah, having completed his prophetic counsel to the exiles, turned to deal with the opposite advice given by Ahab and Zedekiah, whom he denounced on the charge that they were foul livers and false teachers. The falsity of their teaching was proved by its content and character. In vv. 8 f., on the other hand, the prophets are coupled with diviners and dreamers, as though that which Jeremiah blamed in them was the method they followed, rather than the advice they gave. The sentence has the appearance of a gloss which was meant to explain what a false prophet was: and the verses which compose it must be set down as secondary, because of their form, their position in the letter, and their contents.

Is, however, the famous prophecy which limits the period of the exile to seventy years original? Its form is awkward, so awkward that the Septuagint has found it necessary to change 'you' into 'your people', since the translators recognized that after seventy years none of the men who heard the letter could 'return to this place'. But what is of more significance is that vv. 10 and 11 are parallel clauses, each of which gives a reason why the exiles may live quietly in Babylon and work for its well-being; and the two reasons are hardly compatible. In the connexion in which the two clauses at present stand, verses 10 and 11 imply that Yahweh keeps in mind the plans which He forms about the people, plans of peace and not of disaster, to give them a future about which they can hope, but that these plans must meantime remain in abeyance, because only after seventy years can He visit them. He cannot come at present into close relation to them. But, in the thought of Hosea and Jeremiah, God's plans for His people did not rest on the contingency of what was to happen in and to Babylon: they rested on the relation of the people to Him and His relation to them. This relation could be broken by their rebellion: it could not be broken by the accident of an exile which Yahweh Himself had permitted. When Jeremiah was writing to men in new and peculiarly trying conditions, he fell back for their encouragement, not on something which was to happen in seventy years, but on what was ultimate in the purpose of God as he and they thought about God.

Again, when one recognizes that the two verses are parallel reasons for quieting the minds of the exiles, there can be little question as to which forms the better conclusion to v. 7 and the better continuation to the prophet's letter. The sentence which promised return after seventy years could only turn the men's minds away from their present tasks and opportunities. They were not to work for the well-being of their new country in any permanent way: instead they must be so expectant of a better thing from God that the well-being of Babylon became to them a thing indifferent, because transient. On the other hand v. 11, with its assurance that God had them in His mind, dealt directly with the instant and urgent present. Since they were in exile by the will of God and since God had a mind toward them in their exile, the conditions under which they were called to live were not empty of meaning, not mere transient things which must be borne reluctantly: they held for the men an issue and a hope. Life even in Babylon could be more than tolerable, it was rich in fruitful possibilities.[1]

But, further, the assurance that Yahweh bore the exiles on His heart served not only to quiet the troubles in Babylon: it served also to introduce vv. 12–14 with their conviction that, since Yahweh had a mind to them, He remained accessible. They might call upon Him and pray with the confidence that He should hear. Driver[2] has proposed to omit v. 14: 'You shall find me, oracle of Yahweh, and I will turn your fortune and gather you from all the nations and countries to which I have scattered you, oracle of Yahweh, and I will restore you to the place from which I exiled you'. The verse, with the exception of the opening clause, is omitted by the Septuagint; it is patently addressed, not to the exiles in Babylon, but to the whole diaspora scattered across the world: it awkwardly and unnecessarily repeats 'oracle of Yahweh'. Yet the opening sentence in the form 'I will reveal myself unto you' does appear in the Septuagint, and I suggest that the original read: I will yet reveal myself unto you, oracle of Yahweh, and turn your fortune. The last clause was interpreted, as was done elsewhere, to mean 'I will bring you back from captivity'; and this interpretation, which implied that Jeremiah anticipated a return from exile, gave rise to all the interpolations on the part of men who construed the prophecies of the past in the light of that great event. Then the 'oracle of Yahweh' in its earlier occurrence was the original conclusion of the letter, marking it all as a divine revelation.

When the accretions have been removed from the letter, there remains a clear and self-consistent message. The appeal

[1] The promise of return after seventy years appears also in 25 : 12–14, and is equally dubious there ; cf. pp. 113 ff.

[2] *The Book of the Prophet Jeremiah*, p. 171.

of religion was being used among the exiles to prevent them from settling down to face the new conditions of life in Babylon. They were being taught to believe that they could not remain loyal to their faith and peaceable subjects of a foreign power. They must at all costs seek for a return to Jerusalem. So the prophet, who had opposed with all his energy the prophets in Jerusalem who were using religion in order to foment rebellion against Nebuchadrezzar, opposed as unhesitatingly the similar use of religion in Babylonia. When he had assured the exiles that access to Yahweh was not made impossible to them by their captivity, he turned vehemently on the prophets who had misled the unfortunate people. And the vehemence of his denunciation of Ahab and Zedekiah proves that between them and Jeremiah lay a profound difference on the nature of their religion. The difference was one of principle. Had the quarrel between Jeremiah and these two men turned on the fact that the Babylonian prophets looked for and plotted for an immediate return while the prophet of Jerusalem expected the exile to endure for another seventy years, it is incredible that any religious teacher believed the death of his opponents the only adequate punishment for a mistake about a date. Jeremiah's vehemence only becomes explicable if he believed that the gravest issues were involved in this controversy.

A company of Jewish settlers in Egypt found themselves in very similar conditions to those of the exiles. But they acted quite differently. Desiring, like the Babylonians, to maintain their ancestral faith, they built at Elephantine a temple which 'was not a mere synagogue, but a considerable building with an altar and all the appurtenances of sacrifice'. 'After their temple was destroyed in a riot of the Egyptians (in 411) they sent a petition to the High Priest at Jerusalem, asking for help to rebuild it. When this was disregarded they appealed to the Persian governor at Jerusalem. There is no hint of any suspicion that the temple could be considered heretical, and they would surely not have appealed to the High Priest at Jerusalem if they had felt any doubt about it. On the contrary, they give the impression of being proud of having a temple of their own, and as pious devotees of Ya'u (no other god is mentioned in the petition) seriously distressed at the loss of religious opportunities caused by its destruction.'[1]

What prevented the exiles in Babylon from finding a similar solution to their identical difficulty was that between the settlement in Egypt and the exile in Babylon the Josianic reform had made the temple the only legitimate sanctuary, its sacrifices the only valid offerings to Yahweh, its priesthood the only lawful priests. When they turned for guidance to their prophets, these men who held the same convictions could only counsel them to plan for a return to Judah. Chap. 24 has shown the reform producing its inevitable religious result in the minds of men at Jerusalem: chap. 29 brings to light its equally inevitable political reaction in the exilic community. Men who believed that they could not rightly worship their God except at Jerusalem must, if they remained loyal to their religion, count a return to Palestine an essential element in their faith. The new conception of religion which was implicit in the Josianic reform was making every conscientious Jew a bad citizen of the country where he was an exile.

Browne has made the interesting suggestion that the exiles, in spite of the Josianic reform, did attempt to establish a place of sacrifice in Babylonia. He draws attention to the curious passage, Ezra 8 : 15–20, where it is said that Ezra before his return to Jerusalem found a scarcity of Levites among those who were prepared to make up the caravan. Thereupon the leader selected certain messengers and commissioned them to Iddo the chief at the place Casiphia, through whose help

[1] Cowley, *Aramaic Papyri of the Fifth Century B.C.*, p. xx.

he was able to secure a sufficient number of Levites and Nethinim. Noting the unusual and unnecessary description of Casiphia as 'the place', and noting further that the word מקום frequently means a sanctuary, Browne thinks it probable that the exiles attempted to institute a regular place of worship in their new country. And certainly the suggestion does explain the otherwise rather pointless addition to the foreign name, and the fact that Ezra expected to find and did find Levites there.[1] Yet, however probable the hypothesis may be, it is no more, and to build anything on it would be to build on very sandy foundations. Even if such an effort was made, it was evidently confined to a minority of the exiles. The great majority were plainly on the side of the prophets, and as plainly supported the later effort for the return. For, even if we accept Browne's suggestion and suppose that the Levites were at Casiphia because it was a shrine, it will be noted that they instantly deserted it when they were invited to join the caravan which was preparing to set out for Jerusalem.

If now prophets like Ahab and Zedekiah came to control the minds of the exiles, the result was sure. Babylon must strike back against a movement in which it could see nothing but rebellion; and then the gleam of a better life would be quenched in the extinction of the community. Yet, when Jeremiah interfered, what stirred him to action was something larger than the patriotic desire to save his brother Jews from perishing in a pogrom. He was a prophet, and what moved him was the sense that the men were being misled through a poor thought of their God, His power, His grace, His nearness to them. He bade them accept their new condition, because it was the divine will for them. It was Yahweh who had caused them to be carried away into captivity. He had brought them where they were and He must

[1] Cf. *Early Judaism*, chap. iv.

mean something by the deed. The men must so heartily accept their new conditions as to work for the good of the land to which they have been brought. In its welfare they could find their own. Let them marry their sons and daughters in their new settlement, and let them beget and bear children. It is possible that in this peculiar command we can overhear the prophet's counterblast to some extreme utterance on the part of Zedekiah and Ahab. These men may have said that it were better to let the race die out than to rear citizens for the hated Babylon. But, whether this be the case or not, Jeremiah's meaning is clear. Jewish homes could exist and Jewish life be continued in Babylonia. The true faith was capable of being maintained under an alien sky.

That might have been sufficient if Jeremiah's aim had merely been to counteract the disastrous counsel of Zedekiah and Ahab. But the prophet knew that men in the condition of the exiles needed more. What was making the root of all their unrest, what had made them give too ready an ear to their prophets, had been the desolating sense that in their exile they were separated from God. Unless this hunger in their souls could be satisfied, the men would become the ready prey of another prophet after Zedekiah and Ahab had been removed. It is a fine proof of the prophet's insight that he could fling himself into the condition of men in these novel conditions, and recognize the spiritual hunger which was leading them astray. The men needed something which could satisfy and stay up their hearts. As for this need, says the prophet, let them try their God. Let them go and pray to Him where they are, and they shall find Him. 'For I know the thoughts that I think toward you, saith the Lord, thoughts of well-being and not of evil, to give you hope at the last.' They were not and could not be beyond this care. When the men have sought and found Him in Babylon, they shall discover in their own animating and liberating experience that Yahweh is not bound to a land, a temple, a priesthood, a set sacrificial system. He can be found wherever a contrite heart seeks Him. For He is a great God, and the thoughts He thinks toward His people are great and generous thoughts.

The message to the exiles in chap. 29 is thus the complement and fulfilment of the oracle to Jerusalem in the parable of the figs of chap. 24. In the one case Jeremiah, speaking to the men of the capital, told them that their brethren in diaspora were really nearer Yahweh than those who worshipped in the shadow of the temple, but who held false thoughts of Him whom they worshipped there. The shadow of the temple lay over all their worship: and they would not learn liberty, until that was taken away by the act of their God, when He scattered them also among the nations. In the other case Jeremiah, writing to the exiles themselves, was careful to remind them that while they were still able to reach Yahweh in their new condition, they must seek Him wholeheartedly. Exile in itself was no discovery of the width of the divine grace. The men must be diligent to seek their God. But if they did they could not fail to find Him, for He has a mind toward His people. And to find Him in Babylonia will mean to be free for ever from the desolating thought that circumstances, which may rob men of their homes, their habits, and their old associations, must also rob devout men of their God. To find Him also will be for such men as these the dawn of new hope, since they still find themselves in a universe which means well by them, and can go on to build up a new life which has not parted from the best that Jerusalem gave them.

Jeremiah bases his messages about and to the exiles on one simple, fundamental conviction. Yahweh is too great a God to be localized. Now the Josianic reform at least leaned in the direction of the older, cruder idea that Yahweh could only be reached on the soil of Palestine.

IX

JEREMIAH AND THE CONTENT OF YAHWISM

WRITING to the exiles, Jeremiah bade them pray with confidence, because He to whom they prayed had a mind toward them. Speaking to North Israel, he urged them to repent and to return, for He to whom they returned was merciful to the penitent. But in neither case did he expect the men to pray or to return to One whom they did not already know. To him and to them God was Yahweh the God of Israel, who had revealed Himself in the past to His people. Their common religion was the expression of the will and the embodiment of the character of this God. It is necessary to ask whether Jeremiah attached any specific content to this national religion and how he regarded the peculiar relation between Israel and its God.

In 2 : 1–3 he has said: The word of Yahweh came to me: go and cry aloud in the hearing of Jerusalem. Thus speaks Yahweh: I recall in your favour the love you had for me in your early days, a love of the honeymoon, how you followed me through the desert, that barren land. Then Israel was set apart to Yahweh as His property, so select and sacred that every one who interfered with her was to be held guilty and find mischief light upon him. The prophet was referring to the event in which Yahweh first revealed His mind toward the people, the event which also made it a nation different from all other nations, the Exodus from Egypt. The unsown or barren land was the desert in which the men were wholly dependent on their God. They went after Him thither because they were content to be dependent on Him. For that was the period of the first love between Yahweh and His bride. In this time of the honeymoon Israel knew herself to be His and to owe everything to His care. Committing herself to His protection, she found Him to be all-sufficient and she was satisfied to be entirely in His hands. Jeremiah was using Hosea's favourite figure of the nation as the bride of its God. The conception, too, of the wilderness journeys as a period, not of constant rebellion but of faithfulness, is common to both prophets. The idea is no reflection of historic tradition: it is the expression of Hosea's ideal of Israel's religion as a glad and grateful dependence on Yahweh. This is the basis and this is the content of the national faith. It rested on a choice of Israel by Yahweh which sprang from His free grace, and it demanded in return a complete surrender and a loyal allegiance. The people gave itself up to the divine will with so absolute a surrender that it could have no thought for another god, and in His care it found assurance.

According to Hosea, however, no sooner had Israel reached Palestine, the home which Yahweh prepared for His bride, and there discovered that love meant loyalty, than the nation rebelled (9 : 10). The prophet marvelled over the failure. To him this rebellion, with the ingratitude which it implied, was more than he could understand (6 : 4). He made no effort to discover its cause. Again, it seems idle to suppose that Hosea was speaking in terms of history. The lapse of a nation cannot be dated to an exact period like that of the events at Ba'al Peor. The prophet was contrasting the actual with the ideal, the condition of the Israel he knew and lived among with the purpose its God had with it when He brought it into being. Jeremiah took up the same question, but he could not leave it where Hosea had left it. To him Israel's disloyalty demanded an explanation, and it demanded this the more because he found apostacy from the national god to be confined to his own people. 'Go to the lands of the West[1] and inquire, send out East[1] and make full inquiry, find out whether anything of this kind has ever happened. Has any nation ever changed its god, nonentity though that was? Yet my people has put in place of me who am its glory a helpless idol' (2 : 10–11). Any or all of these peoples might have apostatized without loss, for the gods they chose to worship were equally futile. To desert Yahweh was to make the only change which really made any difference. It was to leave a fresh spring and dig cisterns, which at their worst could hold nothing, and which at their best could only hold stale water flat with age and foul with dust (2 : 13). Yet Israel was the one nation in the world which had forsaken its god.

Jeremiah found the reason in the very fact which made Yahwism peculiar and great. Men forsook Yahweh, because it mattered to remain, because His service made such far-reaching demands. He, being what He was, must ask much, and did claim more than Israel was prepared to give. Hence the prophet could say: it has been an old habit of the people to break the yoke, to burst the bonds, to say, I am not going to be a slave to any one (2 : 20).[2] The word he used for bonds is the same word which Hosea used for the bonds of love by which Yahweh drew Israel to Himself and made it His peculiar people. But Jeremiah has given the word a slight turn which serves to show what was in his mind. For the same bond which drew Israel to Yahweh, making it His own, kept it apart. Above all, it involved separation from all other allegiance. It is when men realize that love means more than privilege that they begin to rebel. When Israel realized that Yahweh had a yoke, that He imposed standards and required submission, it forsook Him for the easier religions of heathenism. Out of His mere grace Yahweh had chosen the nation

[1] M.T. Kittim and Kedar. These represent to the prophet the Mediterranean and the Arabian desert respectively.

[2] Reading with R.V. margin.

and given it His name. Through the new sense of unity and self-confidence which the common faith had brought, it had won Palestine and nationhood. Everything which Israel possessed had come from its faith. But the grace which gave much asked much: it demanded self-surrender. And without self-surrender on the part of those who received it, grace became an empty word. No other nation changed its god, nonentity though that was. The reason for the constancy was that it all meant so little. There was no cause to forsake such gods, because it involved so little to follow them. Israel forsook Yahweh, because the relation to Him was full of ethical content. Its national history was a record of apostacy, since the people had to deal with a God who had a character and a purpose which He had not failed to make known to them. Yahwism had this iron core in it. The iron core was that Israel could only have Yahweh on His own terms. And these terms He had made known through Moses and through the constant succession of prophets who had continued the work of Moses. Yahwism was no colourless faith which was simply the expression of the people's pride in itself and in its destiny. It laid a curb on men, it had a yoke and bonds. The bonds were those of love, but love's bonds are the most enduring and the most exacting. Against these Israel had always fretted. The people preferred to make gods for themselves, gods which could lay on no yoke and set up no standards, because they were ultimately the reflection of men's own desires.

Jeremiah knew this, not merely because he had watched the conduct of his own people and looked with a curious interest at the habits of other nations. He had discovered it in himself; and that is the only place where it is wholesome or safe to make such discoveries.

'O Yahweh[1] remember me and give me some heed, avenge

[1] With LXX omit 'Thou knowest'.

my cause on those who persecute me; delay not thine anger, recognize that I am bearing insult and reproach from men who despise thy words.[1] As for me, thy word is my joy and my heart's delight, for I am wholly dedicated to thee, O Yahweh. I never sat in the company of mockers nor found any pleasure there: under thine awful power I sat lonely, for thou didst fill me with indignation. Why then is my grief unceasing and my wound incurable? Art thou becoming to me a stream that runs dry, a spring that fails?

Thus then spoke Yahweh: if you surrender to me and I restore you, you shall be my servant; if you make clear the difference between good and evil, you shall be like my mouth. Then it will be for others to turn to you, not for you to turn to them (15 : 15 ff.).'

A prophet, like the nation to which he belonged, had the privilege of having been brought into a peculiar relation to Yahweh. This, too, was neither self-chosen nor self-created; it came to him through the act of God, who elected him to be His mouth-piece and His representative. He, therefore, could be assured of the divine support in all his work, and might be astonished should it seem to fail. Yet everything which thus came to him must be on the divine terms. And the terms were that he must continue to maintain the divine standards. He must surrender his own will, and utter only what was delivered to him. Only on condition that he made the distinction between the vile and the excellent could he expect to continue God's servant. For him, too, there were a yoke and bonds.

Jeremiah found the reason for the nation's apostacy and for his own rebellion in the characteristic feature of their common faith which formed at once its repulsion and its attraction. It held a moral standard for man's conduct in the character of its God. Hence in his message to Northern

[1] Following LXX.

Israel[1] he made their sin consist in their having forsaken Yahweh and having worshipped strange gods, as he made the first condition and basis of all renewal consist in a repentant return to the God of their fathers. To him and to Hosea apostacy was the root from which every other evil grew. They could not say with Amos 'for three transgressions of Israel and for four I will not turn doom away' (2 : 6), and then proceed to a list of the special sins which were bringing down the divine wrath. Amos saw Yahweh stand with His plummet beside the wall His people had built, and test their building by a standard which came *ab extra*. The sins, too, which he condemned were anti-social, and therefore could be catalogued, tested, condemned. Hosea and Jeremiah saw one sin, the fruitful mother of many: the people knew not Yahweh, they had forsaken Yahweh. Yet it would be a mistake to suppose that Jeremiah showed himself less conscious of the presence of social wrong in his own generation than the prophet of Bethel, or less terrible in his denunciation of it. When he went, another Diogenes, through the streets of Jerusalem seeking for a man, the man he could not find, whose presence would have sufficed to turn back the divine wrath, was one who acted justly and who sought truth (5 : 1). Jerusalem was ripe for doom because it was lacking in these qualities. But the prophet realized that Israel's failure in the common relations of life, with the resultant treachery and unseemliness in all national and private relations, had one root. Men did not recognize any standard for human conduct, or, if they did, it was not the immutable standard of Yahweh. As he stated (2 : 8), they who handle torah or the law do not know Yahweh. The meaning of the accusation was not that the priests who had the task of guiding men's piety and conduct were not themselves religious men. It was

[1] Cf. pp. 60 ff., *supra*.

something at once more simple and more dangerous. The men who had control of so much in the national life did not know the character and mind of Him whose perfect will all torah was meant to express and whose judgements all their decisions ought to embody. The life of Israel was tainted at its source.

Yet even these men could not fail to realize the unique power which lay in their national faith. They might be able to ignore it, so long as things went well with them. But they were driven to acknowledge it as their one hope in every day of distress. As the thief is disappointed when he is found out, so is Israel disappointed—king, leaders, priests, and prophets together, who say to a wooden idol, thou art my father, and to a stone image, thou art my mother. They turned their backs to me instead of their faces: but, let evil days come, they cry: Up and save us (2 : 26 f.). It is true that men who could expect this revealed their idea of their God. They believed Him to be as indifferent to moral standards as themselves, and ready to take them back on any terms. He could be touched by a cry which was born out of distress, but which held in it no repentance. Yet the fact that in their day of need the people fell back on their ancient faith was in itself a confession on their part that Yahwism held something of which the other faiths were destitute. They fled back to it when other hopes and supports failed. Most of them were thinking of mere temporal distress and of deliverance from outward troubles which beset their nation and their life. But their instinctive appeal to their own God meant more than they themselves realized. Yahwism held the secret of strength in all apparent defeat. A religion which implies no yoke in the day of success can bring no support in the day of adversity. Only that which is capable of controlling holds also power to maintain when everything else has failed. Only the religion which men did not make for themselves and which was not the reflection of their own desires, which they did not invent but which they discovered, could at once restrain and uphold. It was the God who issued orders who also sustained. Jeremiah, like all the prophets, believed that Yahweh had revealed Himself to Israel and chosen it to be His servant. They believed this as no tradition from the fathers, but because He had revealed Himself to them and chosen them for His service. It was this steel core in Yahwism, the demand that men must submit to the claim of their God, which caused their revolt, which made them perennially uneasy in their revolt, and gave hope of recovery The feature in their religion which made its repulsion formed also its permanent attraction.

Throughout these oracles the prophet's message was simple and direct. He was urging on the men of his generation the unique character of the God in whom he and they alike believed, with the resultant uniqueness and magnitude of His demands and the consequent reality of His guidance and support.

But the guidance and support were not dependent on the outward conditions in which the nation found itself, its continuance in its own land, its independence, its organized kingdom. They depended on the mind Yahweh had towards this people which He chose, and on the temper and attitude which these brought to His demands. Jeremiah has expressed this in general terms in a little oracle, the meaning of which has been obscured, because a later generation added an unhappy comment to its original terms. Fortunately the secondary matter has been merely added at the close, so that it is easier than in other cases to distinguish between the authentic and the unauthentic sections.

In 18 : 1–6 the prophet was bidden go down to a potter's workshop with the promise that there he should receive a revelation. 'So I went down to the potter's workshop and found him at work with his wheel. Whenever the article he was making went wrong, as clay is apt to do in a potter's hand, he would remake it in a different shape, such as he thought suitable.[1] Thereupon the message of Yahweh came to me: Am I not able to act towards you, O Israel, like this potter? You are in my hands, as clay is in the hands of the potter.'

All that follows is an expansion of the original oracle by a later hand, which has seized the familiar image of the potter and the clay in order to bring in a discussion on the ultimate relation between the divine purpose and man's free will. The writer had reason to use the parable in the way he did because the figure came to be so employed. But he failed to notice that his addition clashed hopelessly with Jeremiah's peculiar use of the figure. For the whole point of the little later sermon turned on the possibility of repentance. Yahweh held man in His hands and controlled human destiny. But He might change a threat into a promise or a promise into a threat, if the recipient changed his mind. Now obviously clay cannot change its mind.[2]

What was revealed to Jeremiah, as he watched the whirling wheel, was that Israel was in the hands of Yahweh, and in no other. Its life depended on Him and His purpose with it, not on what Egypt or Babylon might do with it or towards it, not even on the plans of its rulers and priests. Yahweh had a mind toward it, which could not be altered or turned aside by any other agent. And, while the divine purpose was one and immutable, it was not bound to any fixed plan.

[1] There is no need for any change in the M.T. What is needed is closer attention to the meaning and force of the Hebrew imperfects.

[2] Volz is able to write, ad loc.: 'Dagegen offenbart sich hier eine gewaltige Weltbetrachtung. Es gibt nur einen Willen in der Geschichte: den Willen Gottes, und nur eine Bedingung des Geschehens: das sittliche Verhalten der Völker: die Weltgeschichte dreht sich in diesen beiden Angeln.' That is excellent as a summing-up of vv. 7 ff., and for that very reason makes clearer its incompatibility with all that precedes, for unfortunately clay has no *sittliche Verhalten*.

A potter might find that a certain lump of clay could not be shaped into a vase. Well, he could make something of it. He could mould it into a bowl or some coarser dish. But he need not throw away the lump which he had kneaded and designed to use. Yahweh had taken one way with Israel, and had tried whether it could answer His design. He had planted it in Palestine and made it into a kingdom. Under David He had made it great and powerful. The issue had not been all which He had desired, for Israel had failed Him. The people were too untempered, too petulant, too weak in purpose to fulfil the divine plan with and for them. 'I planted you a choice vine from a first-rate stock: what a change has come upon you, turning you into a wild and degenerate plant!' (2 : 21). But Yahweh was not defeated, nor was His purpose bound to one method. He would try another way with Israel. For it cannot escape now out of His hands. The kingdom may go, the land may go, temple and sacrifice may disappear. These are accidents, like the shape of the first pot. There remained the clay and the eternal Potter. The relation between these two was too intimate to be broken by outward circumstances, for it rested on nothing less than the purpose of the Potter.

Because Jeremiah so conceived of the permanent relation between Yahweh and His people, he could not only speak a parable about it. He could give practical and direct advice in the name of Him who had instituted and was maintaining this relation. His fellow-countrymen in North Israel were defeated men who were subjects where they had once been rulers: they were seeking for something which might give them back self-reliance. Their prophet bade them recognize that they might have everything which made Israel what it was and which would remake it, if they returned to Yahweh. The exiles felt themselves to be undone because they were delivered over to the power of heathen Babylon. He told them that they were in the hands of Yahweh, and they would discover what He would do with or for them, if they would try Him. The Potter could mould them to His will in Babylon as well as in Jerusalem. The men in Jerusalem counted themselves secure because they had the temple: it was the guarantee of the divine grace. There was a day coming, said the prophet, when the sanctuary of Jerusalem should be a heap like that at Shiloh. In that day they should discover that, when Yahweh brought their fathers out of Egypt, He gave no orders about burnt offerings, but He gave this order: listen to my voice and I will be your God and you shall be my people and you shall walk in the way which I command. Israel might be in Ephraim or in Judah or in Babylon: but when it was in any of these places or in all of them, 'ye are in My hands, as clay is in the hands of the potter'. And the religion of Israel could continue wherever men prayed and did the will of Yahweh.

Jeremiah thought of a relation between Yahweh and Israel which was not at the mercy of outward conditions or circumstances. It could continue though the people had lost their independence. Israel could maintain it, though Israel had become a satrapy of the Empire. Judah could maintain it, though Nebuchadrezzar destroyed Jerusalem with its temple. The kingdom might pass out of existence among the kingdoms of the world: but what made Israel defied a conqueror. Their religion was not dependent on the people remaining in their own land. The exiles could maintain their faith, though they lived in subjection to an alien race. Jewish homes could be nurtured in Babylon, and children could grow up to acknowledge a double allegiance—to the king of Babylon and to Yahweh. Their religion did not disappear when its shrine and its sacrificial system disappeared. The temple might be beaten flat and the sacred vessels might be carried to Babylon and be used to grace the triumph of the conqueror. Yahwism could make its new shrines, as it did after Shiloh disappeared, and could constitute its new means of devotion. For it needed no more than prayer and obedience. Everything else was an accessory. Its devotees could rear a synagogue for mutual prayer, or climb to an upper room with an open window toward Jerusalem. And in the Jewish homes which he urged them to rear, and in Babylon which he bade them serve, they could practise obedience.

One might wish that the prophet had developed more largely what the obedience to Yahweh involved. Yet there are two reasons for his comparative silence on the subject. The one is that all through his life he was in opposition, and spoke in the character of one who had to posit his demands against the men of his time. And the bane of all, even necessary, polemic is that it thrusts into the background the positive elements in the teaching of those who are engaged in it. The other reason, however, is that Jeremiah was speaking to men who had some knowledge of all that was involved in obedience to Yahweh. Behind him was his own nation's law, the code of Deuteronomy. And most of its contents were concerned with how men who feared and loved their God should live together in the common relations of their daily life. There is no law in the Old Testament so rich in ethical teaching, so conscious above all that everything which an Israelite does or does not do is the outcome of that relation he holds first to Yahweh.

Meantime it remains to add that the elements of Yahwism and the institutions needed to continue it, on which Jeremiah lays emphasis, are those which tended to constitute it, not a national, but a universal religion. And, whether he was conscious of it or not, the prophet was preparing, as all the great prophets prepared, for this new conception. He was laying stress on all the elements in Yahwism which pointed in that direction. He did this in two main ways. On the one side he knew himself to be a prophet with a commission to all nations. The standards which it was his to set up and the judgement he had to declare concerned the world. Yahweh had a word which was of universal significance. On the other side, he thrust into the background everything in Yahwism which made it incapable of becoming the faith of all men. He loosened its hold on one nation set in its own land and worshipping at a national shrine. He conceived it to be able to exist and to do its beneficent work wherever men prayed and offered the sacrifice of their obedience.

Yet Jeremiah was no cosmopolitan with a new-found creed which was to obliterate and take the place of the old. To him God was Yahweh, the God of Israel, who had made Himself known to Jacob, His acts to the children of Israel. He knew that it was this God, whom he had learned to know and reverence in the pieties of his home at Anathoth, who had called and equipped him to be a prophet to the nations. God had made known His mind to Moses, and the prophet stood consciously in the succession of that initial revelation. He could not depart from it, and would not if he could. Yahweh had called Israel out of Egypt and led them through the wilderness into Palestine. Unless He had done this, there would have been no Anathoth and no prophet with a message and a commission.

Skinner[1] criticized with some justice, and in an interesting way, my view of the prophets as thinking in terms of a universal religion, and insisted that they all found their *raison d'être* in a call to deliver Yahweh's message to Israel. Now certainly Jeremiah was no *illuminé*, trying, like Rousseau with his Savoyard Vicar, to discover the irreducible minimum which might form a religion on which all men could agree. As little was he a modern student of Comparative Religion trying to discover the common denominator in all the

[1] *Prophecy and Religion*, p. 291 f.

religions which have functioned in this world. He would have probably pronounced on all the efforts which have been made to discover a religion which all men might accept, but which nobody has ever accepted, that it failed to do what he had discovered in his own. It could not curb men's appetites in the day of their success, and it could give them no support in adversity. The prophet was a Jew, with all the travail and the passion of his race behind him. To him the revelation which had come at Sinai represented the truth. In it the mind of God was made known to the men who heard and received it. And it had moulded the lives and the history of the nation which had then received it. But this very word from God had made Israel: Israel had not made it. It was greater than Israel, it was no national faith. The prophet could therefore strip it of the limitations which had gathered round it with the lapse of time, and conceive it to continue without the institutions which had been its embodiment and even its defence. The faith which made Israel had given it power to win its land and take its place in the world. It had taught the people unity and self-confidence among peoples alien to its temper. It had built for the men sanctuaries, and determined their peculiar type of worship. But they had once practised this faith in the unsown land of the desert, before one of these accessories had come to enrich and to threaten their life. And that time had been the period of the honeymoon, when the people were wholly devoted to their God. What they had once done they could do again. Jeremiah was feeling out after a religion which was not national in the narrow sense of the word, but which was historic and revealed. And because it was the revelation of the nature and will of One who was the God of the world, it must become universal.[1]

[1] The same attitude appears in the psalms, as I have pointed out in *The Psalter*, Lecture II.

The time when the prophet appeared needed this particular message more than any other. On the one side, Israel was ceasing to be a nation settled in Palestine with a polity and with institutions which it could control. The time of the diaspora had come. Before long the larger and not the less intelligent part of Jewry were to live under institutions which did not represent their own ideals, and under a polity which was framed to serve quite alien aims. If these men were to preserve for their children and for the world the Hebrew faith which had moulded all their outlook, they must have it in a form which was capable of being exported. Men must separate between what was adventitious and what was essential. Jeremiah gave them some guidance.

On the other side, the leaders of the nation were straining every nerve to preserve what seemed to them necessary for the continuance of their faith. They were making sacrifice at one shrine essential, and so they tended dangerously to localize their God and His grace in the sanctuary which He chose out of all their tribes to set His name there. Yahweh was to remain the God of Israel in the sense that He could only be rightly worshipped in Israel's land, through Israel's priesthood, after Israel's rituals. Jeremiah could but say that men who led their people that way were turning back from the great road to which their prophets had set their face.

X

JEREMIAH'S POLITICAL ATTITUDE

AFTER Nebuchadrezzar had deposed Jehoiachin and carried away to Babylon the first body of exiles, he set another son of Jehoiakim, Zedekiah, on the throne of Jerusalem. Judah remained a vassal state subject to Babylonia, but with Egypt in the background seeking to extend its influence over Syria and, with this in view, stirring up trouble in the border states. It was easier to do this, because Western Asia had not quietly acquiesced in accepting the domination of the new Empire. Among the little kingdoms there were movements for liberty, which the Egyptians could use for their own purposes. Accordingly the throne to which the new king had succeeded was an uneasy dignity. And what made matters worse for Zedekiah was that in Jerusalem itself there was no unanimity as to the policy which the little kingdom should follow in the new conditions, just as some of Jehoiakim's courtiers had been out of sympathy with their ruler's attitude.

It is easy to dismiss these recurrent rebellions among the petty states of Syria and to call them futile struggles against the overwhelming power of the new Empire which had risen on the Euphrates. Then one must pour contempt on the men at Jerusalem who dreamed that their tiny principality was of any significance in the clash of the Empires which decided their fate. It is likely that prudent politicians held the same views when Greece made its heroic resolution to resist Xerxes. Marathon no doubt was a success, while the Syrian coalitions failed. Yet is success the final test of any stroke for liberty? If so, it is curious to note that the world has remembered Thermopylae, which was a failure. In the same way it is easy to write Zedekiah down a weakling and to dismiss him with this ready condemnation. He ought at once to have accepted the verdict of Jeremiah and to have carried out his counsel without hesitation. Yet here was a lad of twenty-one, who owed his throne to the foreign power which had deposed his brother. It was true that Jeremiah, speaking in the name of Yahweh, advised submission to Nebuchadrezzar. But another prophet, Hananiah, appealed to the same august authority in support of rebellion. How could the young king tell which was the true and which was the false prophecy? It has pleased God that we all must answer that question in some form. Even if he personally leaned to the policy which Jeremiah advised—and clearly he protected and consulted the prophet—it was by no means certain that he could have carried his state with him. The record of his dealings with Jeremiah leaves the impression that he was set over a body of men who were stirred by something very like fanaticism and who had taken the bit between their teeth so that they were beyond control. Jeremiah himself always speaks with some sympathy and kindliness of the man in whose uneasy reign Judah lost its independence.

How difficult the whole situation was appears at once in chaps. 27 f., which bring vividly to light the conditions in Jerusalem shortly after Zedekiah's accession. The chapters are sometimes grouped with chap. 29 and taken to belong to one source. The reason for deriving them from a common author is that they depart from the practice of the rest of the book of Jeremiah by calling the Babylonian king Nebuchadrezzar instead of Nebuchadnezzar, and that they speak about Jeremiah the prophet. The question could only be adequately discussed in a full examination into the extremely perplexed problem of the composition of the whole book. Yet it is noteworthy that the two chapters differ in one cardinal point. Chap. 27 introduces Jeremiah in the first person. Chap. 28 begins in v. 1 with the first person, and then suddenly and unaccountably breaks off to speak about Jeremiah the prophet. That rather points to an editor having united the chapters and having imperfectly carried out the blending of the first and third personal narratives. To him may be due the slight change involved in the correct spelling of Nebuchadrezzar's name throughout. Then it cannot fail to appear that the two chapters are related to one another much in the same way in which 7 : 1–15 is related to chap. 26. Chap. 27 reports in full an oracle of the prophet, as 7 : 1–15 reports the temple address, and each prefaces the message with a brief historical introduction which serves to indicate the circumstances in which the words were spoken. On the other hand chap. 28, like chap. 26, compresses the oracle into very brief compass and dilates on the effect it produced on the prophet's fate. In the time of Jehoiakim Jeremiah's utterances about the temple brought him into collision with the priests: in the time of Zedekiah his attitude about Babylon resulted in a breach with the prophets. And as the earlier story gives a vivid picture of conditions in palace and court under the one brother, so the later story introduces us to the no less vivid picture of the clash between prophet and prophet under the other.

The resemblance, however, between the temple address in 7 : 1–15 and the oracle in chap. 27 extends even to their present form. They have both been subjected to revision. In the case of the earlier message the proof needed to be sought in a careful examination of its contents. In the case of chap. 27 it lies on the surface, for the chapter has reached us in two recensions. The Greek text is entirely different from the Masoretic in one important particular. From v. 16 it reads: I spoke also to the priests and all the people. Thus speaks Yahweh: Do not listen to your prophets when they tell you that the temple vessels shall be brought back very soon from Babylon, for they are prophesying a lie. If they do prophesy and there should be a message of Yahweh with them, let them plead with Yahweh. For thus speaks Yahweh about the other vessels, which Nebuchadrezzar king of Babylon did not take when he carried Jechoniah into exile from Jerusalem, they shall be taken to Babylon, oracle of Yahweh. When this text is contrasted with the M.T. or read alongside the R.V., it is patent that the two are irreconcilable. In the Hebrew text Jeremiah and the other prophets are equally interested in the fate of certain temple vessels, and equally eager to see them restored. The only difference between them is that, while the other prophets demand an effort for their instant return, Jeremiah bids the priests expect that return after the lapse of certain years, when it pleases Yahweh to visit His people. The debate between the prophet and his opponents is reduced to the question of a date.[1]

There can be little question but that the Septuagint has preserved the original text. For, if the Masoretic text was the original, it is more than difficult to explain how the Greek translators came to transform the passage into its present form. There was no motive for introducing so profound a change into the prophet's message. On the other hand, a later generation which set great store by the temple vessels was loath to believe that interest in their fate was confined to men who were called false prophets. Their great prophet must have foretold the ultimate return of the sacrificial vessels. They utterly failed, as such men are always apt to fail, to recognize that they thus ascribed to Jeremiah an anxiety about the fate of the temple vessels which was directly

[1] In the same way the debate between Jeremiah and the two prophets in Babylon is reduced, in the present form of chap. 29, to the question between an immediate return and a return after seventy years; cf. p. 175, *supra*. But the prophets are made to agree in principle.

opposed to his whole attitude on such matters. The prophet who declared that Yahweh gave Moses no commands about burnt-offerings and sacrifices, and who also stated that Yahweh would destroy the temple as He had destroyed Shiloh, was bound to count it wholly insignificant whether the temple vessels were returned at all. The difference between him and the prophets who erected the restoration of these vessels into a question of state policy was too radical in character to be explained away into a mere debate over the time when the vessels were to be restored. Yet, in spite of its having thus been retouched, the passage makes it clear that Hananiah and his colleagues were controlled by other than merely political motives in connexion with the policy which they were pressing on Zedekiah. They were appealing to their people in the name of religion. And the religious minds to which they appealed were deeply interested in the temple and its sacrifices. Priest, prophet, and people were equally stirred by the loss of the temple vessels, as men who had accepted the Josianic reform could not fail to be. Yahweh could not leave what was consecrated to Him and necessary for His worship in heathen hands.

Here, then, was the situation. An effort was afoot to combine several of the minor states of Western Asia in a league against Babylon. Ambassadors from these had come to Jerusalem to win the support of Zedekiah. A strong body of opinion in the capital, headed by Hananiah and other prophets, was in favour of joining the league. Jeremiah alone opposed this step. The question was one of public policy which was mixed up with, if it was not raised by, the principles of religion. And the guides of the national religion took diametrically opposite views.

It was this opposition between Jeremiah and the other prophets of his time which interested the writer of chap. 28. He has confined his whole attention to that side of the situation. One can almost see the bewilderment in the mind of the young king in his brief picture. How shall he decide, where men who equally claim divine authority for their words disagree? And especially how can he venture to decide, when Jeremiah himself shows signs of embarrassment? For it is apparent that the prophet was at first brought to a pause. Whether the unanimity or the confidence of his opponents staggered him, or whether he was overwhelmed by the gravity of the occasion, he could only appeal to the fact that behind him was the prophetic tradition. All the prophets of the past, he thought, had spoken as he was speaking. And he only ventured to return to the charge when he was convinced that he had received a new revelation. But the situation had needed it. When it did come there was no more hesitation. He denounced Hananiah with the same fierceness with which he denounced the prophets in Babylon.[1]

The man who wrote that account was interested in the fate of Jeremiah, but he was also interested in the perennial question of how Israel could distinguish between true and false prophecy. On the other hand, the writer of chap. 27 was content to set down the oracles he had received, dividing them into three sections, the message to the foreign ambassadors (vv. 2–11), the message to Zedekiah (vv. 12–15), the message to the priests and people (vv. 16 ff.). Before the ambassadors Jeremiah appeared wearing a symbolic yoke, and bade them take a message[2] to their masters to the effect that Yahweh had delivered over the world to the rule of Nebuchadrezzar.[3] To Zedekiah he said that Judah's hope

[1] The vehemence of this denunciation serves to prove that something deeper was involved here than a difference about the date for the return of those temple vessels; cf. p. 175, *supra*.

[2] So with LXX: M.T. makes Jeremiah send a yoke to each of these kings.

[3] It deserves attention that here again v. 7, with its promise of an end to the Babylonian dominion, is absent from the LXX.

lay in its submission to the divine will. But he added a special charge that the king must not permit himself to be led astray by the words of the false prophets. Turning to the people and its priests, he denounced the promise of these prophets that by rebellion they could hope to win back the lost temple vessels. The sure result of joining the league must be to bring about the loss of those which had escaped the conqueror at his first attack. It will be noted that the contents of the successive oracles were adapted to the condition of those to whom they were addressed.

Baynes would date this incident in 590 immediately before the final rebellion.[1] In my judgement it must be placed earlier. But, however this may be, it reveals a sharp division of opinion between Jeremiah and Hananiah on the political question of rebellion against Babylon. Both men appealed to religious motives in support of the policy which they respectively favoured. About the same time a similar agitation was troubling the exilic community in Babylon. Two prophets were appealing to men's religious feelings in favour of some action which had a political character, and again Jeremiah interfered with his own advice which he also based on a religious appeal. In both cases the prophet denounced his

[1] *Israel amongst the Nations*, p. 263. He follows Schmidt, *Z. A. W.* 1921, pp. 138–44. I hesitate to differ from a historian on a historical point, but must point out that the judgement rests on three matters which are more in my province. It proceeds on an assumption that the book of Ezekiel is a unity and was all written in Babylon, an assumption which I cannot share. It involves that Nebuchadrezzar before the capture of Jerusalem, but in Zedekiah's reign, deported certain priests and prophets: this Baynes frankly calls a conjecture. But it further implies that Jeremiah's letter in chap. 29 was written to these exiles after the actual rebellion of Zedekiah. That leaves no time for an agitation, such as is described in chap. 29, to spread among these men and for Jeremiah to hear of it. Nor does it explain how the prophet could find opportunity to communicate with them.

opponents as teaching falsely in the name of Yahweh, and did not hesitate to expect the divine judgement on their unworthy message. He told his fellow-countrymen in Jerusalem and in exile that to rebel against Babylon was to go counter to the will of God. Yahweh was using Babylon and its king for His own ends. But the prophet did not give any further reason for this conviction, nor did he explain the end for which Babylon was to be used as an instrument. Yet he must have meant more than the mere general conviction that Nebuchadrezzar was raised up in order to punish Israel for its sins. For he told the ambassadors from the neighbouring states that it was hopeless for them also to rebel, since the world was delivered over into the power of the conqueror. In the same way, when Babylon first appeared as a direct factor in the life of Judah during the reign of Jehoiakim, he had angered his king by the message that the lord of Babylon should come and ruin the country, destroying out of it man and beast (36 : 29). Yet that utterance appears even more isolated than the similar message under Zedekiah, and it receives as little explanation. In both cases we are left in complete uncertainty as to the reason why Jeremiah adopted this strong and in the end unhesitating conviction about the future of Babylon and the attitude his people must take to it.

The threatened troubles blew over for the time, probably more through the prompt action of Nebuchadrezzar than through the influence of Jeremiah. As has been suggested above,[1] Zedekiah may have sent an embassy to Babylon to satisfy the Emperor, and may have lent his influence and helped the prophet to quiet the seditious movement among the exiles. But when Hophra became Pharaoh in 589, he made a more determined effort to stir up Syria; and the Egyptian party in Jerusalem became too strong for Zedekiah.

[1] Cf. p. 168, *supra*.

He rebelled, counting on support from Egypt. It would appear from the king's attitude to Jeremiah through all the trouble which resulted that he personally was far from confident of the wisdom of this action. But whether he was impressed by the manifest sincerity of the prophet or merely governed by political consideration of the grave consequences of rebellion it is impossible to determine.

The result of the rebellion could not long remain in doubt. Nebuchadrezzar acted vigorously and was first in the field, for he besieged Jerusalem before Egypt moved. A false gleam of hope broke on the doomed city, when an Egyptian army advancing to its relief forced the invaders to raise the siege. It gave rise to an act of bad faith on the part of the citizens toward their manumitted slaves which Jeremiah denounced in chap. 34. But the relief was short-lived, and the Babylonian army closed round their prey.

Now, throughout the war, as in the events which preceded it, Jeremiah never wavered in his attitude. Rebellion against Chaldea was not only hopeless: it was wrong, because it was counter to the will of Yahweh. Indeed, he went farther when the siege began. For he declared that the Chaldeans would capture the city and burn both it and the temple. This also was the will of Yahweh. He had warned the prophet that it was in pursuance of His express purpose that the city and the shrine should fall. Naturally, since the prophet was not content to hold this conviction in silence, but persisted in proclaiming it abroad, this seemed dangerous doctrine to the men who were summoning the whole strength of the nation to defend their capital and their native land. They tried to silence him by forbidding him access to the temple, even before the siege began: that is the purport of the letter from Babylon to the priests in 29 : 24–32. They took the opportunity which he offered them by his action in leaving the city on his private affairs to denounce him as a deserter to the besiegers (37 : 11–21). At first he was shut up in a guarded court, but certain courtiers overheard the terms in which he expressed himself to the garrison there and to the populace. They reported in horror to the king samples of what they had heard. Jeremiah, they stated, is uttering things like these: thus speaks Yahweh; the man who remains in this city shall die by sword, famine, or pestilence, but he who surrenders to the Chaldeans shall at least survive and have his life as his share of booty; or again, thus speaks Yahweh; this city shall be delivered into the power of the army of the king of Babylon and captured. And they demanded that, since the only effect of such talk must be to damp down the courage of the garrison and the civilian population, the prophet should be put where he could no longer work mischief. Accordingly he was flung into a cistern, where he would have been starved to death but for the loyalty of a slave and the secretly given help of the king (38 : 1–13).

In all this there is nothing which need cause surprise. Except in so far as our modern manners are milder and we do not employ old muddy cisterns as places of confinement for political prisoners, Jeremiah received at the hands of his contemporaries nothing worse than what many men were prepared to mete out to conscientious objectors during the great war. Men who oppose their nation in a time of patriotic excitement during a war for national existence need never expect different treatment. The real question is not why the statesmen of Jerusalem acted thus toward the prophet, but why he took the course he did and why he counted it his solemn duty to expose himself to their suspicion and fury. Whether he intended it or not, the prophet was using all his authority to damp down the power of resistance in the garrison. And what it is most important to discover is the motive which drove him to this strong action at such a time, and especially why he said the things he did in the name of religion.

It may appear sufficient to some to say that Jeremiah was moved to his action by religious conviction, and that he thus had the high honour of being among the first who were persecuted for their religious convictions. But it becomes necessary to ask why and how it could be a religious conviction to any man that Babylonia must control his native country and burn down the shrine of his people's faith. There are, of course, men who are always with us who count it sufficient to say that they have made this or that a question of conscience, and who after this claim expect to be let alone to do and say whatever may appear to them a legitimate consequence of their position. But there remains always the prior question whether they are justified in making this opinion a question of conscience at all. And the question remains whether Jeremiah had the right to bring in religion to justify his attitude and his action. After that comes the other question whether it is lawful to set him down a martyr to high principle, because he suffered for taking a different view from others in Jerusalem on the possibility or lawfulness of opposing Babylon.[1]

Remarkable, too, is the prophet's silence on the reason why

[1] Further, whenever Jeremiah had occasion to speak about Babylon and its part in determining the fate of Israel, he made it quite certain what he meant. He spoke about Nebuchadrezzar and his Empire, and he called them by their names, as Isaiah had spoken about Assyria and Ephraim and Damascus. All who, like Wilke, believe that the oracles which speak of the foe from the North refer to the Chaldean power, and must be referred to some time immediately preceding this period, ought to be able to offer some explanation for this curious and entire change. And even those who think those oracles early and bring them into connexion with the Scythian invasion should be able to explain the difference. When Jeremiah meant Chaldea he spoke about Chaldea so that no one misunderstood. Yet he hid all reference to Scythia in cryptic and vague phrases.

resistance to Babylon is resistance to the divine will. The fact is the more remarkable because another prophet, belonging nearly to the same period, who also counselled non-resistance, found and gave a reason. In Ezek. 12 : 11–16; 17 : 11–21, it is said that Zedekiah brought his fate upon him through his breach of faith with Babylon. The king who had sworn allegiance to Nebuchadrezzar could not expect the divine blessing in his rebellion. The difference of attitude could not be due to Jeremiah's indifference to the virtue of loyalty. For he showed himself very sensitive to the dishonour Jerusalem brought upon itself through its people's breach of faith to their slaves (34 : 8–22). Evidently he regarded the whole question from a different point of view. He believed that to resist Babylon was to resist the divine will, and did not ask what were the attendant circumstances, such as the breach of an oath, which made that step worse or more guilty.

Again, what makes Jeremiah's attitude in connexion with Babylon more noteworthy is to recognize how he spoke about that nation in chap. 34. During the siege of Jerusalem by Nebuchadrezzar the inhabitants had solemnly promised to free their slaves.[1] When, however, the advance of a relief expedition from Egypt forced the Babylonians temporarily to raise the siege, the people went back on their solemn oath and restored the original condition. Jeremiah denounced this cynical act with strong indignation. Thus speaks Yahweh: You have not listened to me in connexion with the general release which you proclaimed. I proclaim to you a general release (from Yahweh to new masters) to sword,

[1] The account is a little confused, because a later student of the prophecy has misunderstood the special liberation of these slaves and taken the act to be an instance of the regular manumission of all Hebrew slaves at the end of a period of years. It is unnecessary to enter into the question here, but cf. on the subject Volz's excellent discussion of the passage.

famine, and pestilence. And, turning specially to the leaders of the nation who ought to have forbidden such conduct, he added: Zedekiah, too, the king of Judah and his courtiers I will deliver into the power of their enemies who seek their life, even the army of the king of Babylon, which has retired from the attack. The prophet was there regarding the Chaldean army as an instrument in the divine hands for carrying out a well-merited punishment on the guilty leaders of the nation. In the same way Isaiah (10 : 5) called Assyria the rod of Yahweh's anger, the staff in whose hand was His indignation. But it cannot or ought not to escape notice that Jeremiah was seeing in one particular incident of the siege a sufficient reason why Yahweh should bring back against Jerusalem the hostile army. Men who were dead to the counsels of honour and loyalty must be compelled to listen to a more awful messenger. Yet no mere incidental occurrence which attended the war could serve to explain why the besiegers were there at all, and why Jeremiah was convinced that the initial rebellion which brought them there involved opposition to the divine will.

It is a merit in Volz's recent commentary that he has shown himself conscious that there is a question here which demands an answer, since it involves a great deal in connexion with the whole attitude of the prophet. Whether the solution which he has found can be counted satisfactory is another question. He writes: that the rebellion against Nebuchadrezzar is utterly hopeless (*nutzlos*) Jeremiah knows from his healthy political judgement and from his knowledge of history: the prophets whose God was the Lord of history have not faced the events of history with such unreceptive minds as the people: Jeremiah has not forgotten the years 605 and 597 (i.e. the victory at Carchemish and the first captivity) which moved him deeply: he also recognizes fully from history that the small nations were not destined (*bestimmt*) for civil freedom. Yet the prophet offers the statesmen no political wisdom, but a religious message. . . . Politics for the prophet is only a sphere (*Gebiet*) of religion. Therefore Jeremiah says to the ambassadors: Yahweh is not with you, rebellion against Nebuchadrezzar is rebellion against Yahweh.' [1]

This can only mean that Jeremiah has concluded from the victory at Carchemish and from the captivity of Jehoiachin that the power of Babylonia was not only irresistible but was the will of God. He has deduced the purpose of Yahweh from the course of history during his lifetime, and has arrived at something which closely resembles the verdict that is often ascribed to Napoleon: God is always on the side of the big battalions. And certainly what is thus ascribed to Jeremiah is not the authentic note of Judaism. That had a more daring accent. 'O Nebuchadrezzar, we are not careful to answer thee in this matter. If it be so, our God whom we serve is able to deliver us from the burning fiery furnace, and he will deliver us out of thine hand, O king. But if not, be it known unto thee, O king, that we will not serve thy gods, nor worship the golden image which thou hast set up' (Daniel 3 : 16 ff.). The faith has dared to defy the world in the name of Him who controls the world.

But the question thus raised has larger issues which should be recognized. According to Volz, Jeremiah was seeking to persuade his people to submit to the inevitable. He had concluded from the events of history that Chaldea was a world-empire which the petty kingdom of Judah could not hope to resist. The only sane thing for Zedekiah to do was to accept what was so evidently in the nature of things and to make the best terms possible. And he declared that this was the will of God and that he had received a divine oracle to this effect. On the other hand, the ruling party at Jerusalem either believed it possible to make a stand or preferred

[1] *Kommentar*, p. 257.

to go down fighting rather than live the fatted calves of Babylon. And Hananiah their prophet declared that this had with it the divine blessing. The debate between Jeremiah and Hananiah turned round a question of worldly policy. They were both statesmen, advising on a state policy and supporting their different judgements by an appeal to divine authority. I can only see in such an interpretation the confessed bankruptcy of the theory which sees no more in Israel's prophets than men who concluded from the course of outward events, from the rise and fall of kingdoms, to the mind and will of God. This *a priori* theory has led to an impasse in the exegetical interpretation of Jeremiah's book:[1] it now threatens to emasculate the prophet himself and to turn him into a preacher of defeatism without even the excuse for such an attitude that he believed in passive resistance. For the man who cursed Hananiah with such hearty vigour was no passive resister. It even makes Jeremiah a psychological puzzle. A man who heard the voice of God in the dictates of prudence and the verdict of common sense would have held his peace when he saw how hopeless it was to oppose the court and the people. Men who incur the risk of starvation in a stinking cistern have always been men who have set principle above prudence.

Jeremiah was not content to say that since Carchemish Chaldea controlled the fate of Western Asia and especially of Jerusalem. He said that Yahweh had handed over Judah into this control. The power of Chaldea was no mere expression of the inevitable: in its control over the fate of Judah the Empire furthered the will of Him in whose hand are all things. In resisting it Judah was not foolishly rebelling against the inexorable law of its destiny: it was resisting the purpose of its God. And this purpose of its God with the nation was the burden which the prophet was commissioned

[1] Cf. pp. 106 ff., *supra*.

to declare. The dominion of Chaldea, and especially its conquest of Jerusalem with the resultant destruction of city and temple, must be integrally related to Jeremiah's conception of the purpose of the Lord with and for Israel.

To understand the later message it is only necessary to turn back to the temple address which signalized the beginning of Jeremiah's public ministry. The two are essentially allied. In the earlier the prophet declared that in the interest of true religion the temple was doomed and must go: Yahweh meant to destroy it. In the later he recognized that Nebuchadrezzar was the divine servant (27 : 6) whom Yahweh was to employ for this end. The only difference between the two messages is that the later one defined or indicated the instrument of the divine judgement. Both, however, regard the Babylonian as merely commissioned for one specific purpose. The difference can readily be accounted for by the change which had come over the historical conditions. The first message was delivered in the early period of Jehoiakim's reign, before this king was the submissive subject of Chaldea. But already, when Jehoiakim was meditating rebellion, Jeremiah believed that this act would only bring down on the city and temple the doom which Yahweh had already pronounced against both, and that Babylon was the appointed instrument to effect this end. When Nebuchadrezzar was actually thundering against the walls of Jerusalem, the prophet reiterated his early conviction with greater confidence. Here at last was the fulfilment of his earlier oracle.

Judah had turned back from the way in which God through His prophets sought to lead it. It had tied its faith to a building of stone and lime. The temple with its city had been made essential to the divine purpose of the salvation of Israel. The inevitable result was that men believed that Yahweh would intervene to protect His holy city. Prophets in Jerusalem preached rebellion, and could even find support for it in the fate of some temple vessels. Prophets in Babylon preached unrest among the exiles. The Josianic reform was producing its political repercussion in both sections of the nation.

Against all this movement Jeremiah reacted without hesitation. To meet it he brought no hint about the irresistible power of Chaldea. He spoke in the name of Yahweh and in the power of a different conception of Israel's religion. Yahweh had His own great purpose, and that must stand. Since Judah refused to listen to the warning voice of the prophet and persisted in its own course, it must learn through a more awful messenger. Yahweh has made Nebuchadrezzar His servant for His special ends, and has brought up the Chaldean army to besiege and destroy Jerusalem. He will use them to smash the shell in which the nation has attempted to confine His grace. For its religion must be set free to do its own salutary work.

In thus limiting the sphere of Nebuchadrezzar's work, Jeremiah was again following the example set by Isaiah. The earlier prophet, as has been noted, had declared that Assyria was the rod of the divine anger against the people. But he added that, since Assyria had no true conception of the limits of its power, but rather conceived itself at liberty to do all its will, it in turn must suffer in the day of the divine visitation. When Yahweh had performed His whole work He should visit the glory of the high looks of the king of Assyria (Isa. 10 : 5–12). Assyria could judge and chastise: but judgement was Yahweh's strange work; what He delighted in was mercy. And this greater and final fruition of all things, Yahweh's whole work, was something too vast and blessed for any instrument to accomplish. When it arrived, Assyria was brushed aside; it had fulfilled its task, which was a mere preparation. In the same way Jeremiah strictly limited the commission of Babylon. Nebuchadrezzar was

Yahweh's servant, and, so long as his service was needed, he was irresistible. But this service was confined to the destruction of those things in which Israel was placing a false confidence. Neither prophet brought the foreign nation, the advent of which each of them announced, into any connexion, other than external and preparatory, with the final consummation. For to both prophets the consummation was something which no nation, not even Israel itself, could bring in. It was at once too vast in its scope and too blessed in its ultimate results for any human agent to accomplish. It was salvation, and salvation was of the Lord.

XI

JEREMIAH AND THE FUTURE

ISRAEL possessed the most distinctive life, it may be no exaggeration to say the only distinctive life, in the old world. Accordingly it reared sons who were patriots of the nobler type, men who loved the land for what it had made possible, and who felt beyond its bounds a different atmosphere. And all this distinctive life in the nation had sprung from its religion. When the Old Testament says that Yahweh made Israel, it merely expresses in its own language what a modern student would be compelled to say in different language. The nation became a nation because of the common faith, and in every one of its national institutions and customs it differed from the rest of the world because of that faith. Religion strengthened patriotism and gave it nobler elements. Men loved the land which had moulded their souls as well as fed their bodies. It is difficult to conceive any one in that early world except a Jew being able to say: 'they have driven me out that I should have no share in the inheritance of Yahweh, saying, go serve other gods,' and so setting first among the losses of an exile the spiritual loss involved. Alike as a Jew and as a profoundly religious man, Jeremiah could not fail to have a passionate interest in his nation and in its future.

It is not surprising to find this temper breaking out in some of his oracles and embodying itself in memorable and touching language. Perhaps because he saw the fate of his fatherland so threatening and so sure, he has given clearer expression to his feeling on the subject than any of the other prophets. He saw Rachel weeping for her children and refusing to be comforted because they were not. In the stark simplicity of the phrase, 'because they are not', the man, himself unmarried and childless, has summed up the impassive wall which death presents before the reaching hands of love. He too, being of the seed of Benjamin, could see the mother of his race forsaken in a land which was desolate because it was empty of men. A prophet who could feel thus the intimate relation which the race and the land held to the men they had bred had a right to send a letter to exiles; he could understand their distress. Nor was his sympathy confined to the people of his own stock. After Necho had carried away into captivity the young king Jehoahaz he uttered an oracle about his fate. Thus speaks Yahweh about Shallum: weep not nor mourn for him who is dead; weep bitterly for him who is going away, for he shall never return to see his native land. Once he has left this place he shall never return to it, but shall die in the place to which he has been exiled and shall never see this land again (22 : 10–12).[1] There is a note in that which goes to the heart of a Scotsman like the wail of the pipes in 'Lochaber no more'. Alongside it should be set the other vision of the kindly life in that native land, where were 'the voice of joy and gladness, the song of the bridegroom and of the bride, the sound of millstones and the light of a lamp' (25 : 10). What appealed to the prophet in the thought of his country was the historic past with its memories and its inspiration. What appealed no less to the man was the life he knew and loved. And he thought of it as it had continued through the generations, the bridal song which meant the founding of a new home in Israel, the daily meal-grinding which fed every hamlet, the light in cottage windows which meant a home.

All these sayings, it will be noticed, come out of oracles of doom. The fact gives them but a larger significance. Many men can pronounce doom. But those who do not do it with

[1] Following Condamin, *Le Prophète Jérémie*, I have rearranged the verses.

a certain gusto are inclined to justify themselves or excuse themselves for the act by refusing to see anything except evil in the thing they condemn. They dare not allow it any value. Jeremiah could condemn with a vehemence which is sometimes terrifying. But he also allowed himself to linger over the beauty and the worth of that which he must not spare. He could suffer his thoughts to wander tenderly over the loveliness of an Israel which was about to pass away. He has reported in one place that Yahweh forbade him to pray for his nation (14 : 1). A man who takes occasion to state that at one period he gave up praying for his people is one who has made a habit of such intercession. And a man who says that he ceased because Yahweh commanded him shows that only a divine command to the contrary could have kept him from it. Even when he could no longer intercede, he must weep in secret over his people's pride (13 : 17). Some tribute his heart must bring to the vanishing glory of Israel.

To a man of this character, judgement must have appeared, in Isaiah's memorable phrase, Yahweh's strange work. In this connexion there is something peculiarly appealing in the language he used to the exiles: 'Yahweh keeps in mind the plans He has formed about you, plans of well-being and not of disaster, to give you a future for which you can hope' (29 : 11). Yahweh, said the exiles, has shattered every hope here: the proof is in the weight of His judgement which lies heavy upon us. Yahweh, said the prophet, has long, rich purposes with you and yours : and the issue of every judgement which comes from Him is not disaster, but a future with its hope. A prophet whose thoughts about the future had had their origin in his sense of the irresistible power of Chaldea or the hopelessness of resisting the Scythian, might acquiesce grimly in a prospect which held nothing but crushed liberty and prostrate nations. There was no light behind that storm-cloud. Then Marti's dictum is correct;

the pre-exilic prophets foretold nothing but disaster. But Jeremiah had been called and commissioned to proclaim the purpose of Yahweh. His sense of impending judgement came from his knowledge of the character which informed this purpose. Out of that could issue more than judgement, and even judgement, when it came, was the prelude to a future which held hope.

The thought of the greater thing for which judgement merely prepared the way did not occupy the mind of the prophet in the beginning of his public work. That was natural, because he had to proclaim the instant judgement and to summon men to realize why it was so sure and so terrible. Besides, he himself was looking for an immediate intervention of Yahweh, who should in one great act fulfil His purpose. But it has never been found possible for men to remain for any length of time standing on tiptoe, either physically or spiritually. St. Paul plainly began his mission-work in the Levant with the expectation that the Lord's return could not be delayed. But it was not long before he found himself ordering the affairs of his churches, arranging for a central fund to supply the needs of the poor, settling how men must bear themselves to the imperial power, giving directions about Church sacraments. And the plans he made and the orders he issued began to wear a curious air of permanence, as though the men to whom they went were to have a future very like their present. Life is always larger than human theories, and teaches a great deal to men who do not make their theories something which shuts out life's compelling and educative voice.

So Jeremiah found himself writing to the exiles in Babylon. And he who himself had remained unmarried because of the imminent end bade them marry and bear children. He did not hesitate to speak about grandchildren. For they were to live in Babylon and to accept the conditions of the new land and serve it and their God with an equal loyalty. It could be done, and done with happiness and content of heart. There was a real future for the exiles. But what was to be the ultimate fate of Judah? Jeremiah had been commanded to denounce doom on its capital and temple. He had pronounced its people worse than their brethren in exile, and declared that they too must go into exile to learn its lessons. He had learned to believe that in Nebuchadrezzar was the divine instrument to effect all these needed chastisements. But if the end of Yahweh, who brought the first part of the people into exile, was not exhausted in punishment, neither could He mean under Zedekiah to bring the people and its religion to an end.

In this connexion there has been preserved an account of how Jeremiah came, at the very time when the state of Judah seemed on the brink of ruin, to realize that to it, too, was preserved a future. It is the story in chap. 32 of the prophet's purchase of a field near his native village during the actual siege of Jerusalem. The entire account is full of interest in itself, but is of peculiar interest in its bearing on the prophet's anticipation of the future fate in store for Judah.

The chapter has not escaped the hands of later editors, but has received certain later additions. These have not been woven into the texture of the original; they have been simply superimposed and can readily be distinguished. Since, however, they tend to obscure the sense of the whole, they are better removed. Thus vv. 17–23 merely expand into greater length Jeremiah's briefer petition which is found in vv. 24–6. The additional verses consist of liturgical material which closely resembles similar prayers in the psalter, but which, while excellent in itself, is not strictly relevant to the situation in which the prophet found himself. In this respect it contrasts strongly with the following verses, where everything is subordinated to the one need and where the petition rises directly from the situation. Except so far as it turns the attention away from the cause which produced the prayer, it might be allowed to remain, were it not that there are better reasons for suspecting the rest of the narrative to be supplemented. For the original divine reply in vv. 26, 42–4, has been swollen with a statement of Yahweh's purpose in bringing up the Chaldeans and His further purpose with the nation (vv. 28–41). This section betrays its secondary character at the beginning by making an unnecessary fresh start in its opening words, 'therefore thus saith the Lord', which it repeats at v. 36. It then proceeds to instruct the prophet on matters which he did not need to know. The prayer he had offered sprang from his firm conviction that the siege of Jerusalem could have only one end, because the besiegers were there by the divine will. Since the city was as good as delivered into the power of the Chaldeans, and since this was the fulfilment of the divine will which Jeremiah had been ordered to declare (vv. 25 f.), why was Yahweh bidding him of all men to make arrangements about buying a field? It was wholly unnecessary to introduce a long statement to the effect that the city's fate was irrevocable, because Yahweh was bringing its well-merited doom upon it. The post-exilic character of the addition becomes unmistakable in v. 37 with its promise that God will gather the people out of all the countries whither He has driven them in fury. The writer was living after the dispersion. As soon as his standpoint is recognized, it becomes easy to see what led him to make the addition here. The divine response to Jeremiah closed in v. 44 with the assurance that Yahweh should turn the fortune of the nation. That ambiguous phrase, as has been noted, could mean 'bring back from exile'. It could not, however, have been intended in that sense by Jeremiah here. For the words are brought into close connexion with the promise that fields shall be bought in this country about which men are saying that it is a waste without man or beast, delivered into the power of the Chaldeans. And that again is set into close relation to the purchase the prophet has actually effected. Life was still to go on in the territory of Benjamin, the environs of Jerusalem, the towns of Judah, of the hill country, the low country, and the Negeb, for Yahweh had not forsaken men. The later generation, to whom the phrase could only mean the supreme proof of the divine bounty in restoring the people to Zion, interpolated a promise of that return. The original is to be found in 6–16, 24–7, 42–4, or 43, 44. Then, as in most of Jeremiah's oracles, the words are brief and very pointed.

The chapter, thus emended, is of singular interest on account of the all too brief glimpse it gives into the social and religious conditions of the time. It gives the historical student a wholesome reminder of the existence of a world which he is apt to forget because it has left no records. He must try to set Israel in its place among the nations and estimate how its kings set their sails to the winds that blew from East or West. He reads in old Assyrian army bulletins about how the conqueror overwhelmed a town here and carried away a population there. He studies the words of prophets, speaking at the festivals to attentive or careless worshippers, and examines how their religion was related to other faiths that then held the world. And suddenly a chapter like this lifts the curtain to show a different picture, with all the perspective altered. Jerusalem, closely invested by the foreigner, has dropped into the background: the foreground is a corner of the occupied territory. And there the farmers, only two or three miles distant from the city, were rearing crops in fields to which they clung with all the tenacity of the peasant and the Jew. They were carrying out with patient care the transfer of the land which was like a part of themselves. They were regulating the transfer after the ancestral customs of Israel, maintaining in connexion with it the rights of the family. And all this, while Zedekiah in the capital near by was uncertain whether he could keep his crown on his head or his head on his shoulders.

> (For) this will go onward the same
> Though Dynasties pass.

And in this mundane business of fields and their transfer the prophet took a natural and unfeigned interest. That, too, is a wholesome reminder to the student of Old Testament religion.

The prophets appear in Israel's history in a different capacity. They rebuke the worshippers in the court of the sanctuary at Bethel or Jerusalem. They send messages to kings who slit them up with pen-knives, or listen when Zedekiah asks anxiously whether there is any oracle from Yahweh. They wear strange garments, and are heard of in desert places. They seem moved by weird impulses which are apart from the ordinary motives of men. Their life might appear to be separated from the common pursuits of men. But here is a different picture. Jeremiah belongs to a village where his forefathers lived and where he is a burgher with duties and rights. His relatives expect him to fulfil the ordinary duties of a townsman. And he does not fail them. When the matter in hand is the drafting of deeds connected with the transfer of property and the maintenance of the old practices which have always governed Anathoth, he sees to it that these are duly witnessed and sets down the name of the man who kept the deed. His mind is full of the visions and words of the Almighty, but his feet are firmly planted on mother-earth, even on the fields of his native village. For the prophet believed that the Lord demanded obedience, an obedience which reaches into the fulfilment of a man's duty toward his kindred and his neighbours. These things involved human law, detailed, restrictive, very earthly in some of its demands and implications. Life cannot go on without a vision of the Eternal, but it also comes to a pause without law, which is the needed security for decent order and for human society. Perhaps Jeremiah was helped to his prompt action because he had grown up under Deuteronomy, the Israelite law which dictated how Israel should marry and buy and sell and conduct suits after the fashion of those who have a common vision of the Eternal.

Again, the incident has much to suggest about the mentality of the prophets, especially on the question whether they were mere passive recipients of auditions and visions which they never sought to verify and check, which indeed they possessed no means to verify and check. Jeremiah has received a revelation to the effect that his cousin should come from Anathoth and require him to exercise his right of inheritance by buying a field there. Apparently he either ignored this revelation because he failed to realize its significance, or he waited calmly to see what was to be the outcome. But, when he was closely confined in the guard-house for having predicted the inevitable fall of Jerusalem before the Chaldean army, his cousin arrived making the very request which he had been told to expect. Then, he says, I knew that this was the word of the Lord.

The incident, related with such matter-of-fact simplicity, suggests many questions both as to the method of prophetic revelation and as to how it came to be published. Evidently Jeremiah received, in some way which he does not describe, revelations of which he made no use. He needed, before he could accept them for himself or publish them to his people, confirmation of their divine authority. In the same way, when Jeremiah found himself in opposition to Hananiah (chap. 28), he was content at first to say that the position of his antagonist was not in agreement with all prophetic tradition. The great prophets of the past had announced catastrophe; a prophecy of national well-being needed special confirmation before it could claim to be received. With this reminder he left the court, like a man who was himself in some hesitation. It was only when he had received a fresh revelation that he returned to denounce the counter-prophecy as false. The impression left by the two stories is that of a man who did not merely utter what at first appeared to come directly from God. He exercised his own independent thought on these sudden impressions from without.

So it is in the case of the promised arrival of his cousin with a message about the family inheritance. He put the matter aside, probably because it seemed to concern himself personally and to have no special significance for Israel. But when Hanameel arrived, he found his kinsman in the guarded court of the palace where he was confined on account of his prophecy that Nebuchadrezzar must capture Jerusalem because Yahweh had brought him. Then it flashed on Jeremiah that there was a larger meaning in this demand on him to claim land in Anathoth at the very time when the city was besieged and he himself powerless to leave it. He had been commanded to announce the destruction of the city, and he had been also commanded to expect the arrival of the messenger. Both events had been revealed to him in his capacity as prophet, and the two were intimately connected in more than time. He linked them together in his prayer, Ah Yahweh my Lord, siege works are close to the city for its capture, and through sword, famine, and pestilence the city is as good as given into the power of the Chaldeans who attack it. What Thou hast announced is being fulfilled and Thou seest it clearly. Yet Thou hast said: Buy a field with money and take witnesses, when the city is as good as given up. Then came the word of Yahweh unto me:[1] I am Yahweh,

[1] So with LXX instead of M.T. 'to Jeremiah'.

God of all living, is anything too wonderful for me? Fields shall be bought in this country about which you are saying that it is a waste without man or beast, delivered into the power of the Chaldeans. Fields shall be bought for money, deeds shall be written, sealed, and witnessed in the territory of Benjamin, the environs of Jerusalem and the towns of Judah, of the hill country, of the low country, and of the Negeb, for I will turn their fortune, oracle of Yahweh. The siege must result in the destruction of Jerusalem; but that which seemed the end of all things to the people was not the end of Israel or its faith. Yahweh knew the thoughts He had towards Israel to give it a future about which it could hope. When the Dynasties had passed, when nations had toiled for nothing, and the peoples had wearied themselves to feed the flames (51 : 58), life could and should go on. Babylon could burn down a temple and carry away its vessels; that was the task which Yahweh Himself had given it. But it was powerless against religion. For the true faith continued wherever Israel offered its prayers and its obedience.

The matter came upon the prophet with all the power of a revelation. It was a gospel for himself and for his nation. Hence he not only carried through the business transaction with Hanameel, but he set it all down in its full detail, the seventeen shekels of silver and how he weighed them out, the double deed with the earthenware vessel in which it was stored. Nothing seemed insignificant. The act was symbolic, it was a testimony. In it was all the promise God had given the man for the future of his land and its faith. Hence, when the Chaldean general after his victory gave Jeremiah the choice between going down to Babylon and remaining in Judea, the prophet had no hesitation (40 : 1–6). The man who had advised the exiles to be content in their new country could have had no scruples about joining them there. He remained because he had still a word of hope, a gospel of the future, for his countrymen at home. Hence, too, when a discouraged crowd of women and men, terrified by the violent death of Gedaliah, consulted the prophet as to whether it were not advisable to retire into Egypt, he vehemently urged them to remain in Judah. And he did this in his capacity as a prophet, for he gave them an oracle; thus speaks Yahweh, God of Israel: if you remain in this country I will build you up instead of ruining you, will plant you instead of tearing you up, for I have repented of the harm I have done to you (42 : 10). The remarkable vehemence of the protest and the appeal to divine authority in its support demand some such explanation. Jeremiah is conscious that the people are failing to live up to the largeness of the divine mind toward them. If it were certain that 37 : 11–21 refers to the same situation as appears in chap. 42,[1] this incident would reveal the prophet not content with carrying out the business with Hanameel in Jerusalem, but taking the opportunity of the temporary raising of the siege to hurry out to Anathoth and finish the matter there. So full of meaning was every part of it to the idealist. He must share his new hope, too, with his own kindred. But at the Benjamin gate there was a sentry. And he arrested the prophet on the charge of desertion to the enemy. Brought back before the officials, he was clapped up more securely than ever in an underground cell instead of the guarded court. The situation would then have its own flavour of grim humorous tragedy. The dreamer about eternity has often been taken for a deserter from the tasks of the instant present.

Jeremiah's view of the future of his people here is simply the outcome of his oracle in the potter's house. As clay is in the hands of the potter, so are ye in my hands, saith Yahweh.

[1] Unfortunately the essential word in v. 11, which gives the purpose for which the prophet left the city, is a conundrum.

Israel is not at the mercy of circumstances; it is under the control of its God. And the control of that divine care can be exercised anywhere, whether in Babylon or in Palestine. Exile or defeat makes no difference to it. Nor does the shape of the vessel count for much. Israel may live under its own kings, exercising authority over the conditions of its own life, or it may be a subject province in the Empire with its outward institutions bearing the stamp of the conqueror. That means no more than a change in the shape of the vessel. The potter has altered the outward form, but neither the clay nor his purpose with it has undergone any alteration. We should phrase the conviction differently and state the position from a different angle. So long as a nation retains its native temper and refuses to surrender its ingrained character, it is indomitable. It may be conquered and pass under the power of a stronger people. It may lose the institutions which it framed to express and embody its own ideals of life and thought. But if it has not surrendered its soul, it will mould into its own forms the institutions which are put upon it from without. And at any hour it may renew its own independent life and rebuild all that it has lost. The Hebrew, and especially the Hebrew prophet, did not think of anything which made the soul of Israel as being native to it. Everything which made up the inner life of the people and constituted its peculiar genius came from its religion, and that was not native to Israel. It was a revelation, a gift direct from God. Yahweh had made the nation, and, if it refused to forsake Him, Yahweh would maintain it. Its soul remained its own, because it was His; and it was invulnerable. The life which had its source from springs beyond this world could defy the world.

There is, however, a collection of oracles grouped together in chaps. 30 f. which appear to offer a different prospect, since they set a greater value on Israel's possession of its own land.

These constitute what has often been called the book of consolation, and have evidently once existed in a separate form. For they have been provided with a special introduction (30 : 1–4), which states that the aim of the collector was to gather the messages of Jeremiah which related to the time when Yahweh should turn the fortunes of His people Israel and Judah and should bring them back to their own country. Now, whatever may be the date of the individual oracles of which the booklet is composed, the collection itself was made at a late period. For it begins with a promise (30 : 5–11), that Yahweh will make a final end of all the nations among which He has scattered the people (v. 11), thus implying the diaspora; and it ends in 31 : 38–40 with a prediction of the restoration of Zion directly modelled on the second part of Zechariah. A collector who could ascribe these two passages to Jeremiah was working with very imperfect criteria as to the date and origin of the oracles he brought together. To recognize this is to recognize the need for great care in accepting any of his material as authentic. Now, again, the two oracles in 31 : 7–14, 35–7, are either derived from or influenced by Deutero-Isaiah. It might be possible to say that Jeremiah here struck a note which was taken up by his successor, were it not that the description of Yahweh as the One who has scattered Israel once more betrays the post-exilic date. The section 30 : 12–17, with its tender longing over the beloved land, might well be claimed as authentic, since it touches a chord which was natural to the prophet. But it is entirely destitute of any demand for repentance, and it is not easy to believe that Jeremiah could have uttered anything which even appeared to suggest that Yahweh would take back the people on any but His own terms. Yet here He is made to appear promising to bring relief to the hurt of the land and healing to its wound merely because it has been called 'the rejected', Zion for whose state no man cares.[1] Finally, 31 : 2–6 can speak about a nation which has survived the sword, which found grace in its desert exile, and to which Yahweh revealed Himself in a distant land. Naturally, with these evidences of its late origin, it takes the attitude of that period and describes the culmination of the divine favour to men in Ephraim to consist in their summoning one another: Up and let us away to Zion to Yahweh our God. And 31 : 21 f. sees the people turning its face in the direction along which it has already come, the weary road to Babylon, and chides with some who hesitate to accept and welcome the new thing Yahweh has brought to pass. The reader is conscious of the attitude which is in many of the oracles of chaps. 50 f. and which taints some of the finest utterances of Deutero-Isaiah. Every effort is being made to urge the exiles to return: it is even being suggested to them that it is somehow wrong to hold back.

On the other hand, in 30 : 18–22,[2] with or without 31 : 1, Jeremiah has given his expectation about his own people of North Israel. Its people has lost heart and especially has lost

[1] I strongly suspect that here and in several other oracles which have been preserved in the book of Jeremiah, e.g. 12 : 7–13, we have utterances from the period when Palestine was lying derelict after the exile. It is noteworthy that 30 : 17 describes Zion as the rejected for whose state no man cares, and 12 : 7 says that the land is ravaged because no man gives it a thought, and continues with the remark that brigands roam on its bare heights (cf. for these brigands 40 : 7–12). Now neither the men who faced all the power of Nebuchadrezzar in defence of Jerusalem nor the returned exiles who gave up everything for its sake could be said to care nothing for Zion. The question is related to the question as to whether the intimate descriptions of conditions in Palestine which appear in Ezekiel were written in Babylonia. They, too, may derive from Judah. In my judgement Hölscher is entirely right against Herrmann in refusing to maintain the unity of the book of Ezekiel. But he has not faced the consequences of his position, and in particular whether we must continue to maintain the traditional locale for all these prophecies.

[2] Verses 23, 24 have been repeated from 23 : 19 f.

courage to approach its God.[1] Therefore Yahweh will restore them and bring them into close fellowship with Himself, so that they anew become His people and He is again acknowledged to be their God. And with this renewal of their inner life He will restore the homes of the nation and each town shall be rebuilt on its own 'tell', the heap of rubbish which marks the site of so many former villages in Palestine. The community shall be increased in number and in dignity, and their chief shall be no foreigner, but one of their own sons. The note there is one of grave and quiet simplicity. The ideal for the future is that of a people which has won back its self-respect and which is now content with itself and its place. It can rebuild its ruins and restore its homes, and from these shall arise songs of laughter. It is united, because it is conscious of a common ideal. Yahweh has brought it into fellowship with Himself. The little oracle reads like an epitome of the Code of Deuteronomy. A common spirit of joy and wholesome activity and unity is to animate the life of the people, because in Yahweh it has refound itself.

With this is allied the other promise addressed to the same people (31 : 18–20). I heard Ephraim making moan: 'Thou didst correct me and like an untamed colt I accepted correction: restore me that I may be really restored for thou art Yahweh, my God. Now that I grow wiser, I repent me; now that I have learned experience, I regret my folly and am heartily ashamed, bearing the disgrace my early days have brought.' 'Ephraim is[2] my dear son, my charming child. Whenever I must pronounce against him, I cannot but recall how he is this. Therefore my affections are stirred in his favour and I will surely have mercy upon him.' The whole accent here lies upon the moral renewal. The prophet has added nothing about the condition which was to follow.

[1] Cf. the same tenderness toward Israel 3 : 21–5.

[2] With LXX, which has no interrogative.

It is as though he knew that, when moral renewal was made sure, everything else which mattered must follow. And that was sure, as soon as Ephraim repented.

What he promised for Ephraim he could equally promise for Judah. Thus speaks Yahweh Tsebaoth, God of Israel: when I turn their fortune, men in Judah and in its towns shall yet use this expression: 'Yahweh bless thee, thou abode of righteousness, thou holy hill. May He bless also the inhabitants of Judah's towns and all its land, farmer and shepherd alike,[1] when I shall have refreshed the weary and contented the sad' (31 : 23–5; cf. also 31 : 27 f., 29 f.). The clay was in the hands of the potter.

And finally we have the famous prophecy of the new covenant (31 : 31–4). It is unnecessary here to discuss again the question of the authenticity of the passage, since Skinner has with exhaustive caution shown how little reason there is for denying it to Jeremiah.[2] Yet I confess to a certain sympathy with Duhm in his attitude to these verses. It is true that Duhm, after he changed his mind about their authenticity and set them into the post-exilic period, proceeded to belittle their significance. Presumably that was because in his judgement no great or worthy ideal could come from the men of the later time. Yet even his undue belittling of their scope may serve a useful purpose, if it warns against setting them too high. They say nothing more than what was the burden of Jeremiah to his people throughout his life. The relation between Yahweh and His people could always be renewed, because Yahweh could and did forgive the sin which had broken that relation. The covenant relation rested in its beginning on the free grace of God, who called Israel into it. The new covenant rested on the same grace, but this grace now needed to do and had done more than it did at first.

[1] Following the LXX.

[2] *Prophecy and Religion*, pp. 320 ff.

It forgave the breach which had destroyed the old. Therefore it was new, richer in content and far more wonderful than the old. It had all the content of forgiveness. Having this, it could only unfold its meaning to men who understood their need for forgiveness. The covenant relation was old, as old as the grace of God which made the fathers the people of Yahweh. It was new to men who had sinned against that grace, who recognized that the past relation had been destroyed by their own act and needed to be renewed in spite of it. The new relation unfolded its meaning to their new experience. Because it involved this experience, it was inward and it was incommunicable. Men could not learn it from one another, as they might learn the terms of a law which God ordered and man obeyed. There was something there which involved a personal experience of sin and grace. And the only thing which men cannot hand on in this world is their experience.

In all this Jeremiah was bringing to its full expression and its inevitable conclusion the fundamental thought in Hosea. The relation between Israel and Yahweh was a love which answered the divine grace. That was too intimate and deep to find its full expression in a law. Though Yahweh, in anxious care that the people should know what He required of them, should write His law in ten thousand precepts, these are counted as a strange thing (Hos. 8 : 10). It was the loyalty of love which produced the law and which could alone supply the desire to keep it and the sense of how it arose out of the intimacy of the relation. In the same way the depth and intimacy of Hosea's conception of religion burst through the narrow shell of the nation. No nation, as nations are and have always been constituted, could exercise a loyalty which readily gave everything. Hosea was preaching in shackles, the shackles which the past bound on him; he must speak in terms of the relation between Yahweh and Israel. But his conception of religion implied a relation of such a quality as could not be posited of a nation. Only the individual soul could desire to fulfil the demands which Yahweh's love made or could rejoice in its austere loveliness. When Jeremiah made the new covenant individual in its terms, he was only bringing out what was implicit in the thought of his master. And when he added the note of forgiveness and taught that the divine grace won new meaning through the divine pardon, he was following the way Hosea had taken in his parable of Gomer. The unfaithful wife could be restored after she had learned in the school of discipline. And while her relation to her husband could not be the old one, but was shot through and through with the tender and terrible experience of her past, it could be very real and fruitful. There could be a new covenant, because God could forgive.

There is another collection of prophecies about the future in chap. 33, but here I am compelled to deny the whole to Jeremiah. All the oracles centre round and are concerned with Jerusalem. And they reveal a strong interest in the beloved city which is to form the rallying-point and the pride of Israel through its institutions of the Davidic kingdom and the priesthood. I find it impossible to believe that a prophet who had declared that the sacrificial system formed no integral part of its religion could have stultified himself by erecting this and the restored Davidic line into the leading factors of the community's restored life. The only passages there which can claim to be comparatively early are the two oracles 33 : 10–13, and these appear to me to date from the time when Judah was lying waste after the exile.[1] A prophetic voice holds out a new hope before the scattered and broken villagers, but he makes that hope culminate in the expectation that the temple shall be restored and that its courts

[1] Cf. p. 227, *supra*.

shall echo with the old cult hymn: Praise ye Yahweh Tsebaoth, for He is good, for His mercy endures for ever. The note is that of Haggai.

The chief feature in all Jeremiah's vision of the future is its calm simple dignity. There is no anticipation of a transformed world, where the wolf shall dwell with the lamb and the leopard lie down with the kid. There is not even a prospect held out of new conditions in the recovered land, where the sower shall overtake the reaper and where the mountains shall run down with new wine. There is no hint of the advent of Messiah who is to maintain these new conditions after Yahweh has instituted them. Life shall continue in its old conditions. The one change which is to appear shall be in the men who live it, since they are to accept it from the hands of their God and so to transcend it. Whether their lot was cast in Babylonia or in Judea, it was enough to know that they were where they were because Yahweh had brought them there. Yet while Jeremiah has no Messiah in his view of the future, it would be a mistake to suppose that he has dropped all thought of the consummation. In reality he retains all that is central in the Jewish conception of the consummation, for he looks forward to the continuance of a community which is secure and blessed, because it is in the keeping of Yahweh. It may need to surrender all the outward marks of independence and royalty which have hitherto distinguished it. But it cannot pass away, because it is the sphere in which Yahweh manifests His righteous will and because it commits itself to Him. In its new humble condition among the fields of Judah, which it seems to hold at the will of a conqueror, it can await with confidence the consummation which shall bring to their destined end all the conquerors and vindicate those who have refused to surrender their souls to oppression. In the same way a later prophet bade the people of Yahweh: 'enter into thy chambers, and shut thy doors about thee: hide thyself for a little moment, until the indignation be overpast. For behold the Lord cometh forth out of his place to punish the inhabitants of the earth for their iniquity' (Isa. 26 : 20 f.). The victory of Babylon is a mere interlude to Jeremiah in the great drama of the divine purpose. Babylon has been used by Yahweh for His particular ends with His people: but the issue of His whole long design is His people, 'a people of God chosen to be the vehicle of God's purpose, so that the ultimate consummation is a communal bliss, the community redeemed, blessed and glorious'.[1] This blessed community or kingdom of Yahweh was what was in the divine mind. All that was involved in true blessedness it was for God to reveal in His day. But the kingdom itself was the one reality beneath the falsities which must disappear before it came. And whatever else might be in it and however vast and wonderful its full revelation might be, its essence was that all who shared it were in complete agreement with its eternal standards and content that God do with them what He willed. And that, said Jeremiah, is possible for repentant men now. They could commit themselves into the hands of their God and live in dependence on His care. They were in His hands as the clay was in the hands of the potter. Nor need the memory of an evil past unduly trouble them, for God forgave, and thus though the old covenant was broken, He could make a new one. It was always possible for men to live in dependence on Yahweh, and when they did it they received or would receive from Him all that was necessary for their real life. In the greatness of this possibility Jeremiah asked his fellow-countrymen to endure the loss of their city and their independence, he asked the exiles in Babylon to endure the loss of their fatherland, he asked the men of Jerusalem to endure the vision of their wrecked temple. None of these things,

[1] Bevan, in the *Legacy of Israel*, p. 50.

however dear and great, was essential. Though they lost them all, they had not lost their God, and having Him they held also all which He might count necessary for their full life. It was an amazing demand. But, as Abrahams has said,[1] 'daring is a note of Apocalypse, which would attract our venturesome age, were it not that, while we dare to doubt, we do not dare to do in spite of doubt'. Read for Apocalypse prophecy, and the remark is equally true.

[1] *Permanent Values of Judaism*, p. 24.

XII

CONCLUSION

ONE thing renders and always will render the work of Jeremiah of special interest to students of the Old Testament. We know much more about him and his time than we do about any of the other prophets. It is true that our information even here is all too meagre, and that there are great gaps in our knowledge of the historical events and the social conditions in Judah. But how much more has come down than in connexion with the life of Isaiah or Amos! We are able to trace Jeremiah through the reigns of three kings of Jerusalem—to omit the two pale phantoms, Jehoahaz and Jehoiachin; and we know the attitude taken to him by the leading men in Church and State during this period. Against this setting and in this environment it is possible to place certain of his more momentous utterances. The years, too, of the prophet's activity are peculiarly significant years. During their course Judah underwent one of the profound changes in its history. It lost its land and its independence. Henceforth one half of its people, not the less intelligent or the less religious half, was to live beyond Palestine in diaspora. If these were to be retained for the nation's life, it must be by new means. Nor was it the State alone which was completely altered; the nation's religious life was finding its way into a new channel. Judaism had begun. The older, freer life where the prophet could preach against the temple in the temple itself had passed. The new prophets, like Haggai, will support the settled order. The time was big with change.

It is the last factor in the situation which is most significant in the study of Jeremiah. He came at a time when the leading men of his nation were interested in religion to the extent of seeking to reform it. They might not know, any more than it is given to every man to know, what was to be the outcome of the step they took. But we know what the step was which they took, and that they took it in the interests of their people and of its religion. We know what was in the minds of the men who formed Jeremiah's audience when he spoke about religion. There also the situation is so much clearer than it is in the case of Amos. We do not know what was in the minds of the men whom the man from Tekoa addressed at the Bethel festival. We do not even know whether they were greatly interested in their worship or were merely going about the routine services. Yet a knowledge of how his hearers were thinking about their worship is of immense importance to a right understanding of the prophet's sermon, because he rebuked them for the things they were doing. We must supply, as best we can, the audience and the ideas. That is more easily done in the case of Jeremiah, because the religious aims of the men of the time are partly known. It is also known that he was in opposition all his life, and the opposition he met extended to all classes in the community. These men, who were deeply moved about their religion, would have nothing to do with the most religious man of their time.

All thoughtful men recognized the need of some action to keep their nation loyal to its distinctive faith. They had planned and carried through a national reform of religion. And the Josianic reform was in itself simple to effect, since it involved no more than making the temple *de jure*, what it was already on the fair way to become *de facto*, the only legitimate shrine. It was also planned on generous lines which appealed to many. It promised to undo the fatal act which had divided Israel since the days of Jeroboam's revolt, and to reunite the nation under the Davidic house under whose leadership it had once found its glory. Such a prospect could not fail to appeal to every patriotic Jew. By concentrating worship at one centre under the supervision of a priesthood which had preserved the purity of the ancient ritual, the reform would prevent abuses which were apt to creep in at the local shrines. How real these abuses could be and how far-reaching their influence was apt to become, has become clear through the evidence from the temple at Elephantine, where Yahweh was worshipped alongside other gods. It is not impossible that some such syncretistic worship was practised at Bethel in spite of the returned priest, and formed Josiah's excuse for abolishing the sanctuary there. As the earlier motive appealed to the patriots and especially to the court-leaders, so this must have commended the movement to religious men and especially to the priests whose position and power were enhanced. And any such reform would carry with it the large body of opinion which exists in every community, made up of those who call themselves practical men, who recognize that something really needs to be done and who are impatient and in a hurry. Such men refuse to listen to the suggestion that the something which is proposed may make matters worse instead of better. All the most influential elements in Judah's life could unite to support the Josianic reform.

That was the movement and these were the religious ideas which were filling the thoughts of the men to whom Jeremiah was called to be a prophet. And it is necessary to repeat that, whatever may be the reason, he was in opposition to them all his life. Courtiers, priests, most of the prophets, and finally the populace, would have none of him and of his message. The reason was that he denounced their plans and would have none of them. And he took this position because he was a prophet, one of a great succession. It was his task to judge the reform of his time, not in the light of what was immediately useful or practically convenient, but by the standard of whether it continued or ran counter to the fundamental principles of the Jewish faith. One of the interests in the study of Jeremiah is the opportunity it gives to watch a real mind at work on the inherited past of his people's thought about religion, seeking to correlate these contributions and to determine their implications. And the man was required to do this, not in the calm hours of ordered thought in a study, but in answer to and in relation to an actual situation. As the consequences of the Josianic reform developed themselves with the remorseless logic of every principle, he recognized and condemned it.

Men were making the temple and the sacrificial system essential to the full covenant-relation to Yahweh and to the enjoyment of the divine grace. Jeremiah told his fellow-countrymen in Northern Israel who were being won over to join Judah on these terms that there was only one thing essential to divine grace and that was a right repentance. He went up to a festival in Jerusalem and declared that to give such a position in their religion to the sacrificial system was only to make sure that Yahweh must destroy the temple as He had already destroyed Shiloh. The new demand contradicted the whole prophetic message which had insisted at least that these things were not primary. Now, since they were making sacrifices essential, he had to say that they had no divine authority. In making one shrine the only place where true worship could be offered, the false reform localized Yahweh; men could come into full fellowship with God only on the soil of Palestine. Therefore, when the first exile fell on the nation, men in Judah could only believe that their brethren in Babylon were through that fact rejected of God and cast off from His grace. He would intervene to bring back some temple furniture which was holy and necessary for His worship; but as for their brethren in exile, they were rotten figs. Jeremiah told the men that the exiles had an opportunity to discover how near their God was in Babylon. No conqueror could separate men from the purpose of Yahweh. Again, since the exiles believed, like their fellows in Jerusalem, that the temple and its worship were essential to worship, the men were driven to waste their lives by hopelessly dashing themselves against their prison bars. Their religion became a mere irritant. The prophet bade them see Babylon, not as a prison, but as a divinely given opportunity. Babylon might hold their bodies, but could not imprison their souls. In Jerusalem the courtiers and priesthood made sure that Yahweh could never suffer the sacred city and its temple to fall into the power of the heathen. He would protect what was necessary for His own honour and worship. So they could recklessly plan rebellion and make religion a cloak for a somewhat vulgar chauvinism. To these men Jeremiah declared that Yahweh Himself would make Nebuchadrezzar His servant, and through him destroy temple and city alike.

Yet, while there is a peculiar interest in thus watching a prophet at work developing his thought in the life of action, there is also a certain loss. It is given to few men to stand in opposition to the trend of their own time and not to fall into exaggeration in their polemic. The temptation is constant to ignore what is giving the opponents their force, and to press unduly the mistakes into which they fall. In the heat of controversy, too, a man who is possessed of a large and generous ideal can easily commit himself to extreme utterances which he might not have spoken in calmer hours. And it is difficult to acquit Jeremiah of having made these mistakes. His denunciation of the temple came perilously near making it a religious duty to do without any such help to worship. Yet the religious life needs more for its full culture than repentance and prayer. There is a place in it for common prayer, for disciplined observance, for a sacred place with hallowed associations. There is need for festival and ritual where soul quickens soul in mutual self-dedication, where the past helps the present to realize the life which has helped and guided all the generations. Again, to say, in the connexion in which Jeremiah said it, that Yahweh gave no command about sacrifice came dangerously near saying that the true faith counted such service wrong. His polemic drove him beyond what other prophets had said on the subject.[1] Yet, if it was an exaggeration to make sacrifice an essential, it may be an equal exaggeration to demand its total abolition in the interests of purity of worship.

All who see in the prophetic movement a revolt against settled civilization and a desire to maintain the old simple practices of the desert can find a ready explanation for Jeremiah's rejection of the temple. To them the dislike of the temple dates back to its building, and reveals both a hatred for all the arts of culture and a revulsion against the Phoenician symbolism which Hiram's workmen must have brought with them. And they can find a certain support for their view in the interest the prophet took in the Rechabites and the sympathy he showed with them (chap. 35). For it is well known that these men were devoted to the nomadic ideal. The sect was marked by a refusal to use wine or even to cultivate a vineyard. But their objection to wine was not due to its intoxicating power: it was due to the vine being the sign of the settled life. It is possible for nomads to sow a crop in a place where they have temporarily settled, to reap it and to move on. But the vine needs more than one year to yield its crop. Accordingly a tribe which has planted vines has taken root itself, it has definitely passed from being bedawi to the condition of being fellahin. Its next step will be to build cottages and forsake the houses of hair. The Rechabites only forsook their tents to take refuge in a walled city because

[1] I cannot agree with those who hold that Amos in 5 : 25 took this position. The verse in its connexion does not bear that interpretation.

they were driven to this change (vv. 10 f.). Then Jeremiah would also be a supporter of the unchanging customs of the wilderness period, the time of the honeymoon between Yahweh and the nation. With this it would be easy to join his command to the exiles that they should devote themselves to prayer and find all their religion demanded in prayer and obedience. And the nearest analogy for the attitude of the prophet would be found in one of the reform movements within Islam or even in Islam itself, so far as it can be counted a Puritanic protest.

Yet, on the other hand, one who entered with such gusto into the business of maintaining his family rights over a field and who spoke with such manifest sympathy about the grinding corn-mill and the evening cottage lamps, was plainly no Wahabi or Rechabite. He could conceive of Yahwism making terms with civilization. His sympathy with the sect need go no farther than he himself has defined. He could not but admire their loyalty to the narrow ideals of their founder, and was able to hold it up as at once an example and a reproach to the lax conduct of men in Jerusalem. More probably the reason for Jeremiah's attitude must be looked for elsewhere. Its roots may rather be found in the strong individualism which marked all the prophetic movement. Representatives of such a movement were from their very nature apt to act as a disruptive force, and were specially apt to stand aloof from the currents of practice which swayed the minds of ordinary men. They were themselves not ordinary men and could be both impatient and intolerant of the slow calm life out of which they rose. Besides, as has been said, all Jeremiah's work was done in the electric atmosphere of controversy. Not otherwise than through controversy does it sometimes appear possible to force great principles on the attention of the multitude or to get busy men to think about them at all. But the cost is very great on the temper and the thought of the opponents. Not only do both sides become unable to acknowledge the truth which is always present in the opposite point of view, but they are driven into stating their own position with a sharpness which gives it clarity at the cost of entire accuracy.

Jeremiah's attitude, therefore, cannot be considered the final word in an age-long controversy between institutional religion and prophetic conviction. It may be wiser to see in it a protest. And then it becomes possible to recognize how necessary it was for its time, how wholesome it was in its effects. The time needed such a reminder, for it was the period when the diaspora began. The Jew was no longer to be shut up in his eagle's nest at Jerusalem; he was to be a citizen of the world. If he was to carry his faith with him to be his own strength and a blessing to the world, he needed something more than the principles of the Josianic reform. For that tended to localize Yahweh. It localized worship and so nationalized Yahwism, and cut off all the diaspora as rotten figs. It was the prophetic principles, taught by the last great representative of that movement, which made a better thing possible.

Yet the effects of Jeremiah's vehement protest seem at the first sight hard to discover. The last scene in which he appears might rather be symbolic. Before the curtain drops, the stage reveals the prophet a defeated man among the group of fugitives who took refuge in Egypt. The people he had tried to serve were there against his advice and were refusing to listen to him, now that they had forced him into exile. They told him with stubborn defiance that it was better with them when they served the queen of heaven as well as Yahweh. And he told them in reply that life on these principles meant that within a generation there would not be a Jew left in Egypt. The core of their national life was their religion, and their religion meant the acknowledgement of no other god beside Yahweh. Yet, significantly enough, the men refused to leave their intransigent mentor behind them in Judah, and did not fail to consult him even in Egypt. That was Israel's inveterate habit. They would neither commit themselves absolutely to their prophets, nor would they let these wholly go. So, because he though dead continued to speak, the community in Egypt survived. The temple at Elephantine with its goddess beside Yahweh passed, and left a handful of papyri. But the Jews of Alexandria built a synagogue for prayer, and translated their Scripture into the Greek which their children could understand. They lived without sacrifice, but they could not live without prayer and the eternal word which prescribed for them their way of Jewish obedience. They became citizens of Egypt who owned an allegiance beyond that claimed by its kings. Because the prophet had his hold upon their life, they bred Philo, Greek and Jew.

The other centre of Jewish life in diaspora, which dated from the period, was the community in Babylonia. That colony, which afterwards rose to power and influence in the life of Jewry, derived directly from the first transportation from Jerusalem. For, while many of those exiles returned to the holy city, an appreciable number remained in the country of their compulsory adoption. Some of these, it is probable, were indifferent to their religion and merely lapsed into heathenism. But the others who elected to remain were not disloyal or indifferent to the claims of their faith. They were simply men who found it quite consistent with their duty to remain in Babylon. That is made clear by the terms of some of the oracles which have been preserved in the series against Babylon (Jer. chaps. 50 f.). Such utterances as 50 : 1–5, 6–10, 17–20; 51 : 1–6, 7–10, were plainly intended to rouse the exiles and interest them in the first Zionite movement. They appeal to the men by motives of patriotism and religion to take the opportunity which Yahweh has brought within their reach. Others (50 : 35–40; 51 : 20–4) were designed to make Babylon appear hateful to God and man, and to urge flight from a place on which the divine wrath perpetually rested. The writer of 50 : 1–5 could speak of turning with tears to seek Yahweh and count this synonymous with turning toward Zion and inquiring the way thither. One main purpose of Deutero-Isaiah was to rouse his people to seize their God-given opportunity and join in the return to the holy land. He could even speak of the restoration of Zion in terms which made this restoration equivalent with the final consummation. All that is evidence of an ardent propaganda among the exiles in the interest of the return to Jerusalem. But no one writes propaganda to convince believers. Propaganda is written to persuade the unconverted. And the men who preserve the propaganda are those who believe in its worth. Behind these oracles we become aware of a body of men for whom they were needed, some of whom did not construe their duty along these lines at all.

It is of some importance to discover, if possible, the spirit which animated these men in the course they took at this great period of their people's life. They were not very articulate. Their action did not have the fine dramatic quality which attended those who surrendered everything in order to return to Jerusalem at the summons of religion. Above all, they did not represent the dominant tendency of the time, so that their records rather fell into the background and were overlooked. But fortunately they have not disappeared without leaving some sign. For it is now commonly recognized that the early chapters of the book of Daniel belong to a much earlier period than the visions to which they have been prefixed, and that they were written in Babylonia itself, with life in which they are concerned.[1]

[1] Cf. Hölscher, *Studien und Kritiken*, 1892, pp. 113 ff.; Haller, *St. Kr.* 1893, pp. 83 ff.; and Montgomery, *Daniel*, I.C.C. pp. 88 ff.

The author who issued his visions under the name of Daniel incorporated in his book certain stories which were current about the life of that leader of Israel. This material derives from Babylon, not from Palestine. Hence, whatever historical value it may possess, it is of extreme interest since it reveals the ideals and the attitude of the men who did not return to Jerusalem after Cyrus permitted the restoration of the temple.

What is of special interest in these tales is the religious temper they reveal. Thus they take a wholly different attitude to the heathen world among which their heroes live from that taken by the author who wrote in the Maccabean age. In the stories Daniel is able to call the Chaldean kingdom the head of gold, and to write without a qualm about it: the leaves of the tree were fair, and the fruit thereof much, and in it was meat for all ; the beasts of the field had shadow under it, and the fowls of the heaven dwelt in the branches thereof, and all flesh was fed of it (4 : 12). Daniel has no hesitation about accepting office under the Empire and serving it with a loyal devotion. He can so far identify himself with its life that he is represented as having asked mercy for the Chaldean magicians (2 : 24) and even as having become their head (2 : 48; 4 : 9). But this attitude contrasts strongly with that of the writer of the rest of the book of Daniel. To him the great empires are a succession of brute powers which have all been antagonistic to the kingdom of the saints. If the Macedonian kingdom is the worst of the four, it is only the last of a vile series, which the Babylonian began. All heathendom is fitly symbolized in a series of wild beasts. But the stories do not merely contrast with the visions; they clearly reflect a different outlook from that of the oracles which appear in Jer. chaps. 50 f. There Babylon is accursed of God and is about to be reduced by Him to a waste and a desolation. The only thing the loyal Jew can do, if he is not to be involved in its fate, is to take the opportunity God has given him to escape from the fated place. Daniel, on the other hand, can and does loyally serve Babylon. He takes his complete share in the life of the new world into which he has been thrown. He serves its interests so well that its people acknowledge him and honour him. He becomes a councillor of its king, serving Babylon with all his strength. That was the courageous attitude of Jeremiah. For he had written to the exiles that their presence in Babylon was due to something higher than the fortune of war, it was due to the will of God. Therefore the foreign land meant something and could give something to them, and they in turn must seek the well-being of the land to which Yahweh had caused them to be carried away captive. The men in Egypt took Jeremiah with them and gave him a grudging and unwilling respect. Hence they gained nothing from him but a trouble to conscience and an irritant. The men in Babylon accepted the message of the prophet with a ready mind. They gained from him a positive gospel.

Yet, while Daniel and his companions became citizens of the Empire, they remained loyal Jews. And wherever the demands of the state conflicted with the requirements of the faith, they could only break with Babylon. For they acknowledged other standards which were absolute and ignored the standards by which the nations lived. In their breach of the imperial law they knew why they must not go with the rest of the world. Daniel appears challenging the heathen king: 'thy kingdom shall be sure unto thee, after that thou shalt have known that the heavens do rule. Wherefore, O king, let my counsel be acceptable unto thee, and break off thy sins by righteousness and thine iniquities by showing mercy to the poor'. The rule of the Most High is the rule of justice and mercy. Any authority which ignores them cannot build up an enduring human society, and any king who does not bow to them is only fit for the company of the beasts. These standards are the yoke and bonds of the God of Israel. For the want of them the heathen kingdoms are rotten at the base. And Yahwism shall prove itself supreme, because it holds and can bring to men these elements, not of a local or national religion, but of the universal faith. That is a prophetic message.

Yet a faith cannot live by mere negation and refusal to submit to alien demands. It is no doubt necessary that a higher form of religion, especially when it has to live among baser forms, should be conscious of its own superiority. To do its full work among its own people, it must also create its own forms and offer to those who profess it some means by which it may be confirmed and renewed. Accordingly Daniel is known in Babylon, not less by the things he does than by the things he refuses to do. The things a man refuses to share in are occasional, and may be the outcome of special circumstances among which he happens to be thrown. The things which he always does at the dictate of his faith are the constant and richer evidence of the manner of man he is. And so 'when Daniel knew that the writing was signed, he went into his house, . . . and he kneeled upon his knees three times a day and prayed and gave thanks unto his God as he did aforetime'. The terms in which the act is described are significant. In the connexion in which the picture of Daniel's devotion appears, it was unnecessary to mention that the man offered prayer three times a day. For the purpose of convicting him of disobedience to the royal edict it was enough to prove that he had done it once. It was equally unnecessary to add that he had done it aforetime. His accusers did not need to bring proof of what he had done before the edict was signed. His contempt of the royal authority consisted in what he had done after this was issued. Evidently we are being given a representation of the religious practice of certain devout circles in Babylon. These men have elected to remain when their fellow-Jews returned to Jerusalem, and yet they have no desire to be indifferent to their faith. Only they have not counted temple and sacrifice essential for access to Yahweh, because they could reach Him where they were. That also they learned from Jeremiah. The prophet had bidden the exiles try their God, and had said that, if they did, they should find Him, because He was accessible everywhere. The men in Babylon have done it. And because they have found the prophet's word true, because they have also found how blessed and helpful prayer is, they have regulated it and not left it to the mercy of a casual impulse. It has become their habit to pray three times a day.

Jeremiah was the spiritual founder of the synagogue. That, of course, does not mean that the institution dates back to his time. We know too little about the inner life and early history of the diaspora to be able to say when or where the organized synagogue-worship began. It may have been unknown, when the description of Daniel's act was written, for there the man has his oratory in his own home. But the conviction which gave vitality to the synagogue—that the Jew could live a loyal Jew without sacrifice, but could not so live without prayer—derived directly from the prophet. And through it he preserved the diaspora for Judaism and the world.

At a somewhat later period the authorities at Jerusalem accepted an institution which they could not themselves have created, and even ventured to supply it with a new *raison d'être*. They called the morning and evening prayers surrogates for the temple sacrifices which were offered at the same hours. That is the familiar practice of every official and centralized authority. Powerless itself to create, it can adopt and reinterpret something which has proved itself helpful and blessed for men's religious life. In reality the synagogue needed no *raison d'être*; it justified itself. And so deeply did it sink into the mind of Jewry, and so large a place did it make for itself there, that men transplanted it to Jerusalem itself and set up their houses of prayer under the shadow of the temple. The smoke of the sacrifice and the chant of a prayer which was called a mere surrogate for the sacrifice rose together into the morning and evening air. For Judaism never wholly followed its prophets and never entirely disowned them.[1]

Yet there was a strong body of opinion in the nation which was not prepared to abandon sacrificial worship with temple and priesthood and the recurrent festivals. Even in Northern Israel, where the prophetic influence was most powerful, the system remained. The Code of Deuteronomy gave a large place in the life of the nation to the sanctuary with its opportunities for communal worship in the annual feasts and the

[1] Daniel and his three companions were represented as typical loyal Jews living in the novel conditions of exile. But why did such pious observers of the law ignore the opportunity to return and take part in the restoration of the temple? The men of the return evidently recognized the incongruity, and tried to turn its edge. For we find in Neh. 8 : 4, 7 Mishael, Hanan, and Azariah in the list of those who returned with Ezra, while a priest named Daniel appears Neh. 10 : 7 and Ezra 8 : 2. Further, the Septuagint gives at Dan. 4 : 1 the eighteenth year as the date of Nebuchadrezzar's dream, and thus makes the king's rejection and madness synchronize with his destruction of Jerusalem. It also makes this act part of the indictment against the king in v. 19. Nebuchadrezzar's madness was thus explained as the divine chastisement for his treatment of the holy city. Again the Hebrew chapter, which prefaces the Aramaic stories about the four faithful Jews, makes Daniel continue, i.e. remain where he was until the first year of King Cyrus (1 : 21). The suggestion is that of course he resigned all his offices and returned to Jerusalem whenever the proclamation of release was issued. It was easier, however, to insert these slight points of agreement than to get rid of the broad incongruity between the view taken of Babylon in the stories of the captives and the attitude of the men of the return.

sacrificial ritual. Hence it was natural that the temple at Jerusalem was restored, whether by the exiles who took advantage of the imperial permit under Cyrus, or by the remanent Jews in Judea. And it was restored on the terms of the Josianic reform. The temple at Jerusalem was to be the one legitimate shrine for Jewish worship. Certainly, if the sacrificial system was to be restored at all, centralization was the only practical policy in the circumstances. To permit each local centre of Jewry to set up its own shrine, even if it had been possible for this to be done, would only have led to ugly abuses. The Elephantine papyri are enough to prove that. The book of Tobit shows how superstition of a pretty coarse type could make its way into the minds of Jewish settlers among the heathen. Had these been allowed to filter into the cult and to harden into ritual and rubric, the effect would only have been worse. There was some guarantee that the ritual worship of the Jew could be kept pure from heathen influence, and be practised after ancient forms, when it was confined to Jerusalem. For the men who restored it there had given up much which men value to maintain the tradition of their fathers.

And Zion thus restored became an emblem, a flag to scattered Judaism. It meant much even to the men who did not count it essential and who did not return to rebuild it. They were not in conscious antagonism to it. Daniel, it is said, went into his house to pray, but the window before which he kneeled was open toward Jerusalem. The thought of the holy city appealed to imagination and could quicken devotion. From the beginning the men of the diaspora contributed liberally to the sacrifices and festivals in which they took no direct part.[1] That grew into the system of the temple tax, by which the sacrifices at the central shrine won a certain efficacy for all Israel. Those who were able went

[1] Zech. 6 : 9 ff.

on pilgrimage to the holy city to take reverent share in its festivals. How passionate an affection the ancient home of the race could rouse in those who visited it can be recognized from some of the later psalms. And how early this began can be gathered from the fact that one of its utterances has even found its way into the book of Jeremiah. Ah, glorious throne, high-pitched, venerable, our holy sanctuary! Yahweh, Thou hope of Israel, all who forsake Thee shall be disappointed, all who rebel against Thee in the land shall be brought to shame, because they have forsaken Yahweh, the well of living water (17 : 12 f.). Zion has there become a symbol, an ideal. And no man who knows what religion is outside of books and who knows the strange hearts of men will undervalue the worth of symbols.

Yet in itself Jerusalem could contribute little directly to the life of the diaspora in the new lands where their lives were spent. When conditions permitted, men undertook a pilgrimage and had a share in one of the great festivals. But such a visit must have been a rare event in any man's life, and must have been confined to the few who had leisure or money to make the journey. The vast majority never saw the holy city and never had the opportunity to take part in the rites for the restoration of which the men of the return had sacrificed so much. In particular, all the women of the diaspora were practically shut out from any share. To these men pilgrimage was the evidence of an existing devotion to Jerusalem rather than the means of maintaining it. It could quicken a religious sense which was already there: it could not maintain this, far less could it rouse it in the lives of their children. One of the Jewish pedlars Juvenal saw in Rome lived in the corner of a room in one of the *insulae* or barracked tenements along the Tiber. Out of his meagre earnings he paid his temple tax to Jerusalem. The trifling sacrifice could give him, the despised Oriental at whom the

Roman satirist flung a passing sneer, the sense of belonging to a civilization which was older than that of Rome. His people had seen so many empires rise, Egyptian and Assyrian, Babylonian, Persian and Macedonian, and now this youngest of them all. They had suffered under them all and survived them all. And, while the monstrous gods with their strange worships had vanished with those who gave them honour, morning and evening the smoke of the altar-fire rose from the rock of Zion. And in it he had his share. And yet all that could at best fire the man's imagination. What kept his soul alive was the worship he practised in some squalid room or along a stream-side, where St. Paul found him praying with his fellows on the Sabbath to the God of his fathers. In their community life he found, too, the help needed to maintain in an alien civilization his obedience to the dictates of his faith. The men had learned through the travail of their prophets that, where one or two gathered to pray, they could find God. So they built up a Church which could exist wherever a Jewish household was found. By the deed they set the life of their nation and its dearest inheritance beyond the reach of time and accident. The men who counted Jerusalem essential to right worship had run the risk of leaving themselves at the mercy of circumstances. When the enemy defiled the sanctuary, he had their souls at his mercy. And he would have had, if it had not been that Israel was unable to cast out the prophet it had bred and to forget a message to which it seemed to turn a deaf ear. It was the leaven of Jeremiah's principles which preserved the nation under the shock of A.D. 70.

Probably the most amazing fact in the amazing record of Israel is that it not only survived the destruction of the temple, but passed through that loss with little more than a long stagger. And it does seem a somewhat cheap thing to say that Israel only learned to do without a temple when it was compelled by circumstances. To dismiss the matter so easily is to ignore that a people which could thus overcome circumstance and rally after one of its most crushing blows must have been possessed of something very real and very positive in which they found their support. The men discovered where their true strength lay when the outward prop was gone. They could live without their sacrificial system, because they had long been accustoming themselves, even in Jerusalem, to live by prayer and obedience. These, which had long been the unacknowledged support of their devotion, stood out now as sufficient to meet their new need.

Yet such a conviction of how Judaism might continue without temple and sacrifice could only arise in a later generation, which had learned to live by other support. To many men at the period of the exile the disappearance of the sacrificial system must have seemed to threaten the end of all things. Their first aim must be to restore their temple at all costs. It is not easy to determine whether the earliest move in this direction came from the farmers and crofters whom Nebuchadrezzar's generals were careful to reinstate in Judah, or whether the incentive was given by a band of eager exiles who seized the opportunity of Cyrus's permit and returned to Jerusalem. In either case the impelling motive was that the men could not conceive their religion continuing without all for which the sacred shrine stood. And the effort which they made, especially since it proved successful, only confirmed their impression of the significance of the thing which they had done. Men who have sacrificed much for the sake of a particular end inevitably exaggerate the worth of the institution which has claimed and received their devotion. Temple, sacrificial system, and sacred festival became central in the thought and worship of the returned exiles. Things which were at best a means of devotion threatened to become an end in themselves.

But all which these men aimed at and all they succeeded in was a conservative reaction: they sought to restore what had been. It is the failure to realize this fact which vitiates Kuenen's view of the events that attended the return, a view which Wellhausen accepted. According to them the priests busied themselves during the exile in preparing a new law, P., which they were able to bind on the little community at Jerusalem by pledging them to its demands in a solemn covenant. In so acting, the priests were consciously preparing a new situation. And they succeeded in persuading their compatriots to turn their back deliberately on their national ideals and, ceasing to desire independence and a kingdom, to become a Church which centred round the sanctuary and found its leaders in its priesthood. Hence, even when Ezekiel spoke of a prince in Israel, he assigned this official a lower position. The men of their own choice abdicated from a place among the kingdoms of the world.

In reality the men of the return restored everything of the past which they could restore. If they did not bring back the house of David to reign in the old capital, it was because they could not. Our information about the conditions which prevailed at this time in Jerusalem is unfortunately very meagre, and the little which has come down is confused and perplexing. But there are indications that some among the settlers desired to see Zerubbabel sit again as prince on the throne of his fathers. And in this connexion it is significant to note how persistently the enemies of the struggling community represented to the Persian court that a restored Jerusalem must endanger the king's peace in the province, and how the rescript which authorized Ezra to return was peculiarly careful to say that he held authority over none except his fellow Jews, and even with them was only empowered to issue regulations about their religious affairs (Ezra 7 : 11 ff.). These hints point to some effort having been made in the direction of restoring Judah in more than a religious way. And how long the passion after national independence glowed in Judea, and what heroism the memories of David's house could evoke, the story of the Maccabean struggle is enough to prove. But the Persian Empire made Judah a province and forced Israel to become a Church with no other head than a High-priest who was not likely to be politically dangerous. This, however, it was wise enough and generous enough to allow. It went even farther, for it authorized the nation to organize itself in all religious matters under its own law. And the law which the men introduced was essentially their old law, the custom of the fathers, the emblem of the past which meant to them their life.

INDEX OF SCRIPTURE PASSAGES

GENERAL INDEX